PRE-HISTORIES AND AFTERLIVES
STUDIES IN CRITICAL METHOD FOR TERENCE CAVE

LEGENDA

LEGENDA, founded in 1995 by the European Humanities Research Centre of the University of Oxford, is now a joint imprint of the Modern Humanities Research Association and Maney Publishing. Titles range from medieval texts to contemporary cinema and form a widely comparative view of the modern humanities, including works on Arabic, Catalan, English, French, German, Greek, Italian, Portuguese, Russian, Spanish, and Yiddish literature. An Editorial Board of distinguished academic specialists works in collaboration with leading scholarly bodies such as the Society for French Studies and the British Comparative Literature Association.

MHRA

The Modern Humanities Research Association (MHRA) encourages and promotes advanced study and research in the field of the modern humanities, especially modern European languages and literature, including English, and also cinema. It also aims to break down the barriers between scholars working in different disciplines and to maintain the unity of humanistic scholarship in the face of increasing specialization. The Association fulfils this purpose primarily through the publication of journals, bibliographies, monographs and other aids to research.

MANEY
publishing

Maney Publishing is one of the few remaining independent British academic publishers. Founded in 1900 the company has offices both in the UK, in Leeds and London, and in North America, in Boston. Since 1945 Maney Publishing has worked closely with learned societies, their editors, authors, and members, in publishing academic books and journals to the highest traditional standards of materials and production.

MEN CAN DO NOTHING without the make-believe of a beginning. Even Science, the strict measurer, is obliged to start with a make-believe unit, and must fix on a point in the stars' unceasing journey when his sidereal clock shall pretend that time is at Nought. His less accurate grandmother Poetry has always been understood to start in the middle; but on reflection it appears that her proceeding is not very different from his; since Science, too, reckons backwards as well as forwards, divides his unit into billions, and with his clock-finger at Nought really sets off *in medias res*. No retrospect will take us to the true beginning; and whether our prologue be in heaven or on earth, it is but a fraction of that all-presupposing fact with which our story sets out.

GEORGE ELIOT, Epigraph to *Daniel Deronda*, Book 1, Chapter 1

Pre-Histories and Afterlives

Studies in Critical Method for Terence Cave

❖

Edited by Anna Holland and Richard Scholar

LEGENDA

Modern Humanities Research Association and Maney Publishing
2009

Published by the
Modern Humanities Research Association and Maney Publishing
1 Carlton House Terrace
London SW1Y 5AF
United Kingdom

LEGENDA is an imprint of the
Modern Humanities Research Association and Maney Publishing

Maney Publishing is the trading name of W. S. Maney & Son Ltd,
whose registered office is at Suite 1C, Joseph's Well, Hanover Walk, Leeds LS3 1AB

ISBN 978-1-905981-93-9

First published 2009

Printed in Great Britain

Cover: 875 Design

Copy-Editor: Richard Correll

CONTENTS

❖

NOTE ON REFERENCES,
ABBREVIATIONS AND TRANSLATIONS

❖

References in the text and endnotes to Terence Cave, *Pré-histoires: Textes troublés au seuil de la modernité* (Geneva: Droz, 1999) and *Pré-histoires II: Langues étrangères et troubles économiques au XVIe siècle* (Geneva: Droz, 2001) take the form *Pré-histoires I* and *Pré-histoires II* respectively. All references to Montaigne's *Essais* are to the edition by Pierre Villey and V.-L. Saulnier (Paris: PUF, 1965). References list book, chapter and page numbers in the form 'III. 6, 908'. Where the period of composition of the text is relevant to the argument, contributors adopt the scheme developed by Villey: [A] refers to the 1580 and 1582 editions, [B] to the 1588 edition, and [C] to manuscript additions made by Montaigne to the so-called 'Bordeaux copy' of the 1588 edition. In quotations from early modern French, 'i' and 'j', and 'u' and 'v' are distinguished. Translations are the contributors' own unless otherwise indicated.

PREFACE

❖

This volume arises from a symposium on 'Pre-Histories and Afterlives' held in honour of Terence Cave in St. John's College, Oxford on 30 September 2006. Pre-histories and afterlives, methods that have emerged in recent work by Cave, offer new ways of shaping the stories we tell of the past and the critical analyses we offer. The contributors to this volume engage in a dialogue with these two new critical methods, exploring their uses in a range of contexts, disciplines, languages and periods. In respect of its engagement with methodological questions raised by Cave's work, *Pre-Histories and Afterlives* might usefully be thought of as a companion volume to *Retrospectives: Essays in Literature, Poetics and Cultural History by Terence Cave*, edited by Neil Kenny and Wes Williams, also published by Legenda.

We are grateful to the following for their generous financial support of this project: the President and Fellows of St John's College, Oxford; the Faculty of Medieval and Modern Languages, University of Oxford; the Maison Française d'Oxford (ACI–TTT: 'Frontières de la modernité'). We owe a particular debt of gratitude to Agnieszka Steczowicz, who co-organized the symposium with us and played a major role in the early stages of the present volume's conception and preparation. We thank the contributors to this volume for their hard work and unfailing good cheer. We should also like to express our thanks to the following individuals for their participation in and assistance with the project: Kathryn Banks; Jessica Benson; Luisa Calè; Tim Chesters; Richard Cooper; Elizabeth Fallaize; Miranda Gill; Ann Jefferson; Ruth Livesey; Will McKenzie; Martin McLaughlin; Will McMorran; Michael Moriarty; Ritchie Robertson; Angela Scholar; Alexis Tadié; Rowan Tomlinson; Alain Viala; Valerie Worth. We thank Emma Herdman for compiling the index. Martin McLaughlin and members of the Editorial Board at Legenda have offered valuable editorial guidance, while Graham Nelson has guided the manuscript through to publication with admirable efficiency, attention to detail and good humour.

We are grateful to the Bodleian Library, University of Oxford, and in particular to the Keeper of Special Collections, for permission to reproduce as the cover image Emblem XVIII from *Emblemata v. cl. Andreae Alciati* (1618), Shelfmark Vet F2 f.58, page 38. The still from the film *Back to the Future* (Universal) is reproduced courtesy of the Kobal Collection.

Finally, we should like to thank Terence Cave, colleague, teacher and friend, whose work inspired both the symposium and this volume and who has contributed to both with unfailing enthusiasm, patience and care.

A. H. & R. W. S.

ABOUT THE CONTRIBUTORS
❖

Terence Cave is Emeritus Professor of French Literature at the University of Oxford and Emeritus Research Fellow of St John's College, Oxford. His publications include *Devotional Poetry in France, c.1570–1613* (CUP, 1969), *The Cornucopian Text: Problems of Writing in the French Renaissance* (Clarendon Press, 1979), *Recognitions: A Study in Poetics* (Clarendon Press, 1988), *Pré-histoires: Textes troublés au seuil de la modernité* (Droz, 1999), and *Pré-histoires II: Langues étrangères et troubles économiques au XVIe siècle* (Droz, 2001). He is a Fellow of the British Academy.

Marian Hobson is Professorial Research Fellow, Queen Mary, University of London, a Fellow of the British Academy, and a specialist both of the European Enlightenment and present-day literary theory and criticism. Her book on eighteenth-century aesthetics (CUP, 1982) has just been published by Champion in a French translation (*L'Art et son objet: Diderot, la théorie de l'illusion et les arts en France au XVIIIe siècle*). She is the author of many articles on Diderot and Rousseau. She has also published on Derrida, *Jacques Derrida: Opening Lines* (Routledge, 1998) and translated Derrida's early dissertation, *The Problem of Genesis in the Philosophy of Husserl* (2002).

Anna Holland is Lecturer in French at Oriel College, Oxford. She is a specialist in early modern French literature with particular interests in Renaissance humanist culture and the poetic circles of the Pléiade, and is completing *Afterlives of Horace in Renaissance France: 'Imitatio', Identity and Poetic Community*, to be published by OUP. She is currently working on publications concerning literary and sexual identity in the milieu of mid-sixteenth-century humanism.

Neil Kenny is Reader in Early Modern French Literature and Thought at the University of Cambridge. His publications include *The Palace of Secrets: Béroalde de Verville and Renaissance Conceptions of Knowledge* (Clarendon Press, 1991), *The Uses of Curiosity in Early Modern France and Germany* (OUP, 2004), and *An Introduction to Sixteenth-Century French Literature and Thought: Other Times, Other Places* (Duckworth, 2008).

Mary McKinley is the Douglas Huntly Gordon Professor of French at the University of Virginia. She has written two books on Montaigne, *Words in a Corner: Studies in Montaigne's Latin Quotations* (1980) and *Les Terrains vagues des Essais* (1996); co-edited *Critical Tales: New Studies of the Heptameron and Early Modern Culture* (1993); and edited and translated Marie Dentière's *Epistle to Marguerite de Navarre and Preface to a Sermon by John Calvin* (2004) for The Other Voice in Early Modern Europe series.

Ben Morgan is University Lecturer in German and a Fellow of Worcester College, Oxford. His main research interests are in German intellectual history (medieval mysticism, Nietzsche, early psychoanalysis, the Frankfurt School) and German film (Fritz Lang, Leni Riefenstahl). He has also worked on contemporary women's writing (Jelinek). He is currently completing a project which explores how texts from the fourteenth-century milieu of Meister Eckhart can help a re-thinking of modern ideas of personal identity. His next project, 'Heidegger at the Movies', will draw on popular film from 1930 to 1970 to re-evaluate the process of coming to terms with the past in West Germany after 1945.

John O'Brien is Professor of French Renaissance Literature at Royal Holloway, University of London. He is the author of *Anacreon Redivivus* (1995), the editor of the forthcoming *Cambridge Companion to Rabelais* and the co-editor of *Remy Belleau, 'Les Odes d'Anacréon'* (1995), *Distant Voices Still Heard* (2000), *La 'Familia' de Montaigne* (2001) and most recently of *Theory and the Early Modern* (2006). His current projects involve the relationship between law, fiction and narrative, and between speculation, the imagination and the grotesque in early modern French literature.

Richard Scholar is University Lecturer in French and a Fellow of Oriel College, Oxford. His main research interests are in the field of early modern literature and thought, particularly French, but also comparative. He is the author of *The Je-Ne-Sais-Quoi in Early Modern Europe* (OUP, 2005), editor of Blaise Pascal, *Entretien avec Sacy sur la philosophie* (Actes Sud, 2003) and co-editor of *Thinking with Shakespeare* (Legenda, 2007). He is currently completing a book on Montaigne and the art of free-thinking.

Kate E. Tunstall is University Lecturer in French and a Fellow of Worcester College, Oxford. She works on eighteenth-century literature and thought, Diderot in particular, and on the relationships between words and images. She has published on subjects as diverse as Diderot and Chardin, Racine and silent film, Zola and still life, and is currently writing a book on Diderot's *Lettre sur les aveugles*.

Wes Williams is University Lecturer in French and a Fellow of St Edmund Hall, Oxford. His main research interests are in the field of early modern literature and thought. He is the author of *Pilgrimage and Narrative in the French Renaissance* (Clarendon Press, 1999), and continues to explore travel narratives across the period. He is now completing a study of monsters and their meanings from, roughly, Rabelais to Racine (by way of Shakespeare, Montaigne and a few others). He also works on European film and contemporary theatre.

INTRODUCTION

❖

Anna Holland and Richard Scholar

'The past is a foreign country; they do things differently there.'[1] The sentence that opens L. P. Hartley's novel *The Go-Between* (1953) provides, in more ways than one, a fitting point of departure for the present volume. It encapsulates a view of the past which is central to the work of Terence Cave, and what is more, the first half of Hartley's sentence figures as one of two epigraphs to Cave's book *Pré-histoires I* (1999).[2] Cave's work in that book and in subsequent publications might be described as an attempt to pursue the implications for critical method raised by the metaphor that Hartley deploys to such powerful effect. If the past is indeed a foreign country, then how can we enter into meaningful dialogue with its inhabitants, and how can we make sense of the extraordinary things they say if we understand them on our terms alone? 'Pre-histories' and 'afterlives', two critical methods to have emerged in Cave's recent work, offer new ways of shaping the stories we tell of the past and the analyses we offer. The contributors to this volume engage in a dialogue with these two new methods from the perspective of their own work, exploring the meanings and uses of pre-histories and afterlives across a range of contexts, disciplines, languages, and periods. The result is a volume that offers a testimonial to a colleague, teacher, and friend of many people working in the arts and humanities, not by praising his work, but by taking it seriously in its advocacy of method, its combination of historical rigour and speculative inventiveness, and its attempt to formulate better ways of understanding our relationship to the foreign country that is the past.

The past as it appears in Cave's work is foreign without ever being entirely remote. The narrator of *The Go-Between* produces the aphorism with which we started in precisely this situation. He has come in old age upon a diary from the distant past of his own early adolescence recording an episode that at the time he was not equipped to understand. As he reads the diary, that past comes closer, refuses to remain remote: 'I should have to face it, I *was* facing it, the scene, the people, and the experience.'[3] The texts on which Cave generally works afford less obviously immediate encounters but they too, in various ways, bring the past closer. These are texts that may be said to engage their latter-day readers in a kind of dialogue about what they might mean and how they might mean it.

What that dialogue is and how it might best be conducted are questions of critical method. By 'method' is meant here a form of intellectual activity, sandwiched between 'practice' and 'theory', which involves working out an approach that is suited to a particular set of materials, thinking about the uses and the limitations of that approach, and making connections where appropriate with parallel projects. In his individual work, and as a convenor of research seminars at Oxford, Royal

Holloway (London), Oslo and elsewhere, Cave has long advocated reflection on and discussion about method to those who work in the arts and humanities. He has made two points in particular: first, that questions of method are common to all kinds of research, however different the materials and areas of specialization; and second, that they are of particular concern to the many people whose work crosses borderlines between different languages, historical periods or disciplines. In *Recognitions* (1988), and in his current work on the figure of Mignon, Cave crosses such borderlines in inventive ways, moving between different European languages, between the early modern and modern periods, and between the disciplines of history, literature, and music.[4] His emphasis on method — and the same could be said of the present volume and of the symposium from which it arose — is intended not to stifle such inventiveness but to coax it towards a greater lucidity and so to offer people working on different projects a means of discussing shared questions.

What, then, of the dialogue between past texts and their later readers? Cave argues strenuously for methods that, while acknowledging the inevitable presence of those readers in the dialogue, do not conclude from this that their perspective should be allowed entirely to dictate the terms of that dialogue or to fix the meaning of the text. His pre-histories offer a way of listening attentively — from a position that is itself caught in the flow of time — to texts of the past that move and keep moving. So too, perhaps, do the afterlives that Cave has worked on since publishing his two volumes of *Pré-histoires* — or at least this thought occurred to the three of us who co-organized the symposium 'Pre-Histories and Afterlives' in Oxford in September 2006. Cave prompted our thought, it might be said, by publishing articles in 2003 and 2005 both of which use the term 'afterlife' to describe the extraordinary transformations that Mignon, the foundling in Goethe's *Wilhelm Meister* novels, underwent in nineteenth- and twentieth-century European literature and music.[5] We noticed too that, during roughly the same period, Cave was publishing work on Montaigne containing passages that, without using the term 'afterlife', sketch out ways of understanding the dynamic relation between Montaigne's text and its later reception.[6] While differences between these two afterlives are obvious — and should come as no surprise, Montaigne being no Mignon, and vice versa — the attempt seemed to us to be the same in both cases: namely, to examine the 'downstream contexts', as Cave calls them, in which a particular cultural object is received.[7] As with pre-histories, the thought occurred to us that the point of afterlives was not to fix the meaning of the object from a latter-day perspective, but on the contrary to trace the shifting dialogue between the object and its various contexts through time.

What exactly did this thought imply about the relationship between pre-histories and afterlives? We weren't sure. It might be that the two methods, the one looking backwards to an object in a fragmented past and the other looking forwards with an object into an uncertain future, would prove to be perfect mirror-images — with Janus, the god of thresholds and two-way time-travel, presiding. Then again, it might transpire that the relationship between the two methods was altogether less symmetrical, that the part Janus had to play in their pairing was other than that of presiding genius. In any case, it seemed to us that to put pre-histories and afterlives together would provide a useful focus for the symposium and the book we were planning. Useful, we hoped, because it would stimulate reflection and discussion not only about these two approaches and the relations between them but also about the wider value of critical method in the humanities.

I. Pre-Histories

The past that Cave's pre-histories set out to explore survives in particular objects that are firmly rooted in that past and yet seem also to speak to the present. The method of pre-history may be described as an attempt to listen more attentively to the testimony that these objects offer. Cave stresses that large areas of the past are now inaccessible because they are lost to the ravages of time. He places alongside his quotation from *The Go-Between*, as the other epigraph to *Pré-histoires I*, a sentence to this effect in Montaigne's 'Des coches': 'Quand tout ce qui est venu par rapport du passé jusques à nous seroit vray et seroit sçeu par quelqu'un, ce seroit moins que rien au pris de ce qui est ignoré' (III. 6, 908).[8] What remains of the past, then, is not a continent ready to be mastered but an archipelago of fragments waiting to be explored at close quarters by those willing to undertake the journey. Cave characterizes the enterprise of his *Pré-histoires*, indeed, as a form of 'archipelago history'.[9] The journey through that archipelago, like the journey of Rabelais's travellers which inspired the metaphor, is bound to be circuitous and to remain incomplete, but it also contains the promise of rich and strange encounters along the way, as Rabelais's travellers discover.

The comparison with Rabelais is all the more appropriate here in that Cave's pre-histories describe for the most part encounters with particular texts, Rabelais's among them, from that part of the past we call the 'early modern' period. The particular allure — and difficulty — of these texts for us is expressed by their description as 'early modern'. That phrase has come in Anglophone cultural criticism to characterize a series of developments in the period stretching from the late fifteenth to the late eighteenth centuries — the political and economic development and the colonial expansion of European nation states; the rise of vernacular languages, of new forms of literary and philosophical expression, and of a broader reading public; profound shifts in scientific understanding and religious identity; and the emergence of the 'self' as a form of individual secular subjectivity — that seem to announce fundamental features of our 'modern' world. Yet, as Cave has pointed out, 'whatever early modern people may have thought or felt, they could not have thought that they were early modern': the model of history implied by the phrase 'early modern' is, in this sense, 'intrinsically teleological and evolutionary'.[10] We belated moderns need to be wary of projecting on to early modern texts later developments in a story that is familiar to us but of which they can know nothing, of visiting upon them the distortions to which hindsight, unchecked, falls prey. The allure of the 'early modern' *is*, in a certain sense, the difficulty here.

Pre-history, as Cave practises it, does not seek to deny its possession of hindsight. It chooses to acknowledge hindsight's ineradicable presence in the writing of all history in order to limit and control, as much as possible, its inferences.[11] Pre-history offers, as a result, one approach to the question of 'how we read without distortion the signs of a future story'.[12] The precise formulation quoted here post-dates the two volumes of *Pré-histoires* — a fact which merely confirms, in passing, the role of hindsight in the writing of history — but the question is the one that both seek, in different ways, to address. Cave takes various 'signs of a future story' — the emergence of sceptical forms of thought, the 'self', and the notion of suspense in *Pré-histoires I*; the rise of vernacular languages and the economic phenomenon of inflation in *Pré-histoires II* — and uses the pre-historical method in his attempt to read them without distortion. By unsettling and even (in some cases) moving against the flow of history, the pre-historical method seeks to suspend the hindsight that turns these early modern signs into the origins of the story that makes us modern, and encounters them instead in the present tense of their articulation.

The notion of the threshold plays an important role in this respect. The book in which Cave first elaborated the pre-historical method, *Pré-histoires I*, was the first volume in a new series, edited by Michel Jeanneret and Max Engammare at Droz, which took as its title Jeanneret's French translation of the phrase 'the early modern (period)' as 'les seuils de la modernité.' In his introduction to *Pré-histoires II*, Cave spells out his understanding of that translation, stressing that the 'thresholds' of which it speaks are, if not arbitrary, certainly perspectival and time-bound constructions in that they become fully visible only in retrospect.[13] They are for that reason intrinsically provisional, shifting, and — as Jeanneret's translation has it — plural. We are a long way here from a teleological and evolutionary model of history that discovers in the past a source for the origins of the present. It might well be that these thresholds 'cluster and merge to provide the energy for the major turn which carries history into the modern' and that they therefore have a particular role to play in methodologies of the early modern.[14] But he leaves that general question to others. He chooses instead to argue for a 'much more open and flexible map' of the past in general and to stress, in particular, the heuristic value of the threshold as a provisional latter-day construction from which the scattered signs of a pre-history become visible or — to change the metaphor from a visual to an auditory one — as a delicate instrument with which better to capture those 'half-heard voices' to be found in texts of the past.[15]

The pre-historical method remains, as a result, receptive to the affective shock of the texts that it encounters. It characterizes these texts as being often at once 'disturbed' and 'disturbing'.[16] Cave identifies the disturbance that the texts carry with them as signs found in the text of a psychological response to a phenomenon that we latter-day readers view in historical terms: 'ce que j'appelle ici "trouble" se laisse définir comme le signe textuel d'une réponse psychologique à un phénomène qui pour nous est historique.'[17] These signs most often take the form of an abrupt shift at the level of plot, theme, argument, register, syntax or lexis: the sudden arrival in *Pantagruel* (Chapter 9) of a stranger speaking in foreign tongues, for example, or the repeated intrusion of the first-person object pronoun 'moi' in a sentence of the *Essais* dealing with the question of imitation.[18] These signs can be seen as the responses of the individual writer to wider historical phenomena of the early modern period: to the rise of vernacular languages in the emerging nation states of Europe, say, or to new ways of thinking and talking about personal identity. But if they are to be seen as precisely that, signs of an *individual* response, they need to be read in a manner that takes full account of the complex structures — narrative, discursive, poetic, rhetorical, and linguistic — in which they appear. That means studying them in their wider historical context and, at the same time, reading them at close quarters using the instruments of literary analysis. The texts of Rabelais, Montaigne, and others register the shock of developments taking place at the limits of their authors' awareness or understanding. And they not only register it, as the closing pages of *Pré-histoires II* make clear, but also retain the elusive power to transmit something of that shock, that exuberant energy, to their modern readers — Cave among them.[19] Pre-history, as he practises it, offers access to a past that is defined by its elusiveness and its difference from the present. It offers, at the same time, a method of understanding the power of disturbance that texts contain in the rich and strange past to which they belong and that they carry into the present in which we encounter them.

II. Afterlives

Afterlives share with pre-histories the capacity to probe the (often seductive) myths of origin attached to a particular cultural object and to unpick the status of its 'beginning'. In the case of Mignon, Cave has chosen an object of which the first instance in temporal sequence is by no means the most developed. If the appearance of Mignon in Goethe's *Wilhelm Meister* marks the figure's initiatory moment in European literary and cultural history, it remains a marginal, fragmentary beginning: the elements of her story are characterized as 'individual moments of intensity rather than as the manifestations of a fully motivated narrative sequence'.[20] Such a beginning does not constitute a privileged threshold after which successive manifestations are apprehended as 'declensions', so to speak, of the first. Rather, the traditional hierarchy generally assumed between 'real' life and more shadowy afterlife is complicated, even inverted, with Mignon's figure acquiring fresh vitality, power and narrative coherence in a series of new 'lives' — musical, artistic, literary — within European culture in the course of the nineteenth and twentieth centuries. Consequently, the figure moves in the diachronic flow of literary and cultural history across a series of shifting local thresholds, each of which re-calibrates the relation between 'after-' and '-life', as 'Mignon' is incarnated anew in the work of such artists as Balzac, George Eliot or Ambroise Thomas. It is perhaps worth clarifying here the force of the biographical metaphor underpinning the term 'afterlives', which at first sight may appear to be pulling against the archaeological or historiographical implications of 'pre-histories'. In fact, as Cave's studies concerning Mignon demonstrate, afterlives in this sense do not suggest a series of increasingly etiolated existences, or shadow-lives, but rather an astonishingly vital sequence of incarnations or lives made anew. The same is true in the case of Montaigne's *Essais*, which themselves have no fixed point of origin or definitive form, no privileged initiatory threshold. On account of their cultural singularity, it is only in the course of their reception in downstream contexts that their full signifying power is realized.

The afterlives of the *Essais* are not merely 'a discrete series of reinterpretations in alien contexts'; rather, the text's reception 'in some sense completes the meaning of the book, over and over again, without ever exhausting it'.[21]

A second distinguishing feature of the method of afterlives is its receptiveness to objects that are situated at the margins of culture or that cross and re-cross between genres and forms in the course of their temporal trajectory. Both Montaigne's *Essais* and Mignon occupy marginal positions, but of very different kinds. In Montaigne's case, the marginality is generic: the *Essais* resist classification according to the schema of Renaissance as well as modern intellectual disciplines. As a result of what Cave identifies as 'Montaigne's deliberate strategy of positioning himself at the margins of contemporary thought and scholarship', the *Essais*'s afterlives weave to and fro across the boundaries between autobiographical, philosophical, historical and belle-lettristic narrative.[22] In the case of Goethe's Mignon, the object of enquiry is a socially marginal figure at the periphery of the novels' narrative structure, but one who, in her subsequent incarnations within a variety of cultural forms — prose narrative, poetry, theatre, art, opera — occupies a perpetually shifting position in relation to the social and cultural centre. In consequence, her figure assumes a peculiarly unstable, centrifugal, elusive quality and it requires sustained attention on the part of the critic to track the oblique course of her movement through time and to keep the object of enquiry in focus. The critic may find him- or herself in some interesting 'marginal' company — among the eclectic members of a circus community, including Fevvers, Mignon and the tiger-taming 'Princess of Abyssinia', in Angela Carter's *Nights at the Circus*, for example, or with Mirah as a representative of Jewish culture and identity in Eliot's *Daniel Deronda* — and so has the opportunity to render audible, as it were, voices usually only half-heard. This carries a suggestion for critics who are inclined to approach the reception of an object from within the bounds of their own academic specialism or to focus their attention upon limited forms of cultural production: in cases such as that of Mignon it is not possible adequately to trace the object's trajectory without opening up the enquiry to a variety of cultural forms, marginal as well as dominant.

A further characteristic of the method is the open attitude it assumes towards identity and resemblance in both defining and tracking the cultural object. Regarding Mignon, the figure's afterlife is pursued through incarnations in characters such as Eliot's Caterina or Mirah, or Balzac's Modeste whose similarity to Mignon has generally escaped the attention of previous critics, being considered of too delicate and fugitive a kind. The method of afterlives operates within a framework of what might be termed 'familial' resemblances; in effect, the critic is identifying a subtle genetic trace as it re-appears in incarnations downstream. The story of Mignon's afterlives succeeds in restoring to the foundling child a kind of extended family structure. Cave himself confirms the appositeness of the familial metaphor, describing two of George Eliot's fictional characters whom he seeks to reclaim in the context of Mignon's afterlife as 'close cousins of Goethe's foundling'.[23] By recognizing and exploring looser 'familial' similarities, which are not in fact vague but are based upon precise structural and situational parallels, this method is alert to the significance of resemblances that might otherwise slip through the grid of a more rigid framework of likeness.[24] The model of influence being advocated is explicitly adversarial, operating according to a principle of 'oppositional repetition' or 'motivated difference', in which differences and divergences from the model are freighted with significant meaning and so analysed with full seriousness and care. It is legitimate, Cave argues, to seek to trace the connection between objects that might differ in substantial respects from one another because 'the presence of a "model" is more often palpable through the precise way in which it is changed or countered than through more passive procedures of intertextual recycling'.[25] As the framework of resemblance is expanded in this way, so too there is a corresponding proliferation and diversification of the incarnations of the object, and a multiplicity of trajectories plotted through time. The form assumed by the *Essais*'s afterlife in Descartes's writings shows the dynamic of 'motivated difference' at work. It would appear that in making the first-person subject central to his thought concerning the *cogito*, Descartes stands as a direct heir to Montaigne's first-person writing; at the same time, however, he performs a deliberate reversal of Montaigne's method by creating a first-person singular subject with no object and by using a radical sceptical strategy in order to establish a method expressly intended to eradicate sceptical doubt. It is in such a movement of differentiation, suggests Cave, that the force of Montaigne's *Essais* is felt, and in the downstream context of such a generative reversal that, paradoxical as it may seem, the *Essais* have their afterlife.[26]

Just as this method attaches importance to familial similarities in identifying successive instances of a figure or object, so too it acknowledges the central role played by affect — the observer's own shock of recognition in the encounter with resemblance — in any story of reception.[27] It resembles the method of pre-histories in engaging openly with the power to disturb or move carried in the object's trace, as constituting a fundamental way in which that object is freed from passivity and actively participates in an encounter or dialogue with its own future, as-yet-unknown, interpreters. In this respect, the biographical metaphor implied in the term 'afterlife' recovers some of its force: the object, revenant that it is, retains a power to haunt. Indeed, certain objects, including the *Essais*, manifest a perceptible anxiety concerning their own future reception, an anxiety evident in Montaigne's own use of the revenant trope to evoke the possibility of his future return to haunt the interpreter: 'Je reviendrois volontiers de l'autre monde pour démentir celuy qui me formeroit autre que je n'estois, fut ce pour m'honorer' (III. 9, 983). Alert to the echoes of such emotional disturbance, Cave gives them full weight in the story of the object's reception. He draws attention, for example, to the arresting pathos attached to the figure of Mignon, on account of her excluded, foundling status, her physical fragility, her vulnerable youth and the abuse she suffered, a pathos that must be acknowledged in order to understand the extraordinary interest and attention she attracted as a subject in literature, music and the visual arts in the nineteenth century.[28] Other approaches within the field of reception studies also reserve an important place for the workings of affect, most notably perhaps Bloom in his psychoanalytic framework for the interpretation of relations between the Romantic poets and their precursors, *The Anxiety of Influence*, and Greene in his characterization of the relationship between Renaissance authors and their predecessors in antiquity as conditioned by a sense of yearning, vulnerability and loss.[29] However, both Bloom and Greene appear to be concerned with the affective charge and emotional response located *within* and *between* the texts, materials and authors whom they are considering, while Cave is more explicit in acknowledging the force of those emotional reactions that are generated by the dynamic encounter with and complex interaction between the interpreter or critic and the object, and that are situated in him or her as much as in the object's trace.[30] His concern is not with affective responses *per se* but insofar as they suggest or reveal an underlying cognitive dissonance.

So perhaps 'afterlives' may best be understood as ghost stories, albeit of a rather singular kind.[31] They are, as we have seen, revenant narratives, accounts of a haunting of the cultural imagination by figures and objects with a particular power to interest, disturb and move. In the wake of Montaigne (and in dialogue with a powerful strand in modern criticism), Cave tropes his own analysis of Mignon's afterlives as an account of successive 'returns from the dead'.[32] As the characteristics associated with the method of afterlives outlined here suggest, the critic is attempting to trace the progress of a labile, Protean object, as fleeting and evanescent as any ghost, in its oblique and shifting forward progress through time, to track that object as it crosses a succession of thresholds into diverse downstream contexts, metamorphosing as it goes. Afterlives, like pre-histories, seek to resist the teleological drive, and so the critic's path may lead, through unexpected connections and border crossings, to some surprising places. The interpretative goal must surely be to remain sufficiently flexible and fleet of foot to 'move with' the chosen object in its onward path through time.

III. The Contributions

How, then, do the contributors to this volume engage with the methods of pre-histories and afterlives from the perspective of their own work?

Neil Kenny discusses the range of symptomatic affects, including unease and anxiety, that a pre-historian might attribute to his or her source-materials. At the same time, he asks what kind of affect is operating within the pre-historian that might inform the manner in which he or she apprehends and interprets those same materials, and he probes the nature of the connection between affect which is attributed and affect which is experienced. The starting-point for his enquiry is the importance that Cave's method of pre-history attaches to affects betrayed by the source-materials. In Cave's work, such affects are held to be symptoms of experiences or perceptions that a writer cannot quite express, because an adequate framework for expressing them does not yet exist. Kenny goes on to ask how the pre-historian apprehends such affects — whether directly, through a kind of empathetic affectivity, or indirectly, either through analysis which reveals the traces of a now-absent affect, or conversely through arriving at the point at which the pre-historian's analysis reaches its limit and senses something that goes beyond its powers of expression.

Ben Morgan engages in a dialogue with the method of pre-history as it relates to the notion of selfhood. He does so by juxtaposing more recent ways of understanding personal identity with that to be found in talks that Meister Eckhart gave to novices at the Dominican Friary in Erfurt in the closing years of the thirteenth century. Eckhart's advice is disturbing to a modern subject, for whom a sense of agency and responsibility is a defining attribute of identity, since it suggests we leave unresolved the question of who the agent of our action is. One response to the ambiguities of Eckhart's texts has been to see in them a precursor of modern philosophies of identity, such as those of Fichte. But the power of Eckhart's texts for a twenty-first century reading lies precisely in their ability to surprise us out of familiar habits, and make us question what we think we know about our modern habits of individuality. In particular, they draw attention to the shared activity that underpins and qualifies our sense of individuality. The attention to the specific formulations through which identity was lived in Eckhart's milieu, and the desire to escape a teleological account of modern identity, are inspired by Terence Cave's work on the pre-history of selfhood. At the same time, the essay emphasizes the continuities with the present that the revised account of Eckhartian identity draws to our attention, showing modern selves the habits that survive alongside, and call in question, their desire to be agents of their own identities.

Mary McKinley chooses the figure of the sibyl as a paradigmatic point of contact between the frameworks of pre-histories and afterlives. She centres her argument upon the historical particularity of one artistic manifestation of the figure: the cycle of twelve sibyls represented in the early Renaissance carved wooden choir stalls at St Bertrand-de-Comminges in the French Pyrenees. She argues that the iconographic cycles of sibyls in French churches constitute a privileged moment in the long history of representations of the sibyls, at which they can, as pagan figures of wisdom, appear side by side with saints and apostles, in a 'spirit of religious and cultural syncretism' particular to the period. McKinley acknowledges the affective charge of her source-materials and examines how this charge might be understood and conveyed in her work as a historian. By drawing out the enigmatic and vatic qualities of the sibylline figure looking both forwards and backwards in time, she shows how the story of the sibyls of St Bertrand can be cast as both 'pre-history' and 'afterlife'.

Anna Holland engages with Cave's notion of afterlives by focusing upon a single emblematic image that has its origins in Greek and Roman literature and by tracing its afterlife through a shifting sequence of manifestations in Renaissance literary and musical texts. The image she selects is itself the representation of an afterlife — the potential of the poet's literary reputation to transcend death, figured as the poet's metamorphosis into a swan. She charts the transformations and transmogrifications of this figure of metamorphosis, and explores the varying nature of its affective charge in the context of each of its successive incarnations. She suggests that the sensitivity of Cave's notion of afterlife, as of pre-history, to the more disquieting kinds of affect such as anxiety and anguish makes it particularly well-adapted to apprehending the traces of this image of poetic afterlife. For, she argues, the figure retains an enduring capacity to generate unease and disturbance — but disturbance that functions in heuristic and creative, rather than disabling, ways.

John O'Brien suggests that Montaigne's discussion of Epicurus and pleasure can be perceived in the light of the distinction drawn by Cave that Montaigne marks not so much a 'breakthrough' in the intellectual and literary history of pleasure as a 'breakout', one symptom of a slow and complex evolution that a downstream reading will see retrospectively as a source of decisive change. Montaigne creates a challenge to received Renaissance views on pleasure through the naming of Epicurus and the use of paradox (in the early modern sense of that word). But this is no simple valorization of pleasure in which Montaigne might be our ancestor: the gap that he opens up between Epicurus and his significance anticipates the problems in the afterlife of this Greek thinker.

Kate Tunstall is inspired by the close textual analysis so characteristic of Cave's work, in particular his fine-tuned attention to textual *volte-face*, verbal rhythms, and, in particular, intertextual echoes. She takes as her object of study two passages from the eighteenth-century French philosopher and writer Denis Diderot's *Salon de 1767*, in which Diderot writes about portraits of himself, the images that posterity will have of him, that is to say, his own 'afterlife'. Unlike most work on Diderot's art criticism, which tends to adopt a comparative text-image approach, Tunstall focuses here exclusively on the texts. She argues that, in his commentary on his painted portraits and in the narrative and descriptive self-portraits he puts in their place, Diderot makes dense intertextual reference to Montaigne's *Essais*. The intertext is not explicitly acknowledged by Diderot; but close analysis of his themes (the 'moi', friendship, change) and careful tracking of his peculiar logical switch-backs and frequent use of 'if' clauses lead Tunstall to suggest that Diderot's textual portraits are a deliberately paradoxical affair, in which he creates portraits of himself as someone else, as Montaigne.

Marian Hobson argues for the value of bringing to certain texts what she calls a 'rear-mirror view', in other words, an interpretative context which is, in chronological terms, posterior to the text's composition. She specifically distinguishes this method from a reception history or an afterlife, allying it instead with an 'anti-realist' or 'intuitionist' notion of truth expressed in the work of the philosopher Michael Dummett. Like Tunstall, Hobson takes as her example the work of Diderot, though she focuses in particular on his dialogue *Le Neveu de Rameau*. She shows how elements in its future — those found in the work of nineteenth- and twentieth-century philosophers like Hegel and Derrida — may be said to offer a deferred context for Diderot's experimental text.

Wes Williams brings the keywords of Cave's recent work and of this volume — pre-histories and afterlives — into dialogue with a further paired set of terms: dedication and filiation. The focus of this study is upon a particular metaphor animating the work of Montaigne, that of the brainchild; its method is speculative border-crossing and time travel. In encouraging cross-disciplinary travel from *essai* to film, and back again, Williams seeks to engage with two key aspects of Cave's own work: methodological rigour and speculative play.

IV. Looking Backwards, Looking Forwards

The contributions, taken as a whole, cover a wide spectrum of periods (from the late thirteenth century to the twentieth), materials and disciplines (those of intellectual history, iconography and art criticism, as well as literature and film), and languages (Greek, Latin, Italian, French, and German). They may be said as a result to do some kind of justice to the wide range across which Terence Cave has worked in the last four decades — and therefore to offer a fitting tribute to his work. Some gaps, it is true, remain: the area of nineteenth- and twentieth-century literature is relatively undeveloped here, as are the connections between literature and music, both of which are central to his current and ongoing work on the figure of Mignon. But the point of the exercise was never to achieve the illusion of complete coverage. It was — and this perhaps needs to be reiterated on the threshold of the main text — to invite contributors to take part in a collective discussion of method by engaging with pre-histories and/or afterlives from the perspective of their own work.

One result of this invitation is that various questions about these methods return at different moments. A first cluster of questions concerns the applicability of pre-histories and afterlives, while a second cluster explores the role of affect in these methods. If pre-histories amount to a 'method', in other words an approach suited to a particular set of materials, then the broader applicability of that method needs to be considered. Can pre-histories be applied to cultural phenomena other than literary texts? And to periods other than the early modern? And even, more particularly, to the present? The method sets out to recover past testimonies that differ in important ways from present concerns. But could past testimonies, once recovered, not be used to improve our understanding of present concerns? Afterlives, which appear to be more evenly scattered than pre-histories through the field of history, raise similar questions of applicability. What, if anything, does the afterlife of a particular phenomenon reveal about the wider historical moments to which it belongs? And how is the phenomenon inflected by the different media and cultural contexts in which it appears? Like pre-histories, afterlives also raise recurrent questions about the role of affect in critical practice, since they set out to examine the disturbance that certain texts (in the broadest sense of the word) carry with them. To what range of psychological responses in the texts may that disturbance be said to correspond? Moreover, if the texts still transmit something of that disturbance, it seems that the psychological responses of the critic to those texts also have an ineradicable part to play in the analysis offered. How are the psychological responses carried by texts and experienced by their readers to be understood, and what are their cognitive implications? Are they necessarily different because separated in time, or can they sometimes signal a shared preoccupation across time, a meeting of minds? And how does the relationship between them condition, in turn, the dialogue between past and present that pre-histories and afterlives make possible?

Implicit in our invitation was the thought that, while quite distinct in certain respects, pre-histories and afterlives might themselves be brought together in various ways. Some of the contributions that follow focus on one of the methods in an attempt to pursue its implications: the essays of Neil Kenny and Ben Morgan are primarily concerned with pre-histories, for example, and those of Anna Holland and Kate Tunstall with afterlives. Other contributions, such as those of Mary McKinley, John O'Brien, and Wes Williams, reveal connections between these two methods from the perspective of their work or, as in the case of Marian Hobson, suggest an alternative method to suit the particular materials chosen. No overarching conclusions are reached about the relationship between pre-histories and afterlives, except perhaps that both are powerfully implicated in the acts of retrospective and prospective exploration that are central to the arts and humanities, so that the choice of Janus as attendant god was appropriate enough. What matters here, above all, is the process whereby specialists in different areas of the subject come together to take part in a collective discussion about critical method. Terence Cave adds his voice in the epilogue to this book and, in so doing, continues the dialogue he has done so much to foster.

Notes to the Introduction

1. L. P. Hartley, *The Go-Between* (Harmondsworth: Penguin, 1976), p. 7.
2. *Pré-histoires I*, p. 11. The first part of Hartley's opening sentence has also been used by David Lowenthal as the title of a book concerning nostalgia and the manifold ways in which, for better or worse, we respond to the past. See *The Past is a Foreign Country* (Cambridge: Cambridge University Press, 1985).
3. Hartley, *The Go-Between*, p. 21.
4. Terence Cave, *Recognitions: A Study in Poetics* (Oxford: Clarendon Press, 1988). On Mignon, see n. 5 below.
5. The articles in question are 'Mignon's Afterlife in the Fiction of George Eliot', *Rivista di letterature moderne e comparate*, 56 (2003), 165–82, and 'Modeste and Mignon: Balzac rewrites Goethe', *French Studies*, 59 (2005), 311–25. The second article begins by recalling the title of the first: 'Mignon [...] had a European afterlife of extraordinary range and complexity' (p. 311). A further article concerning Mignon, 'Singing with Tigers: Recognition in *Wilhelm Meister, Daniel Deronda* and *Nights at the Circus*', is to be published in the proceedings of a colloquium held at New York University in April 2003, currently in press with Peter Lang; it will also be re-printed in *Retrospectives: Essays in Literature, Poetics and Cultural History by Terence Cave*, ed. by Neil Kenny and Wes Williams (London: Legenda, 2008).
6. See in particular Cave's 'Master-Mind Lecture: Montaigne', *Proceedings of the British Academy*, 131 (2005), 183–203 (pp. 197–202), his article 'Locating the Early Modern', in *Theory and the Early Modern*, ed. by Michael Moriarty and John O'Brien (*Paragraph*, 29 (2006)), pp. 12–26 (pp. 20–22), and the chapter entitled 'Writing for the Future' in *Montaigne* (London: Granta Books, 2007), pp. 106–16.
7. 'Locating the Early Modern', p. 21.
8. *Pré-histoires I*, p. 11.
9. 'Une histoire en archipel' (*Pré-histoires I*, p. 14). Cave notes (ibid., p. 13) that he borrowed the metaphor from Rabelais's travellers via Frank Lestringant's essay 'L'Insulaire de Rabelais ou la fiction en archipel' in his book *Ecrire le monde à la Renaissance* (Caen: Paradigme, 1993), pp. 159–85.
10. 'Master-Mind Lecture: Montaigne', p. 185; 'Locating the Early Modern', p. 13.
11. This choice is in marked contrast to the approach taken in Cave's earlier study, *The Cornucopian Text: Problems of Writing in the French Renaissance* (Oxford: Clarendon Press, 1979), which gives an altogether freer rein to the drawing of inferences and the making of connections. In his Introduction to that study, Cave describes it as the result of 'a convergence between an attempt to deal with the empirical evidence of sixteenth-century writing and an attempt to grasp important aspects of modern critical reflection', insisting on the 'conciliation of different possibilities' that this approach implies (p. xvi). On the difference between this approach and that of pre-history, see *Pré-histoires II*, p. 189.

12. 'Master-Mind Lecture: Montaigne', p. 186.

13. *Pré-histoires II*, pp. 12–15.

14. 'Locating the Early Modern', p. 22.

15. 'Locating the Early Modern', p. 22 (see also p. 13).

16. *Pré-histoires I*, p. 15 ('troublés ou troublants'). Other English translations of these adjectives and of the noun related to them, *trouble*, are possible. 'Unease' is a good choice for *trouble*, for example, but works less well in relation to the pair of adjectives quoted above.

17. *Pré-histoires I*, p. 16. 'Psychological' and 'psychologique' here carry cognitive as well as affective connotations.

18. *Pré-histoires II*, pp. 27–101; *Pré-histoires I*, pp. 15–16 and 110–27.

19. *Pré-histoires II*, pp. 189–91. Cave talks here of 'une énergie de l'imagination qui émane des textes polymorphes de cette période exubérante et inquiète' and notes that his desire to account for this energy connects his *Pré-histoires* with the earlier and, as we've seen, methodologically different project of *The Cornucopian Text* (p. 189).

20. 'Mignon's Afterlife in the Fiction of George Eliot', p. 168.

21. *Montaigne*, p. 114.

22. See *Montaigne*, p. 19.

23. 'Mignon's Afterlife in the Fiction of George Eliot', p. 166.

24. See for example 'Mignon's Afterlife in the Fiction of George Eliot', p. 174.

25. 'Modeste and Mignon: Balzac Rewrites Goethe', p. 321.

26. On the relations between Montaigne's *Essais* and the Cartesian *cogito*, see 'Master-Mind Lecture: Montaigne', esp. pp. 197–202.

27. The powerful affective (as well as cognitive) impact of acts of recognition and their place within the larger discursive frameworks of narrative and plot is an important dimension of Cave's study, *Recognitions*, a work which foreshadows in significant ways his subsequent interest in the figure of Mignon; see *Recognitions: A Study in Poetics* (Oxford: Clarendon Press, 1990), esp. pp. 144–80 and pp. 260–70.

28. Goethe himself acknowledges the pain associated with Mignon's story, fragmentary and episodic as it is, in scenes in the later *Wanderjahre* when Wilhelm is visiting Italy and the place of Mignon's childhood; these scenes are discussed in 'Singing with Tigers: Recognition in *Wilhelm Meister, Daniel Deronda* and *Nights at the Circus*'.

29. See Harold Bloom, *The Anxiety of Influence: A Theory of Poetry* (London, Oxford and New York: Oxford University Press, 1973) and Thomas M. Greene, *The Light in Troy: Imitation and Discovery in Renaissance Poetry* (New Haven and London: Yale University Press, 1982) and *The Vulnerable Text: Essays on Renaissance Literature* (New York: Columbia University Press, 1986).

30. In his studies on Mignon, Cave explores the ways in which the authors of Mignon's afterlives seek in some sense to redress the wrongs done to her, and to compensate for the tragically belated recognitions — of identity and of passion — that in Goethe's narrative come too late, after death.

31. Cave argues that to the extent that the *Essais* succeed in liberating themselves from the constraints of external context and of time, they are 'the best ghost that Montaigne could have wished for: they remain in this world, always ready to speak for him'. See *Montaigne*, p. 107.

32. Evoking structural parallels between Mignon's narrative and that of Caterina in Eliot's *Scenes of Clerical Life*, Cave writes, 'It is exactly as if [...] Mignon, though still damaged, had revived and returned for a while to the world'. See 'Mignon's Afterlife in the Fiction of George Eliot', p. 173.

CHAPTER 1

❖

Passions, Emotions, and Pre-Histories

Neil Kenny

This paper argues that the method outlined by Terence Cave, in *Pré-histoires I* and *Pré-histoires II*, opens up fresh possibilities regarding a question that has vexed some historians over the last few decades: how can one write history in a way that takes into account (what we now call) emotions?

Can historians have any access to the emotions of those whose history they write? For periods or cultures remote from the historian's own — such as sixteenth- and early-seventeenth-century France and Europe in the case of Cave's two books — an initial step might be to provisionally suspend the very category ('emotions') which drives the investigation, since its anachronism risks distorting the categories (such as 'passions' and 'affections') which moulded people's experience and their ways of thinking about it.

But Cave's method also opens up new possibilities for taking into account — and even acknowledging a productive role for — what one might call feelings and intuitions in the historian him- or herself. This prospect might seem alarming, an invitation to sloppy sentimentalism. Indeed, it is because of justified qualms about the threat posed by emotion and intuition to historical rigour that historians have often preferred to distance historiography from them. However, I will argue that Cave's method offers very specific ways of using them to *enhance* historiographical rigour.

I. Tracing Past Passions

Cave's case studies in these two books are of various conceptual, literary, or socio-economic phenomena which arose in the sixteenth and seventeenth centuries and have often been understood retrospectively as harbingers of modernity, thereby helping the period earn the label 'early modern'. They include: Pyrrhonism; the concept of 'the self'; the incorporation of 'suspense' into narrative fiction; the relativist notion that one's own culture is not necessarily a stable, absolute viewpoint from which others can be judged; rampant price-rises and currency devaluation (*l'enchérissement*, which we would today interpret as inflation), at a time of trade expansion; and so on.

Yet Cave's aim is not to write an intellectual, literary, or economic history of these, at least not if one means by that a history that posits the existence of the phenomenon in question — as philosophical method, concept, literary innovation, or economic shift — as something separable from period perceptions of it. Rather, the aim is to discover how those emergent phenomena — philosophical, literary, economic — were *perceived*,[1] how people seem to have *felt* about them, in both a cognitive sense (how the phenomena were interpreted or explained) and an affective one (what passions they aroused).

In other words, the aim is to glimpse people's *experiences* through texts that happen to have survived. Cave argues that even systems of belief, such as Neoplatonism, were experienced in practice not as pristine, coherent sets of ideas but rather as perceptual frameworks that were constantly twisted, battered, altered by their collisions with numerous others, producing endlessly singular results (*Pré-histoires I*, pp. 85–86). But the actual experience of those collisions is largely lost, even to the sensitive historian, whose sources are only 'la forme fragmentaire d'une expérience perdue' (*Pré-histoires I*, p. 13). From them can be retrieved the symptoms (*Pré-histoires I*, p. 178) of an experience that is in itself largely irretrievable.

A crucial part of that experience is what we now call emotions or feelings. Cave focuses especially on symptoms of one cluster of (what we now call) emotions or psychological states — anxiety, fear, unease, disturbance (*inquiétude, angoisse, anxiété, peur, trouble, perturbation*). He suggests that these have a particularly intimate relationship to historical change and so to the question of pre-history (*Pré-histoires I*, p. 180). Phenomena which were experienced as novel — Pyrrhonism, *l'enchérissement*, or the stretching of the first-person grammatical subject in Montaigne's *Essais*, following which *le moi* emerged, especially with Descartes and Pascal — were also experienced as disturbing, unsettling, anxiety-provoking. Viewed retrospectively, this disturbance is a sign that the arrival of, for example, *le moi* (like that of its English cousin 'the self') represented the crossing of a threshold into an unknown territory which, from the point of view of the texts which immediately preceded it, was either entirely unforetold or else only dimly foretold in ways that little resemble what did in fact subsequently emerge (*Pré-histoires I*, pp. 111–27).

This method therefore makes no a priori separation of affect from cognition. To some extent, the anxieties, disturbances, and so on of which texts are symptomatic are cognitive frustrations with phenomena which people experienced as 'étrange[s], difficile[s] à expliquer' (*Pré-histoires II*, p. 13). So, although this method involves vigilant attention to traces of (what we would now call) past emotional experience, it is no more a straightforward answer to recent calls for a 'history of emotions'[2] than it is a continuation of an older 'history of ideas'. Rather, the prey it stalks is the inseparable intertwining of 'emotions', 'ideas', and much else in an 'experience' that is described not directly by the historian, but indirectly, through its textual symptoms.

For Cave, those textual symptoms can, by definition, only be detected by close readings, and by historically informed ones at that, such as ones which, in the case of early modern texts, follow the grooves of the rhetorical practices according to which the texts were composed. One such groove was the attempt to arouse strong passions (*pathè*) and so proffer one kind of persuasive proof (*pathos*)[3] alongside the other two kinds, *logos* (rational argument) and *ethos* (usually involving presentation of the writer's or speaker's character as trustworthy). However, Cave's method does not — any more than the system of rhetoric itself — offer an interpretive key or grid according to which, for instance, a particular figure or technique could be reliably interpreted as a symptom of a given passion. Rather, their interpretation is dependent on context. For example, the humanist rhetoric of copiousness (*copia*) — the profound ambivalence of which Cave famously revealed a generation ago[4] — is variously interpreted here as a symptom of fear or of (ambivalent) joy.[5] Moreover, Cave's search for symptoms of lost *experience* leads him to go beyond any box-ticking application of the period's rhetorical *theory* to his chosen texts. For example, *logos* is scrutinized less for its triumphs than for the moments when it breaks down, for '*volte-face* logiques' such as the one which led demonologist Jean Bodin to both express and deny hatred for Johann Wier and witches, which suggests that confident orthodox attempts by Bodin and others to circumscribe discursively the domain of the diabolic were troubled by gnawing passions.[6]

However, although Cave prioritizes *inquiétude*, *angoisse*, and so on, he occasionally argues that a given text also — or instead — contains symptoms of more positive emotions or psychological states (as we might now call them), such as joy, hope, wonder, happiness. This raises the question whether some areas of affective experience (such as *inquiétude*) are more readily symptomatic of historical change than are others (such as joy).

Cave's own examples suggest that joy, hope, wonder, happiness can indeed be indicative of historical change. For instance, although fear of the Other is prominent in some of Rabelais's writing (such as the *Tiers livre* and *Quart livre*), the fragile happiness glimpsed in Pantagruel's befriending of the emphatically alien Panurge (in *Pantagruel*, 1532) can be interpreted as the crossing of a micro-threshold within a pre-history of the notion of cultural relativism (*Pré-histoires II*, pp. 96–99). Or, to take another example: in the *Quart livre* of 1552, when the travellers stop at the first island (Medamothi) and purchase some marvellous, fantastical objects, 'L'allégresse du voyage se concrétise pour la première fois dans une expérience, à la fois immédiate et symbolique, de l'exotique' (*Pré-histoires II*, pp. 108–09). The fact that this episode introduces into French the term *exotique* pins down its relation to a historical shift which is echoed here by the exhilaration of encountering the unknown.[7] The exhilaration is perhaps connected not only to contemporary voyages of 'discovery' but also to (what Cave shows in *Pré-histoires II* to be) the *hope* which accompanies anxiety when people contemplate purchasing and bartering, as they did on a vast scale in this age of rapid commercial expansion.[8]

So, although positive passions such as hope are not evoked especially often in the *Pré-histoires* books (and, even when they are, remain closely shadowed by their more negative twins), nonetheless Cave has opened up ways of exploring *their* connection to historical change too. Wonder, for example, to which Cave occasionally alludes, which was often considered to be a passion in the early modern period, and which was judged sometimes positively, sometimes ambivalently or negatively, is likely to be particularly closely connected to historical change because it was conceived as a response to new, unfamiliar, often inexplicable objects. The relation of wonder to new experiences that were engendered by travel,[9] and by the study of nature,[10] has indeed been tellingly investigated in recent years. But I suspect that there is still ample scope for pursuing, both in these contexts and others, the specific question of the extent to which expressions of wonder may be interpreted as symptoms of new, puzzling experiences which people may have had as they approached or crossed what Cave calls micro-thresholds — the innumerable, local points of transition from a genre, conceptual framework, or practice to another.

This approach might involve, for example, trying to historicize textual clues that wonder, directed at incomprehensible objects, was bound up with other passions, complicating both them and wonder. Lucien Febvre lists many texts as powerful evidence for the ubiquitousness of fear in sixteenth-century France, including for example a 1577 pamphlet entitled *Sommaire description de l'effroyable météore et vision merveilleuse naguères veüe en l'air au-dessus du chasteau et l'Aubépin, proche de la ville de Saint-Amour en la Franche-Comté de Bourgongne, par M. Himbert de Billy, natif de Charlieu en Lyonnais* (Lyon, Benoist Rigaud).[11] But the familiar collocation of the vocabulary of wonder ('merveilleuse') with that of fear ('effroyable') here suggests that fear was less straightforward than Febvre allows. Only a range of carefully dated contexts, including those of evolving perceptions of meteors (including around Lyon in this case), might help one begin to assess the relation here between the two passions evoked.

Another, related research direction arises from Cave's demonstration that the sixteenth-century pre-histories and emergence of Pyrrhonism had a crucial, inescapably affective dimension (*Pré-histoires I*, pp. 23–35). That dimension was itself a latter-day echo of the anger (at our inability to know anything with certainty) which, according to Sextus Empiricus, had led in the first instance to the ancient discovery of the Pyrrhonist suspension of judgement. Sextus compares that fruitful anger to that of Apelles, who stumbled across a technique for painting the foam on a horse's mouth by flinging his sponge at the canvas, exasperated at his failure to represent the foam in a life-like way.[12] The passions and (what we might now call) psychological factors for which Cave finds textual evidence in representations of Pyrrhonism by Gianfrancesco Pico della Mirandola (1520), Rabelais (*Tiers livre*, 1545), and Henri Estienne (1562) variously include anxiety, impatience, more anger, and even a kind of mental fever which Estienne describes as curing his bodily one homeopathically.[13]

And yet, as this last example and Cave's readings of Montaigne and others show (*Pré-histoires I*, pp. 35–50), Pyrrhonism had curative, enabling, liberating effects that ricocheted back and forth from its disabling ones. So Cave has opened up rich possibilities for researching further what one might provisionally call the 'positive' affective dimension of the reception of Pyrrhonism, as well as the negative one from which it was often inseparable. To what extent might (what were often considered in the period to be) the passions of joy, daring, desire, or love have characterized philosophical investigations that were encouraged by the emergence of Pyrrhonism or, for that matter, by the earlier humanist promotion of Academic, Ciceronian scepticism? It might be fruitful to ask this question even of texts — such as Du Bartas's celebrated philosophical poem *La Sepmaine* (1578) or François Béroalde de Verville's extraordinary miscellany *Le Palais des curieux* (1612) — which do not apply any sceptical method systematically and yet seem to use strategies derived from scepticism as they go about promoting conjecture and speculation, either periodically (Du Bartas) or persistently (Verville).

Beneath and within such specific projects, which would entail examining the possible relation of particular passions to historical change, there lurks an even broader research field which Cave's 'pre-histories' method has helped prise open: the pre-histories of the emotions themselves.

As we have seen, the precise aim of the *Pré-histoires* books is to write histories not of anxiety, fear, and so on, but rather of period perceptions of specific, new phenomena — perceptions which were permeated by (what we might today call) emotions and psychological states such as anxiety and fear. Cave has not primarily set out to write pre-histories of modern categories such as 'emotions' or 'psychological states', but at every juncture his analysis gestures towards the fact that those categories do themselves have pre-histories, that they neither map onto sixteenth- and seventeenth-century categories nor should be tacitly treated by historians as superior, truer, more sophisticated forms of them. Cave's asides repeatedly distinguish between modern and earlier categories in this domain.[14] His own language is often oriented towards the period's: most of his key terms (such as *trouble* and *perturbation*) for the kinds of experience he claims to detect had rich webs of relevant meaning in the period itself (which would indeed lend themselves fruitfully to further investigation); and he emphasizes that, even in the period, people's attempts to identify and categorize passions were often consciously ambivalent and fluctuating (*Pré-histoires I*, pp. 99–106).

All of this opens up further possibilities for the examination of the relationship between modern and earlier categories in this context. Because Cave's method provides a way for historians to train their 'pre-historical' sights on the passions (and on their successors, the emotions), it has the potential to inject greater lucidity into the 'history of the emotions', which has been beset with problems of anachronism or presentism.

The very phrase 'the history of the emotions' implies the use of a modern category — emotion — to study, say, pre-modern experience, for which it is inevitably a distorting lens. As Thomas Dixon has shown, the category of the emotions, while not new in the nineteenth century, became dominant then, largely replacing the passions, appetites, affections, sentiments, and so on. It was not a replacement of like with like. Using a method partly akin to Cave's, Dixon teases out crucial differences between modern 'emotions' and their predecessors. For example, whereas in the nineteenth century emotions were largely secular and amoral, passions were entwined with theological and moral frameworks; whereas many early modern thinkers respected distinctions periodically proposed by St Augustine and St Thomas Aquinas between appetites (such as lust), passions (such as fear), and affections (such as religious love), on the other hand the overarching category of the emotions eroded such distinctions.[15]

In contrast to Dixon and Cave, those historians who are less reticent about retrospectively applying categories like the 'emotions' tend perhaps do so in two ways. Some, with no theoretical fanfare, apply the term 'emotion' in unobtrusive ways that might strike their modern readers as commonsensical, rather than defining the term using modern disciplines such as cognitive psychology. The 'commonsensical' approach has the advantage of not imposing on, say, early modern texts a rigid theoretical framework which might be alien to them, but it may have the disadvantage of applying modern popular psychology to them in tacit, unexamined ways. This was pointed out scathingly by Lucien Febvre in his famous 1941 call for a history of affectivity. Febvre lambasted historians for relying on 'Cette espèce de sagesse un peu prudhommesque, à base de vieux proverbes, de ressouvenirs littéraires fanés, de prudences acquises ou héritées qui sert à nos contemporains de guide dans leurs relations quotidiennes avec leurs semblables'.[16] For those of us who have fallen into this trap rather often, this still makes uncomfortable reading.

A second approach is to put one's theoretical cards on the table, to use the insights of modern cognitive psychologists, anthropologists, psychoanalysts, or even historians and literary critics to adopt a theory of emotion and apply it to past texts.[17] This approach has considerable advantages. It can be more lucid and transparent than the first; it can heuristically lead historians to ask extremely fruitful questions of their sources. Febvre himself advocated it in that article, but the now dated character of the psychological theory upon which he drew (that of his associate Henri Wallon) is a reminder that such theory is always itself situated in history. Even the best informed, most sophisticated and powerful current theory used by historians — such as the one recently developed by William Reddy — will eventually look dated, and will perhaps be seen more clearly than in its heyday to have devoted special attention to those dimensions of the past which seemed to vindicate it most.

In practice, examples of both the commonsensical and the theoretical approach often contain elements of a third approach, which in its purest form involves trying to eschew modern models of the emotions when studying, say, early modern passions. To attempt this, one needs to begin by identifying and making explicit modern models, not to apply them but — as it were — to exorcize them. This preliminary exorcizing amounts to a highly condensed version of Cave's innovative technique of discussing texts in reverse chronological order (practised at several points in the *Pré-histoires* books). Susan James, for example, near the outset of her important *Passion and Action: The Emotions in Seventeenth-Century Philosophy*, writes that the early modern 'category of passions does not coincide with modern interpretations of the category of emotion, from which desire is excluded. Some early-modern writers use the terms "passion" and "emotion" synonymously. But in following their practice, we need to remember that their sense of these terms diverges from common contemporary usage.'[18] James is perhaps writing what are in effect pre-histories of modern concepts of the emotions.

Cave's 'pre-histories' method is not necessarily incompatible with the commonsensical or the theoretical approach to 'the history of emotions'. It can perhaps be used *by* them, to help reduce their anachronism. Instead of applying a modern framework to the past, the 'pre-histories' method attends to those points at which a modern framework (such as the 'emotions') which one might want to apply to the past in fact breaks down as one works one's way chronologically backwards into history ('upstream', in Cave's frequent metaphor), discovering ways in which, for example, passions, appetites, and affections differed from modern emotions. Many practitioners of the commonsensical or theoretical approach do this extremely well already, but the 'pre-histories' method stringently compels one to do it systematically. It involves not necessarily a disavowal or an exorcizing of the modern framework, but rather a curbing of its claims to be able to describe and interpret the past.[19] As Michel de Certeau — acknowledged by Cave to have been an inspiration (*Pré-histoires I*, p. 19) — radically but persuasively argued, historians' modern explanatory models are revealing at those points at which they fail, at which the otherness of the past resists them and so makes itself dimly sensed.[20]

To take a specific example, the 'pre-histories' method could be further applied in this way to the fear and anxiety that is claimed by many historians to have characterized particularly the late Middle Ages and early modern period.[21] At one point in his thoughtful defence of this thesis, William Bouwsma demonstrates how modern English-language translators of writers ranging from Petrarch and Thomas à Kempis to Calvin and Alberti have translated a wide range of terms as 'anxiety'. For example, 'a recent translation of Alberti's *I libri della famiglia* converts *maninconia, affanno, cura, sollecitudine, sospetto, perturbazione*, and *agonia di mente* indiscriminately into "anxiety", *buona diligenza* into "anxious attention", and *stare in paura* into "to be anxious".'[22] Bouwsma's main point here is the 'downstream' one that modern translators are justifiably finding a wealth of anxiety in texts from the fourteenth to the sixteenth century. But implicit in his gentle critique of some of these renderings is the 'upstream' point that 'anxiety' in its current senses (as distinct from those of, say, *anxietas*) has become a privileged modern concept in terms of which we often now understand certain earlier passions and vices, although this risks distorting them. If one thinks of any 'history of early modern anxiety' one is writing as being in fact a set of pre-histories of modern notions of anxiety, then that risk is surely reduced, especially if by 'pre-histories' one means a search for what preceded modern anxiety, in which we try to understand the past on something like its own terms, rather than a search for, say, the early modern sources of modern anxiety — an important project, but a different one, since it involves cherry-picking the past according to current criteria.

The example of anxiety and fear illustrates another problem — that of grand narrative — which besets histories of the emotions and yet can be mitigated by the 'pre-histories' method. As we have seen, retrospective applications — to the pre-modern past — of the modern category of the 'emotions' are tacitly teleological. They tend to interpret the past in terms of a determinate future — our present — which it did not know. They therefore tend to view the march of centuries as a linear progression towards modern understanding — and experience — of the emotions. One of the most flagrant and influential formulations of this view was Johan Huizinga's characterization of medieval people as childlike in their unrestrained subjection to violent, contrasting emotions.[23] As Barbara Rosenwein has shown, Norbert Elias then used Freud to develop Huizinga's thesis into his own compelling and enduring grand narrative of the 'civilizing process', whereby emotional restraint was systematically cultivated for the first time at twelfth-century courts and then even more by early modern absolutist states.[24] Although Lucien Febvre criticized

Huizinga, his own sketch of a climate of ubiquitous fear in the sixteenth century fed into a grand narrative broadly compatible with Huizinga's,[25] since for Febvre this fear (of phenomena such as the Franche-Comté meteor mentioned above) was 'fille de l'ignorance'.[26] It was, implicitly, a pre-Enlightenment phase that humans went through.

By contrast, Cave is more cautious in generalizing from specific examples. As it happens, he and Febvre share some of the same material: both quote from the vivid expressions of fear in Rabelais's description (in the *Quart livre*) of the death of Guillaume du Bellay and in Ronsard's hymn *Les Daimons*.[27] While for Febvre these are two among numerous examples of 'une épopée de terreurs absurdes, mais paniques' (p. 445), Cave's more respectful approach involves reading them at greater length against specific contexts, rather than as symptoms of an age of (more) fear and anxiety (than other ages). And yet for him such clusters of contexts do constantly provide the opportunity to move *somewhat* — but only partially, provisionally, and in connection with specific domains — further away from the particular and towards the general: 'ces inquiétudes s'offrent à lire comme les symptômes d'un monde complexe en mutation, traversé de tremblements sismiques' (*Pré-histoires II*, p. 186).

II. Past Passions Affecting Present Emotions?

According to this model, then, surviving texts can be symptoms of past anxieties that were in turn symptoms of changes taking place in a complex world. But this raises a further question. Do modern historians studying those texts simply *detect and note* the traces of those past anxieties, passions, and so on? Or do they themselves sometimes actually *experience* any of those past passions now, in the present, as (what we would call) emotions?

Cave neither raises the question in such bald terms, I think, nor sets out to answer it definitively or programmatically. After all, he is proposing a method, not a theory. And it seems to me that the method, at least as practised in the two *Pré-histoires* books, implies holding two possible, contrasting answers in the balance. On the one hand, if the experience of which texts can be symptomatic is indeed 'lost' (*Pré-histoires I*, p. 13), then presumably historians cannot share in it. On the other hand, Cave is visibly fascinated by the *continuing* affective force of certain early modern texts, by ways in which, for example, their *pathos* can still affect readers across the centuries. For him this is a mark of what we now call the 'literary' (the pre-histories of which lie in 'poetry' — in the broad senses it used to have — and in rhetoric (*Pré-histoires I*, p. 15)). The theme dominates the moving, closing pages of *Pré-histoires II*, where Cave puts his own affective cards on the table:

> Si j'ai été hanté longtemps par le chapitre 9 de *Pantagruel*, par les fresques mythologiques de Ronsard, par les parenthèses mal fermées de Montaigne, c'est pour des raisons d'ordre affectif. Quelque chose passe dans ces textes, une chose infiniment difficile à saisir, mais le véritable intérêt, le plaisir le plus intense ne sont-ils pas offerts en compensation par ce qui résiste à nos prises? (*Pré-histoires II*, p. 189)

He goes on to describe this something as 'ce vent qui souffle encore, bien que venu de très loin, à travers les grands textes du XVIe siècle' (p. 189). This makes explicit the rationale behind shifts, within Cave's analyses, from descriptions of texts (or protagonists) as *déconcertés* (for example) to descriptions of them as *déconcertants*.[28] He is not suggesting that early modern texts can move us in the same way as they may have moved contemporary readers. But he is perhaps suggesting that we may experience either (and at most) a textually mediated frisson of the fears, joys, and so on out of which they emerged, or else (and at least) a *feeling* that we have narrowly missed out on doing so. In either case, as he intimates here, the pleasure of reading intervenes between past passion and present (possible) emotion, complicating still further the relation between them.

Let me briefly consider the two possibilities. First, if some frisson of past fears, joys, and so on can indeed be textually mediated to the present, does that amount to a tenuous, distant re-enactment of original early modern experience? The question seems worth asking at a time when some historians from various disciplines — ranging from social history to the history of science — have become increasingly interested in the possibility that re-enactment (in various senses) may provide access to dimensions of historical experience (bodily, emotional, technological, and so on) which would otherwise remain inaccessible. Although the term 're-enactment' perhaps suggests a fuller contact between past and present than does the above-quoted passage by Cave, I wonder whether his method might bolster current moves within 're-enactment history' to take a path that is different from the one advocated by its philosophical inspiration, R. G. Collingwood.[29]

For Collingwood, often described as an idealist,[30] 'history is nothing but the re-enactment of past thought in the historian's mind'.[31] Emotions, on the other hand, while they are an important part of experience, and are even acts of thought, are (unlike thought) evanescent, existent only in their immediate context, and as such cannot be re-enacted later. Referring to philosophers or scientists of all periods, Collingwood wrote:

> The first discovery of a truth, for example, differs from any subsequent contemplation of it, not in that the truth contemplated is a different truth, nor in that the act of contemplating it is a different act; but in that the immediacy of the first occasion can never again be experienced: the shock of its novelty, the liberation from perplexing problems, the triumph of achieving a desired result, perhaps the sense of having vanquished opponents and achieved fame, and so forth.[32]

Whereas for Collingwood this para-logical dimension of the emergence of a new 'truth' (or other phenomenon) is wholly inaccessible and so is not part of history, it is precisely what Cave listens out for. What is beneath the radar of the analytical philosopher may after all have a chance of being, if not re-enacted, then at least dimly sensed, thanks to Cave's 'pre-histories' method, with its combination of historically informed literary or rhetorical analysis with precise historical contextualizing.

Secondly, what if the historian experiences nothing more than a feeling that his or her sources are symptomatic of anxieties, disturbances, passions (and so on) which he or she cannot actually experience, even in some empathetic, second-hand way? The strength of the 'pre-histories' method lies in how it turns this apparently bleak feeling into a fundamental starting-point for (limited and provisional) historical understanding. Indeed, for me personally, this method — which I have been fortunate enough to learn from, if in diluting and simplifying ways, over years of conversing with Terence Cave as well as reading him — often boils down to just such a feeling. It tends, in my experience, to be one of unease either at the discrepancy between an argument one wishes to mount and the textual evidence for it, or else at an incongruous detail that refuses to fit into any pattern.

Given the difficulty of illustrating this by second-guessing other historians' feelings, I will resort to some first-person examples. Having initially considered myself to be writing about late sixteenth-century French non-chivalric 'novels' (*romans*), I felt uneasy that their authors and publishers were mostly intent (sometimes with visible unease of their own) on presenting these long prose fictions as anything but *romans*, reserving that label for chivalric romance. Only by eventually acknowledging my unease did I realize that in fact I was investigating a troubled pre-history of what did not emerge until the 1620s as the *roman* (in broader senses — beyond chivalric romance — that are closer to some 'modern' ones).[33]

To take another example: intending to write a history of early modern curiosity, that is (or so I first thought), the desire for knowledge, I felt increasingly uneasy at the many other early modern senses of 'curiosity' — 'anxiety', 'diligence', 'affectedness', and so on — which complicated or negated my initial theses, and about whose relation *to* the 'desire for knowledge' early modern writers too were sometimes visibly uneasy. Only when my unease had made me abandon those initial theses and extend the field to include the more bothersome meanings too did there begin to emerge the changing contours of (what I think of loosely as) early modern pre-histories of modern curiosity.[34]

But the process of registering and acting upon unease is never-ending. Even at that stage, I still felt uneasy at having excluded one set of sixteenth-century human-ist meanings of 'curiosity', so strange and obscure they can only be described as 'lamb-related'. Only acting subsequently upon that unease taught me that the lamb in question — from Plautus's *Aulularia* — far from being a woolly irrelevance in some satisfyingly smooth history of Western curiosity *qua* desire for knowledge, in fact belonged chronologically and semantically to the very earliest pre-history of Western curiosity, and had (like *roman*) apparently been the object of some unease in the sixteenth century, since it was progressively squeezed out of humanist dictionaries.[35]

In each of these three instances, the unease I felt was certainly not the same as that which my sources seemed to betray. Indeed, in some ways it was its opposite — a pale, belated, inverted mirror image of it. For instance, whereas I was uneasy that late sixteenth- and early seventeenth-century long prose fiction did not fit into the modern category of the novel, or even of *le roman*, on the other hand the actual writers and promoters of such fiction seem to have felt uneasy (as well as a touch exuberant at times) that it did not fit in with their own contemporary generic categories. Unease felt by historians can create 'upstream' awareness of a micro-threshold, such as the one that seems to have been crossed when non-chivalric prose fictions started being referred to commonly as *romans* in 1620s France.

For me personally, then, the 'pre-histories' method is less a fixed sequence of steps than a challenge to acknowledge and be led by certain feelings of unease when they arise in historical research, without knowing where they will lead. Far from being unrigorous, these feelings, intuitions, or whatever one wishes to call them, can open up the elusive world of pre-histories precisely because they register, at least in the first instance, failures rather than successes of historical understanding.[36]

Notes to Chapter 1

1. E.g. *Pré-histoires II*, pp. 22, 114, 116, 157.
2. See especially William M. Reddy, *The Navigation of Feeling: A Framework for the History of Emotions* (Cambridge: Cambridge University Press, 2001).
3. See *Pré-histoires I*, p. 95.
4. Terence Cave, *The Cornucopian Text: Problems of Writing in the French Renaissance* (Oxford: Clarendon Press, 1979).
5. *Pré-histoires I*, p. 95; *Pré-histoires II*, p. 110.
6. *Pré-histoires I*, p. 65. For more *volte-face*, see p. 68 (on Girolamo Cardano).
7. Cave attributes this point to Frank Lestringant, 'L'Exotisme en France à la Renaissance de Rabelais à Léry', in *Littérature et exotisme XVIe–XVIIIe siècle*, ed. by Dominique de Courcelles (Paris: Ecole des chartes, 1997), pp. 5–16.
8. *Pré-histoires II*, pp. 139–40. In a cognate example, Cave connects to social and economic change the 'allégresse du commerce' evoked by Henri Estienne in his 1574 paradoxical encomium of the Frankfurt book fair (*Pré-histoires I*, pp. 109–10).
9. Stephen Greenblatt, *Marvelous Possessions: The Wonder of the New World* (Chicago: University of Chicago Press, 1991).
10. Lorraine Daston and Katharine Park, *Wonders and the Order of Nature, 1150–1750* (New York: Zone Books, 1998). On wonder in various contexts, see also *Curiosity and Wonder from the Renaissance to the Enlightenment*, ed. by R. J. W. Evans and Alexander Marr (Aldershot: Ashgate, 2006).
11. Lucien Febvre, *Le Problème de l'incroyance au XVIe siècle: La Religion de Rabelais* (Paris: Albin Michel, 1947), p. 443.
12. *Pré-histoires I*, p. 23. See Sextus Empiricus, *Hypotyposes*, I.xii.28–29.
13. *Pré-histoires I*, pp. 27, 30, 32.
14. E.g. *Pré-histoires I*, p. 65: 'le travail des *pathè* (ce que nous appellerions sans doute une pulsion psychologique).'
15. Thomas Dixon, *From Passions to Emotions: The Creation of a Secular Psychological Category* (Cambridge: Cambridge University Press, 2003). See especially chs 1 ('Introduction: From Passions and Affections to Emotions') and 2 ('Passions and Affections in Augustine and Aquinas'). Although Dixon and Cave share a distaste for progressivist, presentist history-writing, one difference between them is that, whereas Cave seeks to avoid teleologies which culminate in the present, Dixon inverts them, suggesting that the modern framework of the emotions is *less* sophisticated than earlier ones and so represents an impoverishment (p. 2).
16. Lucien Febvre, 'La Sensibilité et l'histoire: Comment reconstituer la vie affective d'autrefois?', *Annales d'histoire sociale*, 3 (1941), 5–20 (p. 12).
17. Distinguished, nuanced examples include Carolyne Larrington, 'The Psychology of Emotion and Study of the Medieval Period', *Early Medieval Europe*, 10: 2 (2001), 251–56; Reddy, *Navigation of Feeling* (which takes the French Revolution as its case study). For critiques of applications by historians of modern theories of emotion, see Barbara H. Rosenwein, 'Writing without Fear about Early Medieval Emotions', *Early Medieval Europe*, 10: 2 (2001), 229–34 and 'Worrying about Emotions in History', *American Historical Review*, 107: 3 (2002), 821–45.
18. Susan James, *Passion and Action: The Emotions in Seventeenth-Century Philosophy* (Oxford: Clarendon Press, 1997), p. 7.
19. See the review article by Adela Pinch, 'Emotion and History', *Comparative Studies in Society and History*, 37: 1 (1995), 100–09 (p. 109): 'Crucial here might be approaches that historicize and

theorize their own epistemologies of emotion in relation to how a culture of the past understood the relations between language and emotion'. Such approaches can perhaps be understood as open-ended dialogues, which, while devoting the lion's share of space to past voices, make the present voice or voices more visible than in the 'commonsensical' approach, and yet do not grant greater authority to either the present voice or the past ones. For an outstanding example — which studies early modern theories of the passions and of other dimensions of psychology, ethics, and epistemology — see Michael Moriarty, *Early Modern French Thought: The Age of Suspicion* (Oxford: Oxford University Press, 2003) and *Fallen Nature, Fallen Selves: Early Modern French Thought II* (Oxford: Oxford University Press, 2006). Variations on this approach have of course been fruitfully applied to many other periods and fields: for example, Michael Baxandall's *Shadows and Enlightenment* (New Haven and London: Yale University Press, 1995) 'juxtaposes modern with eighteenth-century notions about shadows with a view to benefiting from a tension between them' (p. v).

20. See Michel de Certeau, *L'Ecriture de l'histoire* (Paris: Gallimard, 1975), 'Faire sortir des différences: Du modèle à l'écart' (pp. 106–10).

21. E.g. William J. Bouwsma, 'Anxiety and the Formation of Early Modern Culture', in *After the Reformation*, ed. by Barbara C. Malament (Manchester: Manchester University Press, 1980), pp. 215–46; Jean Delumeau, *La Peur en occident (XIVe–XVIIIe siècles): Une cité assiégée* (Paris: Fayard, 1978); Lucien Febvre, 'Pour l'histoire d'un sentiment: Le Besoin de sécurité' [first pub. 1953], in *Pour une histoire à part entière* (Paris: SEVPEN, 1962), pp. 849–53; Febvre, *Problème de l'incroyance*, pp. 443–45; Robert Muchembled, *Culture populaire et culture des élites* (Paris: Flammarion, 1978), ch. 1; *Fear in Early Modern Society*, ed. by William G. Naphy and Penny Roberts (Manchester: Manchester University Press, 1997), in which the editors seek to remain neutral about the 'early modern fear' thesis (p. 1). For a different approach, which argues for changing attitudes to, and notions of, fear over the centuries, see the editors' 'Introduction' in *Fear and Its Representations in the Middle Ages and Renaissance*, ed. by Anne Scott and Cynthia Kosso (Turnhout: Brepols, 2002). For a critique of Febvre, Delumeau, Muchembled, et al. for applying notions of mental structure and collective psychology too rigidly and reductively to what they identify as popular fear, anxiety, and so on, see Stuart Clark, 'French Historians and Early Modern Popular Culture', *Past and Present*, 100 (1983), 62–99.

22. Bouwsma, 'Anxiety', p. 217.

23. J. Huizinga, *The Waning of the Middle Ages: The Study of Forms of Life, Thought and Art in France and the Netherlands in the XIVth and XVth Centuries*, trans. by F. Hopman (London: Edward Arnold, 1924), ch. 1, esp. p. 1 (first version published in Dutch, 1919).

24. Norbert Elias, *The Civilizing Process: The History of Manners and State Formation and Civilization*, trans. by Edmund Jephcott (Oxford and Cambridge, MA: Blackwell, 1994) (first published in German, 1939). For a critique of Elias's grand narrative and of subsequent adjustments made to it by others, see Rosenwein, 'Writing without Fear', pp. 233–34, and 'Worrying about Emotions', pp. 826–28.

25. See Rosenwein, 'Worrying about Emotions', p. 823.

26. Febvre, *Problème de l'incroyance*, p. 443.

27. *Pré-histoires I*, pp. 87–98; Febvre, *Problème de l'incroyance*, p. 444.

28. For this particular example, see *Pré-histoires II*, p. 29 (on ch. 9 of *Pantagruel*).

29. I have in mind a conference entitled 'Re-enactment history and affective knowing' held at the Centre for Research in the Arts, Social Sciences and Humanities (CRASSH), University of Cambridge, March 2007, organized by Peter de Bolla and Simon Schaffer.

30. He did not accept the label.

31. R. G. Collingwood, *The Idea of History* (Oxford: Clarendon Press, 1946), p. 228. See the whole section 'History as Knowledge of Mind' (pp. 217–28).

32. Collingwood, *Idea of History*, pp. 297–98. See the whole section 'History as Re-enactment of Past Experience' (pp. 282–302).

33. Neil Kenny, '"Ce nom de Roman qui estoit particulier aux Livres de Chevalerie, estant demeuré à tous les Livres de fiction": La Naissance antidatée d'un genre', in *Le Roman français au XVIe siècle ou le renouveau d'un genre dans le contexte européen*, ed. by Michèle Clément and Pascale Mounier (Strasbourg: Presses Universitaires de Strasbourg, 2005), pp. 19–32.

34. Neil Kenny, *The Uses of Curiosity in Early Modern France and Germany* (Oxford: Oxford University Press, 2004).

35. Neil Kenny, 'Plautus, Panurge, and "les aventures des gens curieux"', in *(Re)inventing the Past: Essays in Honour of Ann Moss*, ed. by Gary Ferguson and Catherine Hampton (Durham: Durham Modern Languages Series, 2003), pp. 51–71. (Written after *The Uses of Curiosity*, although published earlier.)

36. I am grateful to Miranda Gill, Michael Moriarty, and John O'Brien for comments I found helpful when planning this paper.

or to our preconceptions about the period concerned. We make the effort that this approach involves so as to remain receptive to echoes of the past that might otherwise remain inaudible.[2] Cave's work is driven by an ethic of humility and bearing witness; of avoiding the narcissistic constructions of grand theory for an encounter with the plurality of past experiences.[3] He is well aware that his work will always be informed by his own era; the very idea of a pre-history presupposes a standard account (for instance, a history of the origins of modern forms of selfhood) which the pre-history qualifies or enriches.[4] Nevertheless, I wonder whether the material which a non-teleological account can draw attention to doesn't do more than bear witness to an unacknowledged past variety. The present, from whose perspective we look back, may itself be more varied than the dominant constructions allow. Studying episodes or phenomena which don't fit our familiar narratives might draw attention to aspects of our own present which remain unnoticed because they don't fit our self-understanding, or don't currently count as things that are worth reflecting on. Reconstructing pre-history is potentially a more powerful tool than Cave, with his characteristic modesty, lets on.

If we acknowledge that the encounter with the past challenges our priorities in the present, then an aspect of another, influential approach to the history of modern forms of identity — Charles Taylor's *Sources of the Self* — comes into sharper focus, suggesting that it is more than the simplifying, teleological narrative that it appears to be in Cave's *Pré-histoires*.[5] Where Cave does not explicitly formulate the assumptions that motivate his reconstructions but leaves it to his readers to agree that it is a good thing to be faithful to the complexities of milieux past, Taylor makes taking a moral stand a central part of his argument, and indeed a necessary feature of human identity: 'To know who you are is to be oriented in moral space, a space in which questions arise about what is good or bad, what is worth doing and what not.'[6] Humans are situated, sentient beings who can't not be involved in taking a stand on things, that is to say, in having projects that they care about, and that they think it is a good idea to be doing. Taylor's account of the developments in the understanding of identity since Montaigne is then intended to show that 'we moderns' at a fundamental level care about more things than we can easily reconcile. Since the Reformation, a number of different ways have developed of being in the world and having priorities. To summarize his argument in very broad terms: the Reformation taught us to affirm the value of everyday life, the Enlightenment to aspire to an ideal of self-responsible reason, and Romanticism to appeal to the authority of nature, be it outer or inner nature. This is a package that we inherit in all its multiplicity and we're not in a position to pick and choose between its different elements. In Taylor's view, the different values and ways of living it entails 'may be in conflict, but for all that they don't refute each other. The dignity which attaches to disengaged reason is not invalidated when we see how expressive fulfilment or ecological responsibility has been savaged in its name.'[7] Far from telling a simplifying, linear narrative, therefore, Taylor's account draws attention to the conflicts that have historically accrued, and which we cannot adequately solve by simply affirming one set of priorities at the expense of the others. We should not, in other words, reduce our account of modern identity to a linear story about the development of a single dominant attribute. Although Taylor's frame of reference is chronologically speaking broader than Cave's, he is equally committed to making visible an unacknowledged plurality. At the same time, his plurality challenges readers in the present more directly, as it draws attention to their conflicting allegiances, making the moral issues both explicit and unavoidable. We can't help but take a stand, but in so doing we will inevitably be pulled in different directions by moral habits which cannot be used to trump one other, but which instead can only painfully co-exist.

Taylor finds faultlines in modern forms of identity comparable to those that Cave finds in moments of historical transition as habits change and existing discourses are no longer fully adequate. But the picture is perhaps even more complex than Taylor admits. He tells the history of the aspects of modern selfhood with which he evidently identifies himself. But as Cave's work suggests, there are in any epoch other aspects that don't necessarily make an impact on the developing self-understanding of the society in question. In a footnote, Taylor himself acknowledges the existence of habits of identity, such as those associated with Buddhism, which run counter to the dominant trends of selfhood as they developed in the West and for which it is not 'axiomatic that a self is what we ought to want to have or be'.[8] Taylor looks beyond the West for his counter-example, but such alternatives may equally continue to live a shadowy existence alongside the dominant forms in Europe and North America as a part of everyday life that is rarely talked about or explicitly acknowledged. What would the relation between these unacknowledged survivals and the dominant forms be? The answer to that question will partly depend on which model of the social whole is presupposed. A theory which presupposes an emphatic idea of totality in the Marxian or Freudian traditions might view these unacknowledged parts of modern identity as being in conflict with the dominant views and pushing towards a resolution: the making conscious of a repressed desire; the coming to prominence of an exploited social group. Alternatively, a more pluralistic, Wittgensteinian view of the social whole might think there is no special relation between dominant and less visible forms, they just happen to co-exist as incommensurable ways of living, which have no special bearing on each other and which we document only because we have a commitment to recording what we find as fully as possible; one language game alongside another. Both these approaches to the relationship between dominant and marginal habits of identity ignore the part played by the pre-historian him- or herself in the process of reflection. If we assume that he or she uncovers a form of behaviour because it seems striking or important in some way — there must be some reason why a particular detail seems eye-catching or significant — then the important connection will not be between the form of behaviour uncovered and other phenomena that are contemporary with it, but between the past and the present. The process of pre-historians finding out what matters to them, and why, discloses previously unnoticed aspects of the past which in turn can further the process of self-understanding. What this engagement with marginal forms of behaviour particularly discloses are the limits imposed by the dominant assumptions then and now. Understanding what limited people's behaviour in the past can then be connected to understanding what limits the historian's behaviour in the present. The writing of pre-history is thus potentially an analysis and acknowledgement of contingent limitations we find ourselves to have inherited.

This view of the historical, or pre-historical, enterprise follows Heidegger's reflections on historiography in the second division of *Being and Time*, where he suggests that an encounter with the past which starts from an honest acknowledgement of the constraints of the present and confines itself to as concrete an account as is possible of the constraints of the past will disclose what he calls 'the quiet force of the possible' in both the past and the present.[9] Underpinning this view of the historical investigation is the early Heidegger's collective and constructivist model of human identity. A sense of identity is something we come to as we are socialized in the shared practices of our culture. It is not something we have 'in advance' of our activities or interactions with others but is experienced in and through these activities. Our sense of identity is part of the way we manage what we do, and how we spend time with people.[10] The latter part of Heidegger's argument in *Being and Time* is devoted to explaining how we can appropriate this collective identity for ourselves, overcoming total determination by existing discourses without believing ourselves magically to have escaped the shared traditions and practices that we have inherited. The key moment in this process is an acknowledgement of what Heidegger calls our 'thrownness,' that is to say, an acceptance of the contingent patterns into which, without choosing, we have been born and which will inevitably shape our lives even though they have no claim to be true or right beyond the fact that they are what people in our culture have generally done. Heidegger balances this acknowledgement of the radical contingency of human culture with a sense of human possibilities that can be lived to a greater or lesser extent through the medium of the culture into which we are thrown. We access this potential through a creative and self-critical re-appropriation of the past which approaches the contingencies of the past with no other agenda than an honest acknowledgement of the contingencies of the present. Through this process, we give up what we think we know to discover, in the encounter with the past, what it is that we were already unwittingly involved in. We re-engage with what's actually going on in our own lives, by learning to understand something that was actually going on in the past.

This Heideggerian framework might seem removed from the textual details of Cavean pre-history. Nevertheless, it is useful because it helps to spell out what motivates the encounter with the past, as well as explaining how it is that a culture, such as that of France before 1600, could do without the sense of inner, personal identity centred on consciousness that later generations take for granted. If identity is approached as something we 'do' 'with' people, then the field is opened for us to study the forms in which people related to themselves and to others without confining our attention to a privileged set of introspective practices associated with the cultivation of a 'self'. But if the Heideggerian framework supports Cave's careful distinction of the nuances of self-relating, it also suggests that we need to push even further than Cave does in seeing the texts themselves as inseparable from forms of activity. As Cave emphasizes, a text is part of a speech act 'striving to make certain things happen'.[11] Our focus needs therefore to include the whole interaction of which the text, and the way it is read, is a part. To illustrate how this more practical focus could contribute to a pre-history of modern forms of selfhood that explicitly reflects on the relation between the past and unacknowledged aspects of the present, I want to turn to the vernacular sermons and treatises of the late medieval Dominican, Meister Eckhart. I have shown elsewhere how Eckhart's trial for heresy in the 1320s fosters a culture of circumspection and self-policing out of which there emerge formulations which pre-figure modern languages of selfhood.[12] The historical vignette offered by Eckhart's trial suggests something of the pressures that made it useful or necessary for people to adopt the habits of self-monitoring from which the sense of a 'self' permanently watching over one's activity can develop. What I want to do for the rest of this paper is to reconstruct in more detail the language, and the attendant practices, for cultivating an identity that preceded the circumspect habits of self-monitoring in the mystical milieu of fourteenth-century Germany. Eckhart's German sermons and treatises reveal a culture in which a personalized, inner life was fostered and promoted, but without the focus on self-monitoring, consciousness, or on a distance from the world and from others, that became the hallmarks of the Cartesian subject. This culture gives a glimpse of an alternative model of individuality, the fragmentary history of which, as it shadows the dominant forms of modern identity, still remains to be written.

II. Taking Leave of Yourself in Late-Medieval Germany

In the closing years of the thirteenth century Meister Eckhart was prior of the Dominican friary in Erfurt, a flourishing town in Thuringia in eastern Germany.[13] One of his responsibilities was to lead evening sessions or *collationes* for the instruction of novices, during which the interpretation of scripture and more general questions of monastic and spiritual life would be discussed under the guidance of a senior cleric.[14] A record of these talks survives in the text *Die rede der underscheidunge* (Talks of Instruction, 1294–98). The practical orientation of the text makes it a useful indicator of habits and assumptions that prevailed in the particular milieu in which Eckhart was active.[15] At the same time, it offers a succinct introduction to some of his key concerns.

Eckhart's project is summed up in a sentence towards the beginning of the text: 'Nim dîn selbes war, und swâ dû dich vindest, dâ lâz dich; daz ist daz aller beste' [Examine yourself and wherever you find yourself, take leave of yourself — that is the best way of all].[16] For a modern reader, there are likely to be a number of obstacles to understanding this exhortation to self-examination and self-abandonment, all of which are the product of assumptions about identity unfamiliar to Eckhart and his audience. A key modern assumption is that a thought or action needs someone — a subject — to which to be attributed. Kant, for instance, argued that in order for something to be experienced, there must be a thinking subject to lay claim to it: 'The *I think* must be capable of accompanying all my representations, for otherwise something would be represented in me which could not be thought; in other words, the representation would be either impossible, or at least it would be nothing to me.'[17] Despite years of critique (be it Nietzsche's insistence that a deed needs no doer,[18] or Foucault's dismissal, in *The Order of Things*, of philosophers 'who refuse to think without immediately thinking it is man who is thinking'),[19] this assumption is still deeply ingrained. To give two examples from different traditions: Anthony Cohen, from an anthropological point of view, has defended the 'unique essence formed by the individual's personal experience, genetic history, intellectual development and inclinations' that prevents human actions from being the mere reflex of social or linguistic codes.[20] The philosopher Manfred Frank insists that for the subject to recognize and know itself reflexively, it must have a core of immediate, intuitive, pre-reflexive familiarity with itself.[21] Common to these two disparate examples is the assumption of a barely articulated layer of self without which human creativity, autonomy and rational self-awareness are inconceivable.

Eckhart did not presuppose such a layer. He appeals to personal experience, and indeed to a sense of individuality. But neither of these is indivisibly linked to a sense of self, or to the patterns of self-monitoring and self-control with which later subjects learn to identify. Even events in the individual's inner life do not need to be attributed to a subject; thoughts themselves do not need an 'I think'. If we do not think or act for ourselves, there is always God to think or act for us: 'Enmeine nihtes dan in, und bis unbeworren, ob got dîniu werk würke oder ob dû sie würkest.' [Intend nothing but [God], and have no thought as to whether it is you or God who performs these things in you.][22] There is experience, but it is not necessary for Eckhart to allocate it to a subject.

This difference in approach is recorded in the language used to discuss identity in the thirteenth and fourteenth centuries, and, more particularly, in Eckhart's way of engaging with it. Middle High German at the turn of the fourteenth century did not have an equivalent to the modern word 'self'. It had reflexive verbs, possessives, pronouns, and adverbial forms, all of which included forms of the word 'selb', but it did not have a noun like the modern 'das Selbst', which appeared for the first time in a German dictionary in 1702, modelled on the English 'self'.[23] The closest Middle High German came was the word 'sëlpheit' and its related forms, which, as it was employed in the mystical texts that coined it, had two main meanings. It could be used to describe an attribute of God over and above the divisions of the Trinity: 'dú hoehste glihheit und selbsheit des wesens' [the highest unity and self-identity of his essence].[24] At the same time, it could be used to describe something more like human wilfulness or self-love — not my 'self' but my 'selfness' or self-orientation. This self-orientation is exactly what the mystical literature encouraged its readers to leave behind. Heinrich Seuse (1295/97–1366), a Dominican friar who knew Eckhart probably from the time when the latter was preaching in Strasbourg or Cologne (1313–*c*.1325),[25] describes the spiritual process as the 'dú verlornheit sin selbsheit' [losing of one's self-orientation].[26] The Eckhartian tract 'Von der edelkeit der sêle' [On the nobility of the soul] similarly suggests that the individual must forget his self-centredness: 'Er sol aller vrîest sîn, alsô daz er vergezze sîn selbesheit unde vlieze mit alle dem, daz er ist, in daz gruntlôse abgründe sînes urspringes' [[the spirit] is most free where it forgets its self-orientation and flows with everything that it is into the groundless abyss of its origin].[27] There is a historical link between this form of language and the modern vocabulary of selfhood.[28] However, there is also a fundamental difference between the two. The word 'sëlpheit' refers to something which can be relinquished and with which the individual does not identify, whereas the self, in modern usage, is ever-present as the silent tag which constitutes experiences as my own.

Interestingly enough, forms of 'sëlpheit' are found in texts arising from the milieu in which Eckhart wrote, but not in the sermons and treatises most reliably attributed to Eckhart himself. This could be an accident of transmission. But if it were true that Eckhart eschewed the word available to his followers, that would be an important indicator of his spiritual and psychological programme. Where Seuse, or the Eckhartian author of 'Von der edelkeit der sêle' used the idea of 'selfness', Eckhart tends to prefer alternative formulations, the common factor among which is their dynamism. In the *Talks of Instruction*, he speaks of 'ein lûter ûzgân des dînen' [a pure leaving behind of that which is yours], or of giving up or examining that which is one's own ('sich sîn selbes [verzîen]').[29] When in a sermon, he summarizes his own preaching practice, he says 'daz der mensche ledic werde sîn selbes und aller dinge' [that one should disencumber oneself of oneself and all things].[30] These formulations emphasize activity (the movement of leaving behind or 'ûzgân') whereas the formulations of his followers were more abstract, speaking of loss or forgetfulness. The difference suggests that what his followers saw more passively and more abstractly as the 'forgetting' or 'losing' of 'self-orientation', Eckhart grasped as something more concrete and more active.

A comparison with the Latin model for the *Talks of Instruction* confirms this impression. At a number of points, Eckhart's text reads as a translation into the vernacular of the epistle 'De vita regulari' written *c.*1255 by the former Master General of the Dominican Order, Humbert of Romans (*c.*1200–77).[31] The Latin term used by Humbert to describe what should be left behind is *spiritus proprius* with all the connotations of ownership, property and that which is one's own that the word *proprius* entails: 'Et vere, si per hunc modum evacuati fuerimus spiritu proprio, replebimur non immerito tunc divino.' [And indeed, if by this means we have been emptied of our selfish spirit, we will necessarily be filled by the divine spirit.][32] Eckhart renders this as: 'Swâ der mensche in gehôrsame des sînen ûzgât und sich des sînen erwiget, dâ an dem selben muoz got von nôt wider îngân.' [Wherever a person through obedience leaves that which is theirs and empties himself of his own, God must of necessity go into him.][33] The Latin uses passive constructions, and an abstract noun ('evacuati fuerimus spiritu proprio'). Eckhart speaks of obedience, but at the same time, he suggests that the individual actively contributes to the process, by changing how he or she relates to himself, and so making way for God. Eckhart's reworking of the passage makes the individual an active participant in the process of re-modelling. This activity is not the sign that there is an inescapable 'self' participating in the process of self-abandonment. It shows rather that Eckhart situates the spiritual transformation at the level of activities and practices — the leaving behind of habits and assumptions.[34]

This more concrete approach explains the critical attention that the *Talks* and many of the later sermons devote to ascetic rituals. The surviving autobiographies and convent histories from the late thirteenth and early fourteenth centuries vividly document the culture of self-castigation to which Eckhart was responding. The *vita* of Heinrich Seuse records how, as a young man, he deprived himself of fruit and meat, drank almost no water, wore a crucifix spiked with nails underneath his habit, and carved the letters of Christ's name into his own flesh.[35] Similarly, the autobiographies and histories from convents in the region in which Eckhart was active as Visitor and Confessor describe some of the violently ascetic regimes adopted by nuns. The spiritual autobiography of Christine Ebner (1277–1356) tells of self-flagellation with nettles, switches, thorns, and of her cutting a cross into her chest because she was ashamed after confession.[36] In the case of religious women, such ascetic attention to one's own body has been given a positive interpretation, and read as an attempt by women to establish an element of control over 'religious superiors and confessors, God in his majesty, and the boundaries of one's own "self"'.[37] Eckhart is frequently critical of such practices, but not because they challenge his authority, or, as other critics have suggested, because he wants to impose a rational order on the emotional and bodily excess of which the self-castigation is a symptom.[38] He is critical of them where they replace the breaking down of an attachment to 'that-which-is-one's-own' with what is in effect a further form of attachment, namely a pre-established pattern considered to have an authority and legitimacy in its own right. Eckhart questions ascetic regimes where they become forms of self-justifying habitual inflexibility hindering rather than furthering the process of development towards God: 'Und hindert dich des dehein ûzerlich werk, ez sî vasten, wachen, lesen oder swaz ez sî, daz lâz vrîlîche âne alle sorge, daz dû hie mite iht versûmest deheine pênitencie; wan got ensihet niht ane, waz diu werk sîn, dan aleine, waz diu minne und diu andâht und daz gemüete in den werken sî' [If any external work hampers you in this, be it fasting, keeping vigil, reading, or whatever else, you should freely let it go without worrying that you might thereby be neglecting your penance. For God does not notice the nature of the works but only the love, devotion and the spirit which is in them].[39]

Eckhart's alternative is an individualized programme that engages with the specific attachments of each person:

> Kristus hât gevastet vierzic tage. Dar ane volge im, daz dû war nemest, war zuo dû allermeist sîst geneiget oder bereit: dâ verlâz dich ane und nim wol dîn selbes war. Daz gebürt dir dicke mêr und unbekümbert ze lâzenne, dan ob dû zemâle vastet aller spîse. Und alsô ist dir etwenne swærer ein wort ze verswîgenne, dan ob man zemâle swîge von aller rede.[40]

> [Christ fasted for forty days. You should follow him in this by considering what you are most inclined or ready to do, and then you should give yourself up in that, while observing yourself closely. It is often better for you to go freely without that than to deny yourself all food. And sometimes it is more difficult for you to refrain from uttering one word than it is to refrain from speaking altogether.]

In a way that might appear contradictory, Eckhart's version of self-abandonment encourages an attitude which is explicitly individualized and which lays a greater emphasis on inner life than do the texts of some of his close contemporaries such as those of Seuse or the Dominican nun Margarethe Ebner (1291–1351). Seuse's *Vita* and Ebner's autobiographical *Offenbarungen* ('Revelations') suggest two things about the type of identity that flourished in this milieu. The first is that conscious control could in certain circumstances be easily relinquished. Both authors describe moments when they go into the choir in the church of their respective Dominican convents and are taken into a state of rapture brought upon by the spiritual importance of the choir itself.[41] This form of identity is like that of the crowd subjects described by Freud in *Group Psychology and the Analysis of the Ego* (1921) insofar as the conscious, controlling level of individual identity can be swept away.[42] However, for the medieval mystics, it is not the suggestive power of the group that causes the self-loss, but rather the aura of the ecclesiastical space. This leads to the second feature of the identity type. The individual in Margarethe Ebner's or Heinrich Seuse's texts gives up control, but at the price of becoming attached to particular spaces or particular rituals which generate the sense of rapture. Intensity is experienced through a process of externalization or projection. Eckhart questions such externalization, encouraging practices that strengthen the individual and prevent his or her spiritual experiences being dependent on outside objects or rituals. At the same time, the product of this attention to oneself is not a modern 'self' but a new set of habits that produce a different relationship to oneself, to external practices and to God.

Eckhart describes these new habits by saying: '[Der mensche] muoz ein innerlich einœde lernen' [We must learn to maintain an inner emptiness].[43] To explain what he means by this, he differentiates between the level of conscious thought (thinking about, remembering God) and a more permanent re-structuring of the individual's psyche:

> Diz wærlîche haben gotes liget an dem gemüete und an einem inniclîchen vernünftigen zuokêrenne und meinenne gotes, niht an einem stæten anegedenkenne in einer glîchen wîse, wan daz wære unmügelich der natûre in der meinunge ze habenne und sêre swære und ouch daz aller beste niht. Der mensche ensol niht haben noch im lâzen genüegen mit einem gedâhten gote, wan, swenne der gedank vergât, sô vergât ouch der got. Mêr: man sol haben einen gewesenden got, der verre ist obe den gedenken des menschen und aller crêatûre.[44]

> [This real possession of God is to be found in the heart, in an inner motion of the spirit towards him and striving for him, and not just in thinking about him always and in the same way. For that would be beyond the capacity of our nature and would be very difficult to achieve and would not even be the best thing to do. We should not content ourselves with a thought-about God, for, when the thought comes to an end, so too shall God. Rather we should have an essential God who is beyond the thoughts of all people and all creatures.]

One acquires this 'essential' God through a programme of self-observation and repeated exercises. But the end product should not be a new consciousness. Instead, Otto Langer has suggested the term *habitus* to describe the product of spiritual exercises repeated over and over again until they become automatic.[45] Eckhart compares the acquisition of such a self-relationship, or what could be called a new 'technique of the spirit', to learning to write. The scribe first consciously imitates a pattern, but later he writes freely and automatically.[46] The habit of inner detachment is similarly an acquired *techne*.[47] However, the impulses thus trained are, for Eckhart, almost physiological. If learning to write provides a model for the process of spiritual training, a raging thirst and the feeling of loving something describe the result.[48] Once we have successfully acquired the *habitus*, the relationship to God will accompany the individual everywhere, as do thirst and passionate longing.

III. Situating Eckhart: Some Conclusions

The vocabulary of selfhood from the early fourteenth century is subtly different from the language of today, suggesting different practices of the self. The self is not treated as a centre or inescapable point of reference at either a grammatical or a practical level. One Middle High German translation of the passage from Galatians 2, 20, in which St Paul describes his de-centring by Christ reads: 'Jch leb ieczunt ich nicht, Cristus lebt jn mir' [I live now not I, Christ lives in me].[49] The ungrammatical 'I live not I' highlights the degree of flexibility available in the vernacular for describing a relationship with one's own inner life that did not centre on consciousness or self-control. Grammar could be bent to describe a state that did not have the 'I' as the subject of an individual's actions. Other groups in the fourteenth century undertook a similar grammatical disruption by refusing to speak of themselves in the first person.[50] At the same time, these linguistic habits arise from a milieu in which inner life and personal spiritual experience were actively cultivated. There was subjective experience but not subjecthood.

To a degree, we can reconstruct what this looked like on a practical level. This is not because Eckhart himself gives a direct description of how to behave. Rather, the lifestyle of convents governed by the Dominican rule is well enough documented, as are some of the habits of the lay congregation in the flourishing urban economies of cities such as Erfurt, Strasbourg or Cologne, where Eckhart was most active. During the year and a day of their novitiate, aspiring friars learned to regulate every aspect of their comportment, from where they directed their eyes to how they put on their habit. At the same time, the particular emphasis of Dominican training was learning. When Dominic took over the church of St Romain in Toulouse he added a cloister with cells for study. This promotion of education remained a dominant feature of Dominican life. Offences related to study were written into the order's rule from the very beginning so that mistreating books, sleeping in lectures, reading prohibited texts, behaving disreputably while preaching or working carelessly as a scribe were counted as faults on a par with eating meat or wearing linen underclothes. The rule promoted scholarly qualities, and protected the apparatus of scholarship as much as it fostered humility and obedience, for 'the preacher's intellectual formation was as essential as his apostolic character, and the one merited the same legislative care as the other'.[51] Eckhart's pastoral texts respond to this culture of regulation, attention to detail, self-observation and learning. They work to prevent both the practical and intellectual apparatus from becoming fixed and unchallenged structures, cut off from personal experience. At the same time, they encourage self-observation, and intellectual development; an overcoming of attachments, and a permanent going beyond established certainties, even those that Eckhart uses to start his own arguments.[52]

Eckhart's attitude to the nascent practices of capitalist rationality flourishing amongst his lay congregation is similar to his treatment of regulated life in Dominican convents. The merchants were learning to observe their own behaviour no less than friars, keeping records of income and expenditure, minimizing waste, balancing the books and, by their success, encouraging others to see the virtue of 'the commercial habit of measuring and calculating in monetary terms'.[53] Eckhart adopts the language of trade in his sermons and treatises, describing the overcoming of attachment in economic terms:

> Ez ist rehte ein glîch widergelt und glîcher kouf: als vil dû ûzgâst aller dinge, als vil, noch minner noch mêr, gât got în mit allem dem sînen, als dû zemâle ûzgâst in allen dingen des dînen.[54]

> [It is a fair trade and an equal exchange: to the extent that you depart from things, thus far, no more and no less, God enters into you with all that is his, as far as you have stripped yourself of yourself in all things.]

At the same time, he is critical of economic rationality. Christ cast the merchants out of the temple, and in his sermon on this episode in the Gospel, Eckhart is no less dismissive:

> Sehet, diz sint allez koufliute, die sich hüetent vor groben sünden und wæren gerne guote liute und tuont ir guoten werk gote ze êren, als vasten, wachen, beten und swaz des ist, aller hande guotiu werk, und tuont sie doch dar umbe, daz in unser herre etwaz dar umbe gebe, oder daz in got iht dar umbe tuo, daz in liep sî: diz sint allez koufliute. Daz ist grop ze verstânne, wan sie wellent daz eine umbe daz ander geben und wellent alsô koufen mit unserm herren.[55]

> [See, those all are merchants who, while avoiding mortal sin and wishing to be virtuous, do good works to the glory of God, such as fasts, vigils, prayers and the rest, all kinds of good works, but they do them in order that our Lord may give them something in return, or that God may do something they wish for — all these are merchants. That is plain to see, for they want to give one thing in exchange for another, and so barter with our Lord.]

Eckhart values the habits of self-observation and the monitoring and evaluation of behaviour. But he has little time for purposive action, doing x to produce effect y, in one's relationship to God. Since the individual does not possess his or her actions, there is no trade to be established. God may observe a balance, filling the individual as he or she empties themselves. But the since the individual acts through God alone, he or she can bring nothing to the transaction.

Eckhart's preaching emerges from the context of the friary and the city. He encourages rationalized, regulated behaviour. But he discourages identification with the rules as an end in themselves, and criticizes a possessive attitude to one's own actions, however rational. Externally, it seems that the Eckhartian subject appeared very much like his or her fellow friars, nuns and merchants. Indeed, Eckhart specifically bids his listeners avoid clothes, food or words that would differentiate them from others.[56] At the same time, Eckhart's sermons foster a detachment from the regulating habits, suggesting that the habits are less important than the spiritual experience they promote. It is difficult to assign the resulting practices of the self to a particular period. The outer trappings of the convent or the medieval city are very different from our own, but in both the rule of the friars and the developing account books of the merchants we find versions of rational behaviour that will eventually become the dominant mode. In contrast, Eckhart's spiritual re-deployment of these modes of rational behaviour is neither medieval nor modern. To say this is not merely to acknowledge that twentieth-century writers like C. G. Jung or Erich Fromm promoted an attitude similar to the one that he encouraged in his listeners.[57] Rather, Eckhart's spiritual project is not classifiable because it builds on the 'modern' potential for autonomy that was the by-product of study, self-observation and account keeping, but at the same time it retains the relationship with God. Eckhart's subject resists schemes of historical periodization because the combination of individual autonomy and freedom before God has never been a dominant form of identity in the West.

This kind of non-periodizable identity is just the sort of challenge to our assumptions that Cave's pre-history gives us the tools to uncover. By forgetting for a moment what we think we know about selfhood, and paying attention to the particular ways in which the fourteenth-century language of identity does not match our own, we can lay bare the activity that precedes the establishment of a self. It is an unfamiliar view of identity for two reasons. The first is that it puts activity before consciousness, autonomy and agency. The second is that it allows us to ask what the activities that constitute our identity are doing and why. We need no longer take it for granted that what they are doing is 'constituting identity' as if we all knew in advance what that is. Rather we can ask what sort of identity and then investigate what an identity of a particular sort is for. This last step is one that Cave is less keen to make because he is concerned that this may lead to an agenda being unreflectingly imposed on the material. But it seems to me to be the logical consequence of the historical study of the ways humans have related to themselves and others that we begin to see the contours of our own self-relations, and question their purposes. The purpose of Eckhartian identity is to become one with God. This is not an aim we need to understand theologically. The experience of connection with ourselves, the world and divinity can also be understood in more secular terms. For instance, the anthropologist I. M. Lewis, in his discussion of shamanism and its equivalents, suggests that every society is negotiating the relationship with the spirits, albeit with different behavioural tools and with a different vocabulary.[58] In their own different vocabulary, Horkheimer and Adorno suggest that the management of the sense of connectedness that they call 'mimesis' underlies the practices of modern rationality.[59] If we follow Eckhart's lead, we can see habits of identity as ways of negotiating our relationship with 'God', the 'spirits', with mimetic impulses. The stable, consciousness-centred self of the modern era then appears as a way of structuring this relationship, albeit in the form of keeping the experience of connection at a permanent distance and making 'God' seem ineffable.

Once we have understood that modern habits of identity function in part as a *habitus* to keep at bay the experience Eckhart called being 'in God',[60] the question arises 'what should we do about it?' But 'what should we do about it?' is a modern question which presupposes agency and a sphere of action. Charles Taylor and

Heidegger suggest that whatever we may want to do about it, the situation may not be one that lends itself to our doing anything. The more important point is to acknowledge what we're involved in, namely a set of habits that make us who we are and that simultaneously have been developed to foster a certain sort of distance. These habits do not account for all our behaviour. As Taylor suggests, we will have learnt more than one set of behaving, and have more than one set of priorities. Different situations, or different parts of society will permit more or less connection with others and the world. We don't have to choose between them, but rather acknowledge that that is the case. The point of the encounter with the different habits and different purposes of Eckhart's milieu is not to make a choice, or to embark on a course of action, but rather honestly to engage with the forms of identity we've inherited, and the purposes to which these forms are put.

Notes to Chapter 2

1. *Pré-histoires I*, pp. 120–25.
2. *Pré-histoires II*, p. 16.
3. Terence Cave, 'Locating the Early Modern,' *Paragraph*, 29 (2006), 12–27 (p. 22).
4. *Pré-histoires II*, p. 15.
5. *Pré-histoires I*, p. 113.
6. Charles Taylor, *Sources of the Self: The Making of the Modern Identity* (Cambridge: Cambridge University Press, 1989), p. 28.
7. Ibid., p. 502.
8. Ibid., p. 527.
9. Martin Heidegger, *Being and Time*, trans. by John Macquarrie and Edward Robinson (Oxford: Basil Blackwell, 1962), §76, p. 446.
10. For an exposition of the first part of *Being and Time* that particularly emphasizes these collective and social aspects of Heidegger's argument, see Hubert L. Dreyfus, *Being-in-the-World: A Commentary on Heidegger's 'Being and Time', Division I* (Cambridge, MA: MIT Press, 1991).
11. Cave, 'Locating the Early Modern,' p. 21.
12. Ben Morgan, 'Developing the Modern Concept of the Self: The Trial of Meister Eckhart,' *Telos*, 116 (1999), 56–80.
13. For historical background, see Yoshiki Yoda, 'Mystische Lebenslehre zwischen Kloster und Stadt: Meister Eckharts "Reden der Unterweisung" und die spätmittelalterliche Lebenswirklichkeit,' in *Mittelalterliche Literatur im Lebenszusammenhang*, ed. by Eckart Conrad Lutz (Freiburg, CH: Universitätsverlag, 1997), pp. 225–64.
14. *Meister Eckhart Werke*, ed. by Niklaus Largier and Josef Quint, 2 vols (Frankfurt am Main: Deutscher Klassiker Verlag, 1993), II, 793 (editorial commentary).
15. For a summary of Eckhart's pastoral functions, see Winfried Trusen, *Der Prozeß gegen Meister Eckhart: Vorgeschichte, Verlauf und Folgen* (Paderborn: Ferdinand Schöningh, 1988), pp. 14–19. I follow critics such as Koch, Ruh or Langer who make Eckhart's pastoral concerns, or what Langer calls the 'praktische Zwecksetzung', the central focus of his thought. Scholastic concepts, be they in the commentaries or the sermons, are, in Eckhart's texts, ultimately a tool to help Eckhart and his charges in their spiritual endeavours. Joseph Koch, 'Sinn und Struktur der Schriftauslegung Meister Eckharts,' in Joseph Koch, *Kleine Schriften*, 2 vols (Rome: Edizioni di Storia e Letteratura, 1973), I, 399–428. Kurt Ruh, *Meister Eckhart: Theologe, Prediger, Mystiker* (Munich: Beck, 1985). Otto Langer, *Mystische Erfahrung und spirituelle Theologie: Zu Meister Eckharts Auseinandersetzung mit der Frauenfrömmigkeit seiner Zeit* (Munich: Artemis Verlag, 1987).
16. Eckhart, *Selected Writings*, trans. by Oliver Davies (Harmondsworth: Penguin, 1994), p. 7. *Meister Eckhart Werke*, II, 340 (*Die rede der underscheidunge*, §. 1).
17. Immanuel Kant, *Critique of Pure Reason*, ed. by Vasilis Politis, trans. by J. M. D. Meiklejohn and Vasilis Politis (London: Dent, 1993), p. 99 (B 131–32).

18. Friedrich Nietzsche, *Zur Genealogie der Moral*, ed. by Giorgio Colli and Mazzino Montinari, *Kritische Gesamtausgabe* (Berlin: de Gruyter, 1968–), vol. VI.2, p. 285 ('Erste Abhandlung', §. 13).

19. Michel Foucault, *The Order of Things: An Archaeology of the Human Sciences*, trans. by Alan Sheridan (London: Tavistock, 1971), pp. 342–43.

20. Anthony Cohen, *Self Consciousness: An Alternative Anthropology of Identity* (London: Routledge, 1994), p. 23.

21. Manfred Frank, *Selbstbewußtsein und Selbsterkenntnis: Essays zur analytischen Philosophie der Subjektivität* (Stuttgart: Reclam, 1991), pp. 7, 161.

22. Eckhart, *Selected Writings*, p. 51. *Meister Eckhart Werke*, II, 430 (*Die rede der underscheidunge*, §. 23).

23. Jacob Grimm and Wilhelm Grimm, *Deutsches Wörterbuch*, ed. by M. Heyne et al. (Leipzig: S. Hirzel, 1905), vol. X.1, col. 451.

24. *Heinrich Seuse: Deutsche Schriften im Auftrag der Württembergischen Kommission für Landesgeschichte*, ed. by Karl Bihlmeyer (Frankfurt a. M.: Minerva, 1961), p. 180, ll. 1–2.

25. For the details of Seuse's acquaintance with Eckhart see Alois M. Haas/K. Ruh, 'Seuse, Heinrich, OP', *Die deutsche Literatur des Mittelalters: Verfasserlexikon*, ed. by Kurt Ruh et al., 2nd edn (Berlin: de Gruyter, 1977–), vol. VIII, cols 1109–10.

26. *Heinrich Seuse: Deutsche Schriften im Auftrag der Württembergischen Kommission für Landesgeschichte*, p. 187, l. 22.

27. *Meister Eckhart, vol. 2: Deutsche Mystiker des vierzehnten Jahrhunderts*, ed. by Franz Pfeiffer (Leipzig: G. J. Göschen'sche Verlagsbuchhandlung, 1857), p. 393.

28. Morgan, 'Developing the Modern Concept of the Self: The Trial of Meister Eckhart,' pp. 75–79.

29. *Meister Eckhart Werke*, II, 336 (*Die rede der underscheidunge*, §. 1); II, 40 (*Die rede der underscheidunge*, §. 3).

30. Ibid., II, 564 (Q53).

31. Georg Steer, '*Würken vernünfticlîchen*: Das "christliche" Leben nach den "Reden der Unterweisung" Meister Eckharts', in *Heinrich Seuses Philosophia Spiritualis: Quellen, Konzept, Formen und Rezeption. Tagung Eichstätt 2.–4. Oktober 1991*, ed. by Rüdiger Blumrich and Philipp Kaiser (Wiesbaden: Dr. Ludwig Reichert, 1994), pp. 94–108 (pp. 101–02). For details of Humbert's biography, see Fritz Heinkle, *Humbert von Romans, der fünfte Ordensmeister der Dominikaner* (Berlin: Dr. Emil Ebering, 1933).

32. 'Epistola,' *B. Humberti de Romanis quinti praedicatorum magistri generalis Opera De vita regulari*, ed. by Joseph Joachim Berthier, 2 vols (Rome: A. Befani, 1888–89), I, pp. 1–41, p. 6. Quoted by Steer, p. 102.

33. *Meister Eckhart Werke*, II, 334 (*Die rede der underscheidunge*, §. 1). Quoted by Steer, p. 102.

34. For a reading of Eckhart's use of the Latin 'proprium' and the Middle High German equivalent 'eigenschaft' which emphasizes intellectual insights at the expense of psychological or habitual change, see Alessandra Beccarisi, 'Predigt 1: "Intravit Iesus in templum"' in *Lectura Eckhardi II: Predigten Meister Eckharts von Fachgelehrten gelesen und gedeutet*, ed. by Georg Steer and Loris Sturlese (Stuttgart: Kohlhammer, 2003), pp. 1–27.

35. *Heinrich Seuse: Deutsche Schriften im Auftrag der Württembergischen Kommission für Landesgeschichte*, pp. 39–53 (chs 15–18).

36. *Leben und Gesichte der Christina Ebnerin, Klosterfrau zu Engelthal*, ed. by Georg Wolfgang Karl Lochner (Nuremberg: Aug. Recknagel's Buchandlung, 1872), p. 11.

37. Caroline Walker Bynum, *Holy Feast and Holy Fast: The Religious Significance of Food to Medieval Women* (Berkeley: University of California Press, 1987), p. 193.

38. Winfried Trusen writes of 'der von Eckhart eingeschlagene Weg einer rationalen Erfassung der Mystik' (*Der Prozeß gegen Meister Eckhart*, p. 52).

39. *Selected Writings*, p. 27. *Meister Eckhart Werke*, II, 382 (*Die rede der underscheidunge*, §. 16).

40. *Selected Writings*, p. 30. *Meister Eckhart Werke*, II, 388 (*Die rede der underscheidunge*, §. 17).

41. *Heinrich Seuse: Deutsche Schriften*, p. 10. *Margaretha Ebner und Heinrich von Nördlingen: Ein Beitrag zur Geschichte der deutschen Mystik*, ed. by Philipp Strauch (Freiburg i.B./Tübingen: J. C. B. Mohr, 1882), p. 41.

42. *Massenpsychologie und Ich-Analyse* (1921), Sigmund Freud, *Studienausgabe*, ed. by Alexander Mitscherlich, Angela Richards, and James Strachey, 11 vols (Frankfurt am Main: S. Fischer, 1969), IX, 67–76.

43. *Selected Writings*, p. 11. *Meister Eckhart Werke*, II, 350 (*Die rede der underscheidunge*, §. 6).

44. *Selected Writings*, p. 10. *Meister Eckhart Werke*, II, 348 (*Die rede der underscheidunge*, §. 6).

45. Otto Langer, '*Sich lâzen, sîn selbes vernihten*: Negation und "Ich-Theorie" bei Meister Eckhart', in *Deutsche Mystik im abendländischen Zusammenhang: Neu erschlossene Texte, neue methodische Ansätze, neue theoretische Konzepte*. Kolloquium Kloster Fischingen 1998, ed. by Walter Haug and Wolfram Schneider-Lastin (Tübingen: Niemeyer, 2000), pp. 317–46 (p. 328).

46. *Meister Eckhart Werke*, II, 350–52 (*Die rede der underscheidunge*, §. 6).

47. Otto Langer, *Mystische Erfahrung und spirituelle Theologie: Zu Meister Eckharts Auseinandersetzung mit der Frauenfrömmigkeit seiner Zeit* (Munich: Artemis Verlag, 1987), pp. 174–75.

48. *Meister Eckhart Werke*, II, 348–50 (*Die rede der underscheidunge*, §. 6).

49. The phrase appears in a text called 'Von der anmynnent gnad' in a fifteenth-century manuscript that contains, amongst other things, Eckhart sermons and a Seuse excerpt. Georg Steer, *Scholastische Gnadenlehre in mittelhochdeutscher Sprache* (Munich: Beck, 1966), p. 78.

50. Robert E. Lerner, *The Heresy of the Free Spirit in the Later Middle Ages* (Berkeley: University of California Press, 1972).

51. M. Michèle Mulchahey, *'First the Bow is Bent in Study...': Dominican Education before 1350* (Toronto: Pontifical Institute of Medieval Studies, 1998), pp. 11, 18, 38.

52. Ruh, *Meister Eckhart: Theologe, Prediger, Mystiker*, p. 165.

53. Joel Kaye, *Economy and Nature in the Fourteenth Century: Money, Market Exchange, and the Emergence of Scientific Thought* (Cambridge: CUP, 1998), p. 17.

54. *Selected Writings*, p. 17. *Meister Eckhart Werke*, II, 342 (*Die rede der underscheidunge*, §. 4).

55. Eckhart, *German sermons & treatises*, trans. by Maurice O'C Walshe, 3 vols (Shaftesbury: Element Books, 1979), I, 56. *Meister Eckhart Werke*, I, 12 (Q1).

56. *Meister Eckhart Werke*, II, 392 (*Die rede der underscheidunge*, §. 18).

57. Jung explicitly quotes the phrase from Galatians, 2, 20 'I do not live, but Christ lives in me' to explain the self-relationship that Jungian therapy aims at. C. G. Jung, *Die Beziehungen zwischen dem Ich und dem Unbewußten* (Munich: DTV, 1990), p. 106. Fromm draws on Eckhart in Erich Fromm, *To Have or to Be?* (London: Abacus, 1979), pp. 65–71.

58. I. M. Lewis, *Ecstatic Religion: A Study of Shamanism and Spirit Possession*, 2nd edn (London: Routledge, 1989).

59. For a fuller discussion and critique of Horkheimer's and Adorno's version of connectedness see Ben Morgan, 'The Project of the Frankfurt School', *Telos*, 119 (2001), 75–98.

60. 'You will be at peace to the degree that you are in God, and you will not find peace to the degree that you are out of God.' ('Wan als vil bist dû in gote, als vil dû bist in vride, und als vil ûz gote, als vil dû bist ûz vride.') *Meister Eckhart Werke*, II, 432.

CHAPTER 3

❖

From Cave to Choir:
The Journey of the Sibyls

Mary B. McKinley

Atop the small village of Saint Bertrand des Comminges, the cathedral of Sainte Marie dominates the landscape where the plain meets the foothills of the central Pyrenees. It shelters an enclosed choir with intricately carved wooden sculptures, one of only a few such ensembles remaining intact in France. When I first visited the site over ten years ago the beauty of the wooden figures captivated me, and since then I have felt compelled to return there several times. Included among the prophets, patriarchs, saints, and virtues in the dorsal panels of the choir stalls are twelve sibyls, graceful young women carrying symbolic attributes. Their place in that choir invites consideration of their pre-history as well as reflection on their afterlife, and I present them here framed by details of their past and their posterity. The Saint Bertrand sculptures also raise for me questions of methodology as I, a reader accustomed to analysing words, try to convey the powerful attraction of those images. Sibyls have been appropriated to different ends as they moved from the Eastern Mediterranean west and north across Europe. The Saint Bertrand sibyls allow us a glimpse — albeit a teasingly partial one — into one privileged moment of their journey.

I. Pre-History

Sibyls are female ecstatic seers associated in Antiquity with holy places, often caves. A cave on the coast of Asia Minor near Erythrae, for example, was associated with the Sibyl from a very early date. Initially Greek writers spoke of 'the' Sibyl, one woman, a prophetess and conduit for divine pronouncements. The earliest recorded reference to a sibyl is found in a fragment of the Greek philosopher Heraclitus, preserved by Plutarch in his 'On the Pythian oracles': 'the Sibyl with frenzied lips, uttering words mirthless, unembellished, unperfumed, penetrates through a thousand years with her voice by the God' (397a). Aristophanes and Plato refer almost casually to a single divinely inspired woman, as if the Sibyl needed no introduction.[1] Later, writers began referring to several different sibyls: the Erythraean sibyl and the sibyl of Delphi. In the Hellenistic period the sibyls multiplied, the most famous one in Italy emerging in Cumae, where she would be immortalized by Virgil in Book

VI of the *Aeneid*. Pausanius wrote of a Jewish sibyl Sabbe, and, later, medieval writers conflated her with the Queen of Sheba. The Romans began collecting written versions of the Sibylline oracular pronouncements and kept them in the Temple of Apollo on the Palatine Hill, where they would consult them in times of crisis. Tacitus records that Nero consulted them after Rome burned in 64 CE. The fragments of those Greek hexameters that survive are obscure if not unintelligible; it is hard to imagine what instruction or solace Nero could have found there.[2]

In the early Christian era, the written Sibylline oracles proliferated and were gathered into a corpus of books of various origins: the *Oracula Sibyllina*. Alexandrian Jews were prominent in saving and transmitting those oracular texts. Christian writers saw in them verses foretelling the birth of Christ to the pagan world, and some Christians embellished them by adding details after the fact. Stories arose about the sibyl's role as prophet of Christ. Virgil had referred to the Cumaean sibyl in the fourth *Eclogue*. He recalled her prophecy of a new age with the appearance of a virgin and the birth of a child who would liberate the world from guilt and dread and give rise to a glorious age. Early Christians saw Christ prophesied in Virgil's lines. One famous story told that the Roman senate had offered to make the emperor Augustus a god in recognition of his having brought peace to the world. Augustus went to the Capitoline Hill and consulted the Tiburtine sibyl on the day of Christ's birth. The sibyl saw — or caused to appear — an aura of gold surrounding a beautiful Virgin nursing a child. A voice spoke, saying: 'Haec est ara Coeli', whence the name of the church that now stands on that spot. The emperor understood the words as an announcement to the pagan world of the birth of Christ, and he renounced any claim to divinity — or so Christian writers reported. The story became a favourite of medieval authors and illuminators.

Two Patristic authorities, each drawing on Varro and the sibylline oracles, validated the sibyls' prophecies and thus authorized their passage into Christian tradition. Lactantius (*c*.250–*c*.325) in his *Divine Institutions* frequently evokes one or several of the sibyls, presenting them as a group in Book I, chapter 6. He lists the ten sibyls that were mentioned by Varro: Persian, Libyan, Delphic, Cimmerian, Erythraean, Samian, Cumaean, Hellespontic, Phrigian, and Tiburtine. In each case he names authors who recognized the sibyl's authority and in some cases adds a brief anecdote about them. Lactantius emphasizes the individual character of each sibyl, but he insists that they all proclaimed one God. Augustine (354–430) in *The City of God* (Book X) attributes to the Sibyl of Cumae Virgil's lines in the fourth *Eclogue*. Augustine gathered Lactantius's scattered statements about the sibyls and presented them together in *The City of God* (Book XVIII, 23). There he analysed a poem he attributed to the Erythraean Sibyl, and he concluded: 'ut in eorum numero deputanda videatur, qui pertinent ad civitatem Dei' [she is evidently to be counted among those who belong to the City of God].[3]

In the Middle Ages, Christian iconography associated the sibyls with the Old Testament prophets, the latter foretelling Christ's coming to the Jews, and the former announcing the news to the pagan world. A line from the *Dies irae*, the sequence of the Requiem Mass, summarizes that shared role: 'Teste David cum Sibylla.'[4] Alone or increasingly in groups, sibyls abound in medieval art, literature and music.[5]

A striking example of the sibyl's privileged status is found in Dante's *Paradiso* (xxxiii, 64–66) when the poet evokes the Cumaean sibyl in the final canto of his *Commedia*. Christine de Pizan mentions the sibyls frequently in her writings, and they appear in the manuscript illuminations of her works. She portrays the Cumaean sibyl as her guide in the *Chemin de longue estude*; she tells the story of the sibyl and Augustus in *Epistre Othea*; and she refers to the sibyls' prophecies in both the *Ditié de Jehanne d'Arc* and the *Advision Christine*. Her most striking tribute to the sibyls occurs in *La Cité des Dames* (1405), at the beginning of Book Two, when Dame Droiture praises them above the Old Testament prophets for their priority and clarity in announcing the birth of Christ.[6] Emile Mâle, who devoted his 1899 *thèse d'état* to sibyls, remarked: 'In the course of the fifteenth century sibyls suddenly appeared all over Europe.'[7] Mâle refers here primarily to images of sibyls, but they owe their increased numbers at least in part to the printed word. One of the first three books to be printed in Italy, Lactantius's *Divine Institutions*, was published in Subiaco, in 1465, and at least six new editions followed between 1468 and 1478. Sibyls were an important aspect of Lactantius's work for his late medieval readers, who began rendering them in images. An illuminated manuscript of the *Divine Institutions*, made in Florence around 1460, offers a portrait of Lactantius in the initial letter of Book One, and in the intricate white vine border surrounding that page there are five images, all showing sibyls.[8] Sibyls pictured in illuminated manuscripts soon migrated to the printed page, and those printed sibyls were soon joined by images of sibyls in churches, both in stained glass windows and in sculptures. Among the earliest sibyls sculpted in choir stalls were those in Ulm cathedral, commissioned from Georges Syrlin between 1469 and 1474.[9]

By the early fifteenth century two new sibyls had joined the ten named by Lactantius. They may have appeared even earlier in mystery plays. A group of twelve sibyls, including the new Europhila and Agripa, is mentioned in records about frescoes executed around 1430 in the palace of Cardinal Orsini in Rome.[10] In an appendix to his 1481 study of the differences between Jerome and Augustine, a Dominican, Filippo Barbieri (1426–87), named twelve sibyls, adding Europea and Agrippa to Lactantius's ten. Barbieri systematically described the twelve, noting their place of origin and providing for each of them an attribute, a fragment of their oracular prophecy, and a corresponding prophet.[11] The new sibyls supported the harmony of typological design by raising their numbers to twelve, aligning them with the twelve Apostles as well as with the Prophets. Printed books soon spread word of their privileged status beyond Italy. As they travelled, the sibyls assumed particular characteristics bestowed by the cultures that welcomed them. Italian artists depicting sibyls around the turn of the sixteenth century did not typically represent the group of twelve.[12] In France, however, images of the twelve sibyls quickly became popular. Whereas the Italian sibyls tended to foretell only the coming and the birth of Christ, French sibyls came to represent also the different moments of Christ's passion.

Jennifer Britnell has studied the trajectory of the sibyls in French literature, from early mystery plays through Symphorien Champier's translation of Lactantius in *La Nef des dames* to Ronsard's poetry and beyond. She shows that French enthusiasm for the Italian humanists and Platonists fostered interest in the sibyls and contributed to their popularity as figures of syncretism validating Christian humanist admiration of Ancient authors.[13] In France the twelve sibyls began appearing in printed books of hours and gradually became prominent in church architecture, taking their places among the prophets and apostles.[14] Emile Mâle counted seventeen such sibyl groups commissioned for sculptures or stained glass windows during the reigns of Louis XII and François I. Louis Réau called them 'the College of Sibyls.'[15] We might also refer to them as the Choir of Sibyls, similar to a Choir of Angels, but also because they began to appear frequently in choirs.

II. The Choir of Sibyls

Two of the most striking realizations of the French Choir of Sibyls are found in the south-west in the cathedrals at Auch and at Saint Bertrand des Comminges. At Auch nine sibyls appeared first in the stained glass windows made by Arnaud de Moles between 1507 and 1513. The choir stalls in Auch, 113 in all, were begun shortly before 1520, ordered and supervised by the cathedral's archbishop, Cardinal François-Guillaume de Clermont-Lodève (1478–1538) and completed in 1554 under the episcopate of Cardinal d'Este. The artists are unknown with only one exception, the Toulousain *huchier* Dominique Bertin, who worked only during the last few years of the construction.[16] Among the sixty-seven dorsal figures in the stalls at Auch, the twelve sibyls alternate with prophets, seven on the north side and five on the south side of the choir. Despite their proximity, both in region and in time, the choir stall figures at Saint Bertrand are very different in number, in style and in distribution from their counterparts at Auch.

The enclosed choir and its intricate sculptures at Saint Bertrand owe their existence to Jean de Mauléon (1477–1551), bishop of the Comminges from 1523 to 1551.[17] Perhaps it was during his consecration in Auch Cathedral, where work on the choir stalls had begun, that he first conceived the project. A year earlier, in the cathedral at Saint Bertrand, lightning had started a fire that severely damaged the wooden choir built in the 1330s. Its restoration and embellishment became Jean de Mauléon's mission and legacy. He commissioned the breathtaking ensemble of *boiseries*: enclosed choir, organ, and *jubé*. The choir was completed in the surprisingly short period of about ten years; an inscription beneath the tribune of the *jubé* marks the dedication of the ensemble on Christmas Day, 1535.[18] Earlier that year, Jean de Mauléon is said to have welcomed Marguerite de Navarre, who would have visited the choir under construction. Local legend records that Marguerite came to the area even earlier to pray for fertility. On the tribune of the *jubé*, Saint Marguerite is the first of a procession of twenty saints. The choir and its sculptures are shrouded in mystery because no record remains to identify the artists. That lacuna, while frustrating, has somehow increased their appeal.

The choir stalls consist of sixty-six seats in two rows, thirty-eight places in the upper row and twenty-eight in the lower. The seats for the canons plus the bishop's throne are all supplied with intricately carved *miséricordes*. Behind the upper seats are forty-two dorsal panels with sculpted figures in recessed niches. Capping each niche is a scallop shell, traditional emblem of Saint Jacques, reminding the viewer that this church was a stop on the pilgrimage road to Compostella. The panel figures include prophets, apostles, virtues, saints — and twelve sibyls. In the overall economy of the Saint Bertrand dorsal sculptures, the sibyls claim pride of place; they alone are displayed as an uninterrupted group of twelve, occupying most of the north wall, the gospel side of the enclosed choir. The prophets and apostles intermingle with the saints, evangelists, and virtues, while the sibyls alone stand together, twelve among forty-two, over a quarter of the figures represented. They are framed by the Old Testament Obeth, son of Ruth, and by Michael the Archangel, the last of the dorsal figures. What programme did the artists follow in arranging them in an uninterrupted series? They left no answer to that question.

While the iconographical attributes of the figures at Saint Bertrand are often like those at Auch, their style is very different. Where the figures at Auch are imposing, with sharp, angular facial features, at Saint Bertrand they are engaging. The small scale of the choir allows the visitor to view them in an intimate setting, just a little above eye-level. Moving from the side entrance along the south wall, we meet first the virgin and child, followed by a series of Old Testament figures, all male, interspersed with female virtues. The prophets and patriarchs are mostly aged, stooped over, their brows furrowed and their faces lined. The female figures, Saint Anne apart, are young women, their heads held high, their necks long and graceful. In portraying them, the artists lavished attention on details that suggest lightness and motion. Most of the virtues, like several of the sibyls, have a lock of hair or a ribbon that escapes upward in an undulating line, as if caught by a breeze. That wavy line recurs in pleasing variety: as an end of the knot that holds Charity's headscarf, as a wisp of hair floating away from Prudence's forehead and repeated in mirror image in the figures of Faith and Hope. On the north side of the choir the sibyls of Phrygia, Hellespont, Delphi and Cumea display similar unruly locks of hair. The robes of the female figures add to the impression of lightness: mantles billow; loose folds fall easily from a raised knee or drape softly across an arm. Most of the figures stand in *contrapposto*, their weight resting on one leg as the other knee bends forward and shapes the body into a subtle curve. That posture suggests that the figures are relaxed and supple, ready to move without effort. Some seem caught while executing a graceful dance step. Everywhere there are sensuous curves that reflect the muted light inside the choir. They echo the arabesque motifs found throughout the choir that call to mind the decorations at Fontainebleau or in the recently rediscovered Domus Aurea in Rome.

The artists who carved these dorsal figures between 1525 and 1535 shared stylistic sensibilities with their contemporary, the poet Clément Marot, who was then at the height of his success. His poetry often appears disarmingly light, only to seize the reader with its poignant beauty. We do not know if he visited Saint Bertrand when, in 1537, he travelled with Marguerite de Navarre and her court through the south-west. Around the time of that journey he began an epigram to a young woman by complimenting her 'Jeune beauté, bon Esprit, bonne grace.' Describing another young woman, he wrote:

C'est beauté naturelle
Et grand vertu en forme corporelle [...]
C'est un jardin et clos
Où tout sçavoir veritable est enclost.[19]

Those lines are particularly apt to describe the sibyls, whom I present here in the order the artists of Saint Bertrand assigned to them.[20]

FIG. 3.1: Cimerian Sibyl [Dorsal 31]
SIBILE CIMERIA

She is identified with Cimer, an area to the north of the Black Sea. Here she leans back slightly and points with her left finger ahead to her eleven companions. Her gesture, repeated by several of the sibyls, reminds us that they were prophets, pointing ahead to the coming of Christ. From her forehead arises, like a hair ornament, a cornucopia brimming with fruits. In her right hand she holds a similar object, another horn of plenty or Oliphant. Her prophecy: a child nursed by his mother. She is a nourishing maternal figure. The marquetry surrounding her reinforces that image. Coins are in the pilaster, arch and spandrel surrounding her. They suggest her affinity with Charity, whose image is also surrounded by coins.

FIG. 3.2: Sibyl of Europe [Dorsal 32]
SIBILE EUROPA

She is one of the two newcomers not mentioned by Lactantius. She foretells the Flight into Egypt, and she carries in her left hand a two-handed sword, symbolizing the massacre of the Holy Innocents. She casts her eyes downward, and her inclined head begins the graceful 'S' flow of her body. The drape of her veil continues in her long fluid mantle, delicately raised and held by her right hand as her left knee advances. Here the *contrapposto* is particularly pronounced, almost as if she were about to participate in a stately pavane.

FIG. 3.3: Persian Sibyl [Dorsal 33]
SIBILLA PERSICA

This is the first of the sibyls' panels to include a small detail in a lower corner, a frequent feature in these stalls. The Persian sibyl raises her left foot to step on a claw-footed dragon. By that gesture she prefigures Mary crushing the head of the serpent who tempted Eve in the Garden of Eden. In her left hand the sibyl holds and balances on her left knee a dark lantern, a lantern that conceals or only partially reveals its light. Lanterns are repeated in the border around her. Her right hand holds an elaborate swirl of her mantle, knotted at her hip.

FIG. 3.4: Phrygian Sibyl [Dorsal 34]
SIBILE FRIGEA

She comes from Asia Minor, from western Anatolia. She holds a trefoiled cross with a streamer (oriflamme), whose ends wave like the hair floating from the nape of her neck. She is the first of the bare-headed sibyls; they all appear even younger than the others. The artists captured for each of them an individual quality of hair. Hers is thick, long and slightly wavy, tied back at the nape of her neck. An ornament adorns it just above her forehead, from which another wavy band of hair floats upward. A braided or intertwined geometric band fills the border around her, and two stars, the one on the left a six-pointed star, like a star of David, and on the right eight-pointed, occupy the spandrels. With an elongated index finger she points to her forehead with her left hand, a cryptic gesture repeated by the Libyan sibyl, the next in line.

FIG. 3.5: Libyan Sibyl [Dorsal 35]
SIBILLA LIBICA

She holds a lighted candle whose spiral lines recall the cornucopia held by the Cimerian sibyl. The candle is repeated in the pilasters and the arch above her head. The candle recalls the opening verses of St John's Gospel that announce the coming of Christ: 'the true light that enlightens every man was coming into the world' (John, 1. 9). By her posture, the sweeping arc of her veil, and her downcast eyes, she mirrors the Persian sibyl, the other bearer of light. Like her Phyrigian predecessor she raises her left hand to point her index finger toward her forehead — or perhaps toward the flame of her candle. Her gesture sweeps up her veil, creating spiral folds and a flowing oval movement around her face. Her sleeves are slashed, following a style favoured at the court of François I. A small tree grows from the rocks at her feet. Augé says it is the tree of knowledge. She represents Africa.

FIG. 3.6: Hellespontian Sibyl [Dorsal 36]
SIBILE ELEPONSIA

She represents the meeting of Europe and Asia in the strait now called the Dardanelles. Since the Hellespont was part of the ancient district of Troy, she is considered a Trojan sibyl. Here she holds a cross raised on a rocky hill, foretelling Christ's death on Calvary. She looks back over her right shoulder toward the Libyan Sibyl, as her right arm reaches across to her left, to the cross. She wears no veil, and her short curls mimic the leaves in the wreath that holds them. The wreath seems to end in a knotted ribbon or two long locks of hair whose ends float away — perhaps in the breeze that lifts her cloak from her shoulders.

Fig. 3.7: Tiburtine Sibyl [Dorsal 37]
SIBILE TIBURTINE

One of the most ancient named sibyls, she is the one whom Augustus was said to have consulted on the spot where the church of the Ara Coeli now stands. Because of that legend she was frequently represented in the Middle Ages. She stands here in three-quarter profile, her left knee raised and her foot resting on a rock. In her left hand she holds a severed hand; it represents the hand of the soldier who slapped Christ after he was arrested. Her robes and veil are simple.

Fig. 3.8: Delphic Sibyl [Dorsal 38]
SIBILLE DELPHICA

Originally Priestess of Apollo, she stands here next to another little hill with a tree, like the Libyan sibyl's, apparently a favourite of the artists. She holds a braided crown or wreath that some say represents the crown of thorns (although there are no thorns evident). Perhaps it is the wreath awarded the victors in the games at Delphi. Perhaps both? The braided circular form is repeated in the pilasters and in the spandrel. She stands with her weight shifted to her right foot as though in a delicate sway. Her cloak has fallen from her right shoulder and is draped across her body over her left arm. Her long hair is swirled and caught by a curious ornament with the now familiar errant wisps floating knotted from her forehead and her neck. The knotted shape is repeated by the sash tied above her waist. Her downcast eyes suggest that her gaze is turned inward.

FIG. 3.9: Samian Sibyl [Dorsal 39]
SIBILLE SANNE

She holds an empty receptacle, generally seen as a cradle announcing the birth of Christ. Others see an empty sarcophagus, suggesting the Resurrection. The ambiguity could be intended. She turns her head to look back at her sibyl predecessors. Her headdress includes a scarf that encircles her chin and is tied in a knot in the back. At her feet to her right a plant grows from a leafy mask, like some that appear in the *miséricordes*.

FIG. 3.10: Agrippan Sibyl [Dorsal 40]
SIBILLE AGRIPE

With the Sibyl of Europe, she is the other 'new' sibyl, bringing the group to twelve. The area she represents is uncertain. In her right hand she holds a whip, symbol of Christ's flagellation, and her index finger points beyond the niche in which she stands. The borders repeat the whip, alternating with bundles of birch switches, instruments of corporal punishment. The border of her cap frames her sober face. An arabesque flower adorns an apron-like drape across the front of her robe.

FIG. 3.11: Erythraean Sibyl [Dorsal 41]
SIBILLE ERITHEA

The oldest of the individualized, named sibyls, her place of origin is Erythrae, an Ionic city on the coast of Asia Minor. The Delphic and Cumaean sibyls evolved from her. She traditionally foretells the Annunciation, shown by her attribute, a long-stemmed rose, symbol of the Virgin Mary ('Mystical Rose' in the litany of the Blessed Mother). Roses fill the border and the spandrels. She wears a wreath of leaves and tiny flowers, and her short hair seems almost like a cap of those leaves. At her feet is a tiny naked man on horseback in front of a cave in the rocks. He seems unaware of her presence, but his horse raises his head and looks up at her. Her right hand holding the rose leads her arm and turns her upper body ahead toward her Cumaean sister, while her head turns to look back on the Agrippan sibyl, a position similar to that of the Hellespontian sibyl, although more pronounced. The folds of her mantle suggest that her left knee moves forward, while her cloak billows away from her right shoulder. She seems to have been caught while hurrying to spread the news of Mary's response to Gabriel's message.

FIG. 3.12: Cumaean Sibyl [Dorsal 42]
SIBILE CUMENA

From her grotto in the hills sacred to Apollo at Cumae, she advised Aeneas about his descent into hell in the sixth book of Virgil's *Aeneid*. Here she carries in her right hand a globe, a sphere. Her left arm curls back to point an elongated index finger at herself or, perhaps, back at the series of twelve sibyls. Her gesture would thereby complement that of the first sibyl, the Cimmerian sibyl who points ahead. At her feet appears again a small tree growing from a rocky hill.

III. Afterlife of the 'Choir of Sibyls'

Although sibyls continued to fascinate poets and artists through the sixteenth century and beyond, the ensemble of twelve sibyls, mingling inside churches in harmonious orthodoxy with the prophets, the apostles, and other Jewish and Christian figures, is contained within six decades, roughly the period between Barbieri's 1481 treatise and the 1540s. Jean Dorat's 1586 edition of the Sibylline Oracles includes images of the sibyls and testifies to their continued interest for humanist scholars such as this revered Hellenist.[21] However, by that time the sibyls were no longer welcomed into churches. The same Christian humanist study of Antiquity that had contributed to their growing popularity ultimately led to their decline. Philological scrutiny allowed scholars to question the dates of the Sibylline Oracles and eventually to challenge their authenticity and, hence, their authority as prophecy. Protestant teachers increasingly looked askance at any source of divine revelation not found in the Bible. Post-Tridentine Catholics became less tolerant of pagan inroads into orthodox tradition and doctrine. The Counter-Reformation Church moved to suppress popular visionary movements, including those that involved women prophesying. In the second half of the sixteenth century, women who claimed to channel divine messages and who communicated them in cryptic language were more and more likely to be condemned as witches.[22] A bit like the death of Pan in Rabelais's *Quart Livre* (ch. 28), the disappearance of the sibyls from prayer books and choir stalls marks the end of an era, an era that fostered the co-habitation of wise pagan women with Christ's apostles and saints and his Old Testament forebears — an era when Erasmus could argue that a good Christian could properly pray to Saint Socrates.[23] We might well feel today in our own world a poignant nostalgia for that spirit of religious and cultural syncretism.

IV. Methodology

When I first saw the choir sculptures of Saint Bertrand, I did not have in mind more than a superficial knowledge of the sibyls' pre-history. Researching their past was a consequence of my initial attraction rather than a prerequisite. My attraction to the dorsal figures did not depend on Lactantius or Virgil or even Marguerite de Navarre. In fact, I was unprepared for the intensity of surprised admiration I felt when I first stood in that softly lit space surrounded by the intricately carved warm wood and beheld the figures in their shallow niches. Learning more about them helped to compensate for no longer being in their presence, but it did not explain why I found them so appealing.

My approach was initially historical; research led me back from Saint Bertrand to Erithrea and Delphi, via Barbieri, Lactantius, Augustine, and others. As a student of literature, I hoped to find along the way literary connections, not simply with any sibyls but with this group of twelve. Intrigued by the possibility that Marguerite de Navarre had seen these figures, I kept hoping to find some vestige of that encounter in her works. However, if her visit left a trace in her writings, I have not found it. My investigation of the twelve sibyls draws on the iconographical studies of Emile

Mâle and others. One could continue that line of study, examining in more detail how the attributes of the Saint Bertrand sibyls compare to those in the choir stalls at Auch or to the list in Barbieri's treatise. However, that avenue did not satisfy my desire to convey in words their arresting beauty.

To do that, I had to view the images anew and ask myself what made them beautiful in my eyes. In *Pré-histoires I*, Terence Cave writes: 'chaque texte littéraire est un *hapax*' (p. 12). I realized that the same was true for a work of art, for an ensemble of sculpted figures in the Pyrenees. The appeal of the sibyls of Saint Bertrand resided in the individual qualities their creators had bestowed on them. The unknown artists had made them emerge from their long journey through history and given them with great care and delicate stylistic finesse traits that made them different from their predecessors, even from their neighbours in other French churches. I had to move beyond the familiar, comfortable support of scholarly research, presumed to be objective, and identify the qualities in those sculptures that surprised me with pleasure and admiration. That shift called for another register of language, more personal and subjective.

The identity of the Saint Bertrand artists is only one of the mysteries waiting within that enclosed choir. We should not forget that sibyls, when making their oracular pronouncements, refuse to yield answers transparently. The Persian sibyl's dark lantern, the Samian sibyl's ambiguous cradle–sarcophagus, the recurring gesture of the elongated index finger, all remind us that the sibyls resist iconographical as well as oracular certitude. They are at the same time enticing and elusive. As such, they can stand as emblems for the process of interpretation, inviting it even as they challenge those who undertake the task, be they emperors, exegetes, or modern scholars. Their appeal to me is related to the pull I feel toward an essay of Montaigne, toward a work I find compelling even though — or perhaps because — I do not yet completely understand it. The sibyls' fingers point toward that which is not yet fully clear. They embody an aesthetic principle favoured by the writers whose works I find most beautiful. A few decades after they were carved, a not too distant neighbour in south-west France defended that principle and encouraged his diligent readers with these sibylline words: 'Ce que je ne puis exprimer, je le montre au doigt.'[24]

Notes to Chapter 3

I thank Anna Holland, Richard Scholar, and Agnieszka Steczowicz for organizing the 'Pre-Histories and Afterlives' conference and, along with Rowan Tomlinson, for extending to me their kind hospitality and their insightful comments on my paper.

1. Plutarch, 'On the Pythian Oracle' (VI, 397a). Aristophanes in *Peace* (l. 1095) and Plato in the *Phaedrus* (244b) refer to a single sibyl.

2. H. W. Parke, *Sibyls and Sibylline Prophecy in Classical Antiquity*, Croom Helm Classical Studies, ed. by B. C. McGinn (London: Routledge, 1988). Edwyn R. Bevan, *Sibyls and Seers: A Survey of Some Ancient Theories of Revelation and Inspiration* (Cambridge, MA: Harvard University Press, 1929).

3. Lactantius, *The Divine Institutes*, Books I–VII, trans. by Sister Mary Francis McDonald, OP (Washington: Catholic University of America Press, 1964), p. 34; *Sancti Aurelii Augustini episcopi De civitate Dei, libri XXII*, ed. by B. Dombart and A. Kalb, Bibliotheca scriptorum Graecorum et Romanorum Teubneriana, 2 vols (Stuttgart: Teubner, 1981), II, 287; Augustine, *City of God*,

ed. by David Knowles (Harmondsworth: Penguin Books, 1972), X, 27, p. 411 and XVIII, p. 790.

4. Bard Thompson, 'Patristic Use of the Sibylline Oracles', *The Review of Religion*, 16 (1952), 118–36. Bernard McGinn, '*Teste David cum Sibylla*: The Significance of the Sibylline Tradition in the Middle Ages', in *Women in the Medieval World: Essays in Honor of John H. Mundy*, ed. by J. Kirshner and S. Wemple (London: Basil Blackwell, 1985), pp. 7–35; Arnaldo Momigliano, 'From the Pagan to the Christian Sibyl: Prophecy as History of Religion', in *The Uses of Greek and Latin: Historical Essays* (London: The Warburg Institute, 1988), pp. 3–18.

5. Emile Mâle, *L'Art religieux en France de la fin du Moyen âge en France* (Paris: Armand Colin, 1969), pp. 253–77 (p. 256); trans. *Religious Art in France: The Late Middle Ages. A Study of Medieval Iconography and Its Sources*, trans. by Marthiel Mathews, ed. by Harry Bober, Bollingen Series XC.3 (Princeton, NJ: Princeton University Press, 1986), pp. 236–57; Creighton E. Gilbert, *Michelangelo On and Off the Sistine Ceiling* (New York: George Braziller, 1994), pt. 1, pp. 59–113. In Spain, several regions developed their own haunting renditions of the sibyl's song, El Cant de la Sibilla.

6. *The Divine Comedy of Dante Alighieri*, trans. and ed. by John D. Sinclair, 3 vols (New York: Oxford University Press, 1961), III, 480; Christine de Pizan, *Livre de la cité des dames of Christine de Pisan: A Critical Edition*, ed. by Maureen Cheney Curnow, 2 vols, PhD dissertation, Vanderbilt University, 1973 (Ann Arbor, Michigan: U.M.I. Dissertation services, 1993); *The Book of the City of Ladies*, trans. by Earl J. Richards (New York: Persea Books, 1982), pp. 99–100.

7. Mâle, *Religious Art*, p. 238; Hélène Casez, '*Verbum inuisibile palpabitur*: Les Sibylles dans la seconde moitié du XVe siècle. La Répétition comme poétique de l'oracle', in *The Changing Tradition: Women in the History of Rhetoric*, ed. by Christine M. Sutherland (Calgary: University of Calgary Press, 1999), pp. 73–84.

8. Thomas Kren and Kurt Barstow, *Italian Illuminated Manuscripts in the J. Paul Getty Museum* (Los Angeles: Getty Publications, 2005), p. 57.

9. Mâle, *Religious Art*, pp. 256–57; Michael Baxandall, *The Limewood Sculptures of Renaissance Germany* (New Haven, CT: Yale University Press, 1990), pp. 255–56.

10. Carlo de Clercq, 'Quelques séries italiennes de Sibylles', *Bulletin de l'Institut historique belge de Rome*, 48/49 (1978/79), 105–27. Clercq's series of articles on sibyl groups is extremely valuable, at times correcting or adding precision to Mâle's classic work. On the sibyls in the Orsini palace frescoes, see pp. 106–18; Mâle, *Religious Art*, pp. 258–59, and Gilbert, *Michelangelo*, pp. 69–72. Gilbert (p. 69) refers to a mystery play performed in 1385 in which twelve sibyls are named.

11. *Discordantiae nonnullae inter sanctum Hieronymum et Augustinum* (1481). Clercq, 'Quelques séries italiennes de Sibylles' (pp. 118–24) gives detailed descriptions of Barbieri's text on the sibyls and includes their images.

12. E.g. Pinturichio's four sibyls in Santa Maria del Popolo (1485). On the Sistine ceiling (1508–12) Michelangelo privileged only five: the Delphic, Erythraean, Cumaean, Persian, and Libyan sibyls, along with seven prophets. See Edgar Wind, 'Michelangelo's Prophets and Sibyls', *Proceedings of the British Academy*, 51 (1967), 47–84. Raphaël painted four sibyls (Cumaean, Persian, Phrygian, Tiburtine) beneath the four prophets of Timoteo Viti in Santa Maria della Pace (1514). There are ten sibyls on the marble pavement of Siena cathedral; they were completed in 1482–83, almost contemporary with Barbieri's treatise. Perugino's sibyls in the hall of the *cambio* in Perugia date from 1499–1500.

13. Jennifer Britnell, 'The Rise and Fall of the Sibyls in Renaissance France', in *Schooling and Society: The Ordering and Reordering of Knowledge in the Western Middle Ages*, ed. by Alasdair A. MacDonald and Michael W. Toomey (Leuven: Peeters, 2004), pp. 173–85; and 'Revelation to the Pagans: The Sibyls in Sixteenth-Century France', *Durham French Colloquies*, 2 (1989), 21–35.

14. 'The sibyls, for example, are ubiquitous in the margins of printed Books of Hours produced in Paris in the late fifteenth century'; Martha Driver, 'Picturing the Apocalypse in the Printed Book of Hours', in *Prophecy, Apocalypse and the Day of Doom*, Proceedings of the 2000 Harlaxton Symposium, Harlaxton Medieval Studies, XII (Donington, Lincs.: Shaun Tyas, 2004), pp. 52–67 (pp. 53–54).

15. Mâle, *Religious Art*, p. 506, n.182; Louis Réau, *Iconographie de l'art chrétien*, 3 tomes in 6 vols (Paris: PUF, 1955–59), vol. II, 1, 420–31. Carlo de Clercq, 'Quelques séries de Sibylles hors

d'Italie', *Bulletin de l'Institut historique belge de Rome*, 51 (1981), 87–116, especially (for France) pp. 91–102.

16. Raymond Montané, *Stalles et vitraux de la cathédrale d'Auch* (Auch: Paroisse de la cathédrale d'Auch, 1989); André Péré, 'Les Sibylles de la Cathédrale d'Auch', *Bulletin de la Société Archéologique et Historique du Gers*, 88 (1987), 125–42; Jacques Esterle, 'Les Sibylles associées aux prophètes dans les choeurs d'Auch et de Saint Bertrand des Comminges', in *Pensée, image et communication en Europe médiévale: A propos des stalles de Saint-Claude* (Besançon: Asprodic, 1993), pp. 201–06; Mâle, *Religious Art*, p. 507, n. 189.

17. Jean de Contrasty, *Histoire des évêques de Comminges* (Toulouse: Librairie Sistac, 1940), pp. 279–86.

18. *Saint-Bertrand-de-Comminges: Le Chœur Renaissance; Saint-Just de Valcabrère: L'Eglise romane*, ed. by Sylvie Augé et al. (Graulhet: Editions Odyssée, 2000), is the most complete work available on the church and its choir. It contains images of excellent quality showing in detail each of the dorsal figures, as well as the *miséricordes*. Also very valuable is Jean-Pierre Denis, *Histoires de Chœur: Saint-Bertrand-de-Comminges, les stalles et l'orgue* (Toulouse: Le Pérégrinateur, 1995). See also Emile Gavelle, 'Les Stalles de Saint-Bertrand-de-Comminges', *Revue de Comminges* (1937), 51–54 and 55–60.

19. Clément Marot, *Œuvres complètes*, ed. by G. Defaux, 2 vols (Paris: Bordas, Classiques Garnier, 1990; 1993), II, 265, 295.

20. I reproduce in upper-case letters the identifying label at the base of each sibyl. The spelling of 'sibyl' varies.

21. Jean Dorat, *Sibyllarum duodecim oracula ex antiquo libro latine* (Paris: J. Rabel, 1586).

22. Anthony Grafton surveys the challenges to the authenticity of the sibyls' prophecies in 'Higher Criticism Ancient and Modern: The Lamentable Deaths of Hermes and the Sibyls', in *The Uses of Greek and Latin* (London: The Warburg Institute, 1988), pp. 155–70. Jennifer Britnell argues convincingly that along with the philological evidence that discredited the oracular texts, the sibyls' status as women made them increasingly suspect as fear of witches spread in the second half of the sixteenth century and beyond; see 'The Rise and Fall of the Sibyls in Renaissance France', esp. pp. 179–83. That negative view of sibyls appears already in Antoine de la Sale's *Le Paradis de la Reine Sibylle*, ed. by F. Desonay (Paris: Droz, 1930), a curious fifteenth-century narrative about a pilgrimage to the sibyl's cave in the Apennines. That sibyl is represented as an alluring temptress rather than a virgin prophetess. Winfried Frey discovers sinister sibyls in German mystery plays; see 'Sibylla Led Astray: Sibyls in Medieval Literature', in *Demons: Mediators between this World and the Other*, ed. by Ruth Petzoldt and Paul Neubauer (New York: Peter Lang, 1998), pp. 51–64. Gabriella Zarri chronicles the popularity and then suppression of Italian female visionaries; see 'Living Saints: A Typology of Female Sanctity in the Early Sixteenth Century', in *Women and Religion in Medieval and Renaissance Italy*, ed. by Daniel Bornstein and Roberto Rusconi, trans. by Margery J. Schneider (Chicago: University of Chicago Press, 1996), pp. 219–303.

23. Rabelais, *Œuvres complètes*, ed. by M. Huchon (Paris: Gallimard, Bibliothèque de la Pléiade, 1994), p. 604; Erasmus, 'The Godly Feast', in *Colloquies*, ed. and trans. by Craig R. Thompson (Chicago: University of Chicago Press, 1965), pp. 46–78 (p. 68).

24. Montaigne, *Essais*, III. 9, 983.

CHAPTER 4

❖

Early Modern Swansongs

Anna Holland

What does the idea of an 'afterlife' mean to literary artists in the early modern period?[1] How do they face the prospect of their own demise, and what sort of continuing identity do they imagine for themselves in the form of posthumous renown? I propose to approach these questions by focusing on a particular cultural milieu, that of the French poets of the Pléiade, at a significant 'threshold' moment in the development of vernacular poetry, the 1550s. The cluster of poets whose work I discuss were alert to the perspective of posterity, and took steps to shape as far as possible their own posthumous reputations. I shall be examining the imaginative means through which they conceived of their 'afterlife', and the range of responses it provoked in their work. My aim is to contextualize the particular affective charge that the question of an afterlife carries by tracking closely the textual traces of disturbance — unease, hope, anxiety, exhilaration, fear — in the work of poets face to face with the uncertainty of their own posterity.

My argument centres upon a single emblematic image representing one particular mode of figuring the 'afterlife', that of the poet troped as eluding death and gaining immortality by metamorphosing into a swan. It is a characteristic feature of early modern as well as classical texts that the probing and exploratory 'work' that a text performs may be pursued as much through the development of figures and tropes of discourse as through more openly discursive means, and that metaphors and similes employed in this way may be invested with an affective potential of their own.[2] In the case of the poet-becoming-swan, the image acts as a kind of prism through which the complex responses of French poets in the 1550s are refracted and intensified. The image has a rich history, belonging to a family of figures rooted in both Greek and Latin literature and strongly associated with the genre of lyric in which the poet and the immortality he or she bestows are likened to the majestic flight of a bird.[3] Poets came to be particularly closely linked with the swan, as tradition had it that before death the swan sang with extreme sweetness and was endowed with the gift of prophecy, and so came under the protection of Apollo.[4] The image is found in three subtly different forms, each with its own tonality. The first, elegiac and melancholy, is of the poet–swan as the emblem of grief and mourning.[5] The second, also melancholic, is of the ageing poet whose white hair and proximity to death recall the snowy whiteness of the dying swan.[6] The third and ostensibly most optimistic is of the poet whose metamorphosis symbolizes the achievement through poetic skill of immortal renown the length and breadth of the known world. Yet even in this third and most positive form, for which the *locus classicus* is Horace, *Odes* II.20, the elements of melancholy and mourning, twinned with the ghost of failure (Icarus) are present in shadow, in their very denial, and return in a number of later incarnations of the image. It is this third form of the image which assumes a particular and programmatic resonance within the poetic discourse of 1550s France, and is the principal focus of my argument.

In teasing out the implications of this image of the afterlife, I am also seeking to tell the story of a classical trope and its early modern avatars: the afterlife of an image. For the literary technique of *imitatio*, in which the work of the poet's precursors is the point of origin for each fresh act of literary creation, is integral to the way in which the early modern poets discussed here conceive of their afterlife.[7] From their perspective, the direction of time's arrow that we associate with European modernity is, so to speak, reversed: to project themselves forward from the present into the imagined future of an afterlife is at one and the same time to project themselves backward into the past.[8] In choosing to develop the image of the poet's metamorphosis into a swan as an assertion of confidence in their own poetic powers, they characteristically turn back towards a textual precedent from antiquity, that of Horace imagining his own posterity.[9] By imitating their Roman lyric precursor, they ensure not only their own posthumous renown but also an 'afterlife' for Horace himself, in a form which he himself would have understood.[10] Furthermore, through the example of this gesture of repetition, they invite appropriation of their own text in the work of new poets in the future who will sing the swansong in their turn; in this way, their own literary afterlife will be assured, as a link in the vulnerable yet vital chain of repetition and renewal connecting ancient and early modern culture that is forged through *imitatio*. Participating in the retrospective dynamic of imitation in this way, early modern poets seek to stabilize the uncertain, unknown form of the future by figuring it as the known form of the future-in-the-past.

The gesture of *imitatio* brings with it attendant questions, anxieties, problems: what looks like a movement of repetition is never merely that, as the surrounding context is necessarily different, sometimes dramatically so. For the Pléiade poets, *imitatio* creates a bridge towards the past spanning a millennium and a half — and in the case of their Greek sources, further still. Certain stances, certain personae are no longer possible, or at the very least invite ridicule. If this was true for Horace facing his great Greek predecessor Pindar, then it is doubly, triply so for the belated poets of the Pléiade. To engage in *imitatio* is to invite direct comparison with the cultural archetypes of one's chosen genre, to wrestle directly and textually with the *corpora* of one's precursors. Success appears beyond reach — at one and the same time to *follow* and to *outdo*; failure entails not only one's own 'death' (ridicule and oblivion), but that of one's generic antecedents too. This is the paradox explored by Horace himself, who in his *Odes* qualifies Pindar as inimitable while engaging in explicit and self-conscious imitation of his precursor.[11]

My account of the afterlife of the poet-becoming-swan figure, concerned as it is with the range of affective responses generated by and mediated through Horace's image and implicated in the process of *imitatio*, shares with Terence Cave's work a methodological concern for instances of textual 'trouble' and 'perturbation', as evoked in his work on pre-histories and (more indirectly) in subsequent writing on afterlives, in particular the afterlife of Goethe's Mignon.[12] My approach also shares with Cave's method the attempt to suspend knowledge of the future trajectory of a given cultural phenomenon and to resist the temptations of an 'analeptic' reading, in order to restore to the textual moment its historical particularity (in this case, the perspective of the poet facing a future which is blank and in which manifold future trajectories remain open).[13] However, the aim of my enquiry diverges from Cave's insofar as he is particularly engaged in analysing certain early modern 'threshold' phenomena that foreground developments that we identify as characteristic of modernity. In that sense, the traces of *trouble* in Cave's archipelago of examples indicate cognitive disturbance provoked by a sense of *prematurity*, of being in advance of the age. I too am concerned with anxieties peculiar to a particular historical moment (the mid-sixteenth century) and which mark a significant threshold. However, this is a threshold that faces two ways, towards antiquity and the past as well as towards modernity and the future. My enquiry looks, in Cave's terms, 'upstream' as well as 'downstream': it seeks to articulate the 'troubles' provoked by a sense of *belatedness*.[14] It poses a set of further questions: 'To what extent is the form of afterlife evoked here temporally and culturally specific to antiquity and the early modern period? What afterlives have died with us, late-coming products of the era of modernity, for whom *imitatio* is a distant and dusty practice? And what forms of afterlife have come to replace those that have died?'

I. Back to the Future?

In composing *Odes* II.20, Horace must himself have contended with the anxieties besetting a latecomer to the lyric tradition. The Greek lyric canon had long been fixed at nine consecrated names, and the idea of adding a Roman as a tenth would have seemed extraordinary. There were no vacancies.[15] Yet this ode, placed in a programmatic position at the close of the second book, makes the hubristic claim that the poet has earned his right to immortality and indeed to a place in the lyric canon. At issue is the value of a lifetime of poetic endeavour. Horace shows elsewhere that he is acutely conscious of the stakes for which he is playing: lionization and being pointed out in the street with admiration (*Odes* IV.3.21–24; IV.6.41–44), or the ignominy of his works being judged good for nothing but sordid wrapping paper on some market stall (*Epistles* II.1.267–70). The extraordinary gesture that Horace is making is further compounded by the fact that the poet is claiming the power to confer immortality upon *himself*. While there are examples in extant Greek lyric of poets assuming the ability to render other people immortal, there are few if any examples of them claiming to confer immortality upon themselves.[16] So Horace's gesture is in its self-reflexivity distinctively Roman, and as such, lacks the validating assurance of Greek cultural precedent.

Horace's anxieties of belatedness appear to inscribe themselves within the texture of his ode. For his treatment of the scene of metamorphosis has demonstrated a lasting power to generate unease, the frisson of disturbance, even embarrassment, in succeeding generations of readers, to a degree which places this source-text in the ranks of the 'textes troublés'.[17] It is notable that the poem's modern editors Nisbet and Hubbard, for example, qualify aspects of the poem as 'bizarre', 'surprising' and 'grotesque'; they single out the 'ironic whimsicality' of the third stanza for especial mention.[18] I should like to offer a brief analysis of the ode, drawing out those elements that have provoked most puzzlement and disquiet. I have adopted here the translation by David West, which seems to me to capture best the poem's curious tone.[19]

The poet's stance of prophetic confidence is undercut from the outset by notes of self-disparagement. The poet is presented as a strange sort of binary hybrid, a 'biformis [...] vates', figured at the moment of transition as existing in a 'zone médiane' between man and bird, mortal and immortal, earth and air — and also by implication between Greek and Latin, between 'lyricus' and 'satyricus'. Tension is created between the poet's relatively humble social origins and his high poetic ambition, and attention is deliberately drawn to the risk that he is running:

> Non usitata nec tenui ferar
> penna biformis per liquidum aethera
> vates, neque in terris morabor
> longius, invidiaque maior
> urbis relinquam. non ego pauperum
> sanguis parentum, non ego quem vocas,
> dilecte Maecenas, obibo
> nec Stygia cohibebor unda. (1–8)

[This is no ordinary, no flimsy wing which will bear me, half-bard, half-bird, through the liquid air, nor shall I longer remain on the earth, but, grown too large for envy, I shall leave its cities. I, who am of the blood of poor parents, I who come at your command, my beloved Maecenas, shall not die, nor be confined by the waves of the Styx.]

In stanza three, the poet offers a graphic description of the physical process of transformation that sits most uneasily within the generic conventions of Pindaric lyric that are observed elsewhere in the ode. There appears to be generic *contaminatio* from the ultra-realist strand within Hellenistic Greek art and literature in which metamorphosis was an established subject. For Horace's later readers, it is as if the poet's lyric voice is transmogrified for a moment into that of his younger fellow-poet Ovid:[20]

> Iam iam residunt cruribus asperae
> pelles, et album mutor in alitem
> superne, nascunturque leves
> per digitos umerosque plumae. (9–12)

[Already, even now, rough skin is forming on my legs, my upper part is changing into a white swan and smooth feathers are sprouting along my fingers and shoulders.]

Critics, both early modern and modern, find the third stanza particularly problematic. The fifteenth-century Italian humanist Landino, for example, author of the first printed commentary on Horace, is moved to chart in extraordinary physiological detail the stages of the poet's physical transformation, as if obliged to go toe-to-toe with Horace in graphic description; he expounds on the difference between the scaly, fleshless legs of the bird and the man's fleshy ones, and focuses on the sequence of physical changes, beginning in the legs and then moving along the upper extremities, that lead from man to bird.[21] Modern critics find the stanza equally disturbing. Fraenkel in the twentieth century does not mince his words:

> This detailed description, appropriate to the kind of tale which we know from Ovid's *Metamorphoses*, is in the context of this ode repulsive or ridiculous, or both: repulsive, because the lofty idea of the transfigured *vates* leaves no room for the crude zoological precision in *residunt cruribus asperae pelles*; ridiculous, because the person who undergoes this metamorphosis is not some poet or a typical poet but a definite individual, represented in the reality of his personal life [...] Picture this plump and bald little man turning into a swan, complete with *asperae pelles* and all.[22]

In the following stanzas, the process of metamorphosis is complete and the poet tropes the prospect of his posthumous renown reaching the furthest outposts of the known world as the swan's flight to distant lands:

> Iam Daedaleo notior[23] Icaro
> visam gementis litora Bosphori
> Syrtisque Gaetulas canorus
> ales Hyperboreosque campos.
> me Colchus et qui dissimulat metum
> Marsae cohortis Dacus et ultimi
> noscent Geloni, me peritus
> discet Hiber Rhodanique potor.
> absint inani funere neniae
> luctusque turpes et querimoniae;
> compesce clamorem ac sepulcri
> mitte supervacuos honores. (13–24)

> [Already more famous than Icarus, the son of Daedalus, I shall visit, a harmonious bird, the shores of the moaning Bosphorus, the Gaetulian Syrtes, and the Hyperborean plains. The Colchian will know me, and the Dacian who pretends not to fear a cohort of Marsians, the Geloni at the ends of the earth, the learned Iberian, the Rhône-swigger. Let there be no dirges or squalid mourning or lamentation at my corpseless funeral. Check your cries of grief and do not trouble with the empty honour of a tomb.]

In these lines, Horace appears deliberately to allude to the lowering clouds of poetic failure through the gratuitous allusion to Icarus, that simulacrum of true metamorphosis and symbol of hubris whose wings failed.[24] As Nisbet and Hubbard, following the late-seventeenth-/early-eighteenth-century editor Bentley, note dryly *ad loc.*, '[I]t is an awkward circumstance that Icarus was famous for his fall rather than his flight.'[25] Awkward indeed. The shadow of failure is carefully enfolded by Horace within this ostensibly self-confident assertion of posthumous fame. Grief and mourning are present too, in spite of the apotropaic presence of the subjunctive 'absint'.

Successive generations of readers and critics have been alert to the discomfiting elements of the poem, and some have sought to smooth over the sites of disturbance in the text by emendation, or even excision. In the line referring to Icarus, for example, Bentley proposed 'tutior' ['safer'] in place of 'ocior' ['swifter'] in order to render the reading of Icarus himself 'safer', while in the early nineteenth century Peerlkamp proposed simply excising stanza three. More recently, others have suggested that the poem's provocative elements fundamentally alter its rhetorical function and import. W. R. Johnson has argued that the poem should be considered parodic, a poetic hoax, 'because the extravagance and the naiveté of the simile get on [Horace's] nerves; because this boast evokes the demon Superbia and the demon Cupiditas by whom he is already sufficiently beset.'[26] Although I disagree with Johnson's interpretation, because it seems to me another way of 'smoothing over' the anxieties that the text generates, I would suggest that if the poem makes us uncomfortable, it is because Horace willed it so. In other words, I would argue that our responses result, not from cack-handed poetic ineptitude, but from deliberate aesthetic strategy, perhaps in order to suggest that the domain occupied by the lyric poet's voice of hubristic self-confidence is adjacent to, and perhaps overlaps, that of the ludicrous.

On this analysis, the image of the poet's metamorphosis fulfils a performative as much as a descriptive function in stirring up in the reader the potential unease and embarrassment experienced by the poet contemplating the prospect of his own afterlife. My contention is that a number of early modern French poets were fully aware of the performative dimension of Horace's image and its potential for generating unease, and that they deliberately chose to exploit the provocative qualities of that source-text in their own attempts to represent their prospective afterlife. By doing so, those late-comers to the lyric tradition could re-vivify a cluster of images — of poetic flight, of winged inspiration — which risked becoming, through their ubiquity and their too-convenient assimilation into Platonic and Neoplatonic conceptual frameworks, so trite and banal as to lose their signifying power. Instead, the imitators of Horace's image of the poet-becoming-swan were able, if they so chose, to re-invest the trope of the poet's metamorphosis and flight with heuristic possibilities: they could draw attention to uncomfortable contradictions inherent in this model of poetic identity and the afterlife, and could employ the figure to probe as well as reassure. The process of *imitatio* itself became a heuristic one, as the imitators of Horace's image flirted with risk.

II. Crossing the Threshold

It seems to me that at the heart of the unease generated by the image of the poet's transformation into a swan is anxiety, even anguish, at the prospect of ending, non-being, silence, death. In Horace's poem the drama of the physical description of the process of metamorphosis (that troublesome third stanza) occurs just after the unambiguous reference to, and protest against, death ('non [...] obibo' ['I shall not die']), and thus serves, I would suggest, as a diversion and as a means of concealing the threat posed by the prospect of non-being. However, the image of transformation itself conceals a logical aporia: metamorphosis into a swan is offered as a symbol of the poet's deathless fame and continued existence in the afterlife. Yet the song that the poet–swan sings is, inevitably, culturally loaded with death: it is, as we have seen, only the dying swan that sings. In the early modern period, we find the tradition of the swan's impending death linked to the power of prophecy expressed in Rabelais, drawing on Erasmus and a number of Classical loci, as follows:

> Les cycnes, qui sont oyseaulx sacrez à Apollo, ne chantent jamais, si non quand ilz approchent de leur mort: [...] de mode que chant de cycne est praesaige certain de sa mort prochaine, et ne meurt que praealablement n'ayt chanté. Semblablement les poëtes qui sont en protection de Apollo, approchans de leur mort ordinairement deviennent prophetes et chantent par Apolline inspiration vaticinans des choses futures. (*Tiers Livre* Ch XXI: 'Comment Panurge prent conseil d'ung vieil poëte François nommé Raminagrobis') [27]

The prophetic power of the dying swan, the ability to look ahead to 'choses futures', is the faculty that can bring about the marvellous transmutation of grief, agony or fear into hope, joy and exultation.[28] This is the point made by Plato in the *Phaedo*, in which Socrates, facing clear-sightedly his imminent death, compares himself to the swan: swans do not sing at the approach of death through pain or fear, but rather because, being prophetic birds belonging to Apollo, they foresee the blessings of Hades lying ahead. So too he, Socrates, rejoices at the approach of death.[29]

So the figure of the metamorphosis of the poet into a swan simultaneously serves to conceal the prospect of death, and to reveal it, to draw attention away from the fear of non-being, and to underscore it. Thus, the instant at which metamorphosis is about to begin represents a privileged threshold or crossing-point, an instant of psychological suspense between fear and joy, disquiet and anticipation. It not only captures the moment of greatest risk and potential vulnerability within the process of metamorphosis, but it also represents from the poet's point of view the riskiest part of Horace's poem to imitate, because closest to the ludicrous.

In France in the early 1550s, at a significant period in the history of the development of vernacular literature, imitation of this particular textual moment acquired for a brief period the status of a threshold or 'seuil' in poetic initiation, and became a mark of belonging and a test of both allegiance and skill in imitation.[30] Du Bellay is one of the initiators in this development. In a programmatic position at the close of his collection, *La Musagnoeomachie et Aultres Oeuvres poétiques* of 1550, Du Bellay chooses precisely this potentially embarrassing moment to imitate. He fuses the first-person, subjective mode of his lyric persona with that of Horace, and thus by projecting himself forward into the afterlife, he is at the same time inhabiting Horace's future-in-the-past:

> D'ou vient ce plumâge blanc,
> Qui ma forme premiere emble?
> Desja l'un & l'autre flanc
> Dessous une aele me tremble.
> Nouveau Cigne, ce me semble,
> Je remply l'air de mes criz.[31]

The context of this passage within Du Bellay's poem, entitled 'Contre les envieux poetes, à Pierre de Ronsard', is itself programmatic and polemical; Du Bellay is developing an antagonistic relationship also sketched out in the *Deffence et Illustration de la Langue Françoyse* between certain 'unreconstructed' poetic opponents, troped, in accordance with the topos, as 'corbeaux' ['crows'] and those poetic allies whom he identifies as members of a new community, 'Les nouveaux Cignes'.[32] The passage from Horace, representing a threshold moment, serves as one means of discriminating between 'swans' and 'crows'.

The programmatic force of this comparison is further confirmed by Du Bellay in the preface to *L'Olive augmentee depuis la premiere edition* (1550). He evokes the hostile reaction given to the *Deffence* by the 'rhetoriqueurs', and in the context of this polemic establishes an oppositional relation between swans and crows, drawing on the Erasmian adage, 'the swans will sing when the crows cease', i.e. good poets live on after their insignificant rivals have sunk into oblivion:

> Or ay-je depuis experimenté ce qu'au paravant j'avoy assez preveu c'est, que d'un tel oeuvre [i.e. the *Deffence*] je ne rapporteroy jamais favorable jugement de noz rethoriqueurs François: tant pour les raisons assez nouvelles, et paradoxes introduites par moy en nostre vulgaire, que pour avoir (ce semble) hurté un peu trop rudement à la porte de noz ineptes rimasseurs. Ce que j'ay faict, lecteur, non pour aultre raison, que pour eveiller le trop long silence des cignes: et endormir l'importun croassement des corbeaux.[33]

Here Du Bellay explicitly associates the swan, along with its dark shadow the crow, with provocation, and with the desire to jolt his contemporaries from their complacency and to awaken again the voices of those swans silent for too long. It is in the context of such a desire to provoke that, I think, Du Bellay's imitation of *Odes* II.20 must be understood.

The programmatic association of Du Bellay with the difficult moment of metamorphosis described in stanza three of *Odes* II.20 receives remarkable confirmation from Du Bellay's fellow-poet Jacques Grévin. In his poem 'Pour le tombeau de Joachim Du Bellay', published in 1560 in the wake of the poet's untimely death, he imagines himself impelled by divine influence to contribute to his friend's 'tombeau' by sculpting in relief the emblematic representation of Du Bellay in the process of becoming a swan:

> Puis je fay à demi-bosse
> Un corps qui se convertit
> Desja petit-à-petit
> En un Cygne qui s'esgaye
> Voyant sa celeste voye.[34]

It is on the awkward moment of transition that Grévin fixes. Grévin's poet-swan figure is, significantly, a joyful one; so, the image of metamorphosis here clearly becomes a means of transmuting grief at the poet's tragic death into a more positive affirmation of a posthumous 'second' life guaranteed by his own poetic oeuvre — and that of his friend.

Looking back at Du Bellay's original choice of the poet-becoming-swan image, it seems clear that it is richly overdetermined: it does not result from developments in the literary tradition alone, but emerges, I would suggest, from a serendipitous confluence of Horace's popularity in the textual domain with artistic and musical strands of influence. In Alciato's emblem-book, for example, which was first printed in France in 1534, and which enjoyed great popularity throughout the sixteenth century, we find the armorial bearing of poets represented as a swan.[35] The delicate moment of transition between man and swan was also attracting significant artistic attention: in Aneau's *Picta poesis* of 1552, for example, 'Facunda Senectus' (The Eloquence of the Old) is represented by the figure of Nestor as a curious swan–man hybrid, still clothed and wearing a crown, with human legs but with a swan's head, wings and webbed feet.[36] Icarus, that simulacrum of metamorphosis, was another favourite subject for the creators of emblems throughout the sixteenth century.[37]

Complementing the strands within visual culture in the early 1550s is a popular song from Italy which, along with its composer, Jacques Arcadelt (*c.*1505–68) crosses the Alps to France and to the French court at this time in the entourage of Charles de Guise, Cardinal de Lorraine, a great patron of the arts and closely linked to the Pléiade poets.[38] The song is Arcadelt's madrigal setting of 'Il bianco e dolce cigno'.[39] Erotic in tone in its comparison of the bliss of the poet–lover with the swan's impending death, it enjoyed great popularity, becoming perhaps the best-known and most widely sung Italian madrigal of the sixteenth century.[40] The Cardinal de Lorraine encountered Arcadelt in the papal musical establishment during one of his frequent visits to Italy in the late 1540s, and induced him to work in his service at the French court, where he stayed until 1562.[41] Although the record of his activities and surviving compositions is fragmentary, while working for the Cardinal de Lorraine he is known to have set a number of Horace's odes to music; he also composed settings for poems by Baïf, Magny, Ronsard and Du Bellay.[42] Given the popularity of 'Il bianco e dolce cigno' and Arcadelt's close association with the Pléiade poets and their most influential patron, it is possible at least that musical swansongs contributed to the popularity and programmatic force of Horace's poet-becoming-swan and the enterprise of the 'Nouveaux Cygnes'.

III. Unstable Metamorphoses

Over the threshold of metamorphosis lay the prospect of entering a new life and of belonging to the privileged group of those whose immortal fame was assured. But the image of the poet poised on the cusp of metamorphosis was also exploited by Du Bellay and certain of his contemporaries to express the fraught and potentially hazardous nature of the crossing. Charles Fontaine, an older contemporary of Du Bellay who in the early 1550s was seeking recognition and acceptance from members of the nascent Pléiade around Ronsard, appears to recognize the programmatic status of the image of the poet's metamorphosis, and to engage in imitation in order to gain acceptance in this new poetic community.[43] However, his imitation suggests that he is alive to the full possibilities of the process of transformation, the darker as well as the lighter. He invests his Muse with powers of metamorphosis and rejuvenation that belong to the ambiguous realm of magic. The presence of those powerful shape-shifters Medea and Circe hints at the idea that the revivifying forces of transformation may also entail a loss of freedom, self-determination, even identity.[44] In Fontaine's poem, identities — avian and poetic — become confused: the Muse changes Pindar, the swan of Dirce, into an eagle (and also a phoenix(?)), while the poet himself undergoes multiple transformations that leave him with a voice that has been rendered strangely impersonal, no longer quite his own, but that of 'un doux Poëte':

> Mieux que Medee, & que la Circe
> Tu rajeunis, & tu transmues:
> Comme le hault Poëte Dirce
> Qu'en un aigle, ains Phenix, tu mues.
> Encor, pour un evident signe,
> Tu me transmue en Aloëte,
> En Rossignol, en un blanc Cigne,
> Qui a la voix d'un doux Poëte.[45]

Ronsard had already used the figure of the poet's multiple metamorphoses and its potentially perplexing consequences to express certain anxieties concerning the integrity of identity. In a curious sonnet addressed to Dorat in which he imagines his tutor's afterlife, Ronsard develops the idea contained in Horace's ode of transformation into a dazzling display of the potency of metamorphosis (and poetry) that leads to the creation of a monster. Rather than a single metamorphosis, he conjures up a bravura sequence of five successive transformations. The poet, Ronsard suggests, might risk transformation only to find himself, not a swan, but a cicada, a bee, a nightingale, even Echo — or a monstrous combination of all those previous metamorphoses that results in a being impossible to imagine, a 'beau monstre nouveau':

> [S]i tu n'es changé tout entier en quelqu'un,
> Tu vétiras un cors qui te sera commun
> Aveques tous ceus-cy, participant ensemble
> De tous (car un pour toi sufisant ne me semble)
> Et d'homme seras fait un beau monstre nouveau
> De voix, cigne, cigalle, & de mouche, & d'oyseau.[46]

It is no accident that this poem should itself undergo profound metamorphosis, being almost entirely re-written for the 1578 edition of Ronsard's work.

Unsurprisingly, perhaps, certain poets are unwilling to allow their identities to be drawn into such hazardous territory. Sometimes it is better to be a goose in the afterlife than a swan, as the well-established neo-latin poet Jean Salmon Macrin suggests in the poem that he composed for Du Bellay's *L'Olive augmentee* of 1550. In his poem, Macrin contrives to acknowledge the programmatic force of Du Bellay's chosen figure of the poet as swan, while self-depreciatingly but firmly resisting the flattering analogy, and claiming for himself, via a little reverse metamorphosis, a safer identity as a poetic 'goose' instead:

> Anserem raucè strepentem
> Inter Apollineos olores.
> Dulci tuo effers carmine me tamen,
> Inter poëtas atque aliquem facis,

> De musca avens barrhum videri,
> Metior at modulo meo me.[47]

[[I am] a goose with raucous cry among the swans of Apollo. However, by your sweet song you enlist me among the poets and you make me one of them, from your heartfelt desire that, a gnat, I may pass for an elephant. But I rate myself by my own measure.[48]]

In laying claim in this way to the identity of a goose in the afterlife, Macrin is affirming the continuity and integrity of a literary identity established twenty years previously. For in a programmatic position at the conclusion of the first book of his *Carminum Libri IV* of 1530, closely modelled on Horace's *Odes*, Macrin had already marked himself out from the 'swans of Apollo':

> Sat si [...]
> vatum sacratum extremus in ordine
> adscribor, ut Tarpeius anser
> inter Apollineos olores.[49]

[It is enough for me if I am numbered among the sacred poets, though in last place, like the Tarpeian goose among the swans of Apollo.]

The apparent self-depreciation is, as is often the case with Macrin, deceptive: by describing himself as a 'Tarpeius anser', Macrin is associating himself with those sacred geese who, when the citadel of the Capitol was attacked at night by the Gauls, gave warning to the Roman people: Rome was saved, in fact, not by the swans of Apollo, but by those cackling geese.[50]

IV. Icarus / Anti-Icarus

The image developed by Horace of the poet's metamorphosis allows his imitators to explore more far-reaching anxieties concerning the relationship between nature and art, and appearance and reality in poetic identity. The prospect of the afterlife raises the spectre of ultimately failing in what one has undertaken, or being judged a fraud. The figure of Icarus that is glimpsed frequently in the narratives of metamorphosis developed by our early modern poets alerts the reader to the distinct possibility that the figure of the swan is not a natural bird whose element is air, but merely an effect of artifice, a boy with a swan's wings attached, doomed to fall. Du Bellay in particular, as Peter Sharratt amongst others has shown, appears haunted by the prospect of the potential failure of poetic metamorphosis and the difficulty in distinguishing borrowed from natural wings.[51] In Sonnet 115 of *L'Olive*, he congratulates Ronsard on avoiding Icarus's fate, and yet his use of the interrogative and his choice of the verb 'prêter' hint at the tension between apparent and true metamorphosis latent in the image of the swan:

> Quel cigne encor' des cignes le plus beau
> Te prêta l'aele? et quel vent jusqu'aux cieulx
> Te balança le vol audacieux,
> Sans que la mer te fust large tombeau?[52]

Ronsard in turn reflects upon the ambiguous status of the swan's feather, the 'plume':

on the one hand, the individual feather, separate from the wing, can represent the artificial nature of Icarus's power of propulsion through the air, ever threatening to become detached and precipitate his fall. On the other hand, in the *Odes* of 1550 Ronsard repeatedly draws attention to the feather as a vital link between the swan's flight as a symbol of immortality and the material agency of the feather in the physical act of writing that guarantees poetic immortality — that is, the scratching of the feather, the 'plume', across the page. In this way, he ascribes to the poet's 'plume' its own power of metamorphosis, a power that can even reverse the fall of Icarus. He suggests, in a cunning conflation of Horace *Odes* IV.9 and II.20, that the poet can by his Daedalian skill as an artist rescue those worthy of immortality and save the hero (in this case Achilles) from a watery fate:

> Si la plume d'un Poëte
> Ne favorisoit leur nom,
>   [i.e. the names of past heroes]
> Leur vertu seroit muete,
> Et sans langue leur renom [...]
> Les plumes doctes & rares
> Jusque au ciel ont envoié
> Araché des eaus avares
> Achille presque noié.[53]

V. Doubling and Splitting

The figure of metamorphosis, once the threshold of change has been passed and the process of transformation has begun, is employed by early modern poets in order to convey a complex set of concerns centred upon the consequences of 'doubling' and 'splitting' (to borrow Marina Warner's categories) for poetic identity.[54] On the one hand, the trope of metamorphosis implies the threat of diminution. Within Classical and Renaissance cosmology, any change of state affecting the spirit is generally heralded by a diminution or lightness in the body, and at such privileged, as well as vulnerable, moments, the bonds between body and soul are loosened in readiness for imminent separation, thus allowing the spirit greater licence to travel: to be able to get off the ground at all, the swan–poet must necessarily be diminished.[55] Poets frequently represent such diminution as the subjective experience of a loss of identity, as we see here in the case of Fontaine describing the poet's experience of change in his poem with the charmingly descriptive title 'L'Auteur presagit, & quasi prevoit son immortalité, par sa Muse':

> Dieu qu'est ce-cy?
> Je sens icy
> Hors & dans moy
> Un grand esmoy:
> Une mutation étrange
> Entierement tout mon corps change.
> Chantant mes vers
> En tons divers,
> Suis mué tout,
> De bout en bout.

> Ma teste haulte, s'appetisse
> Et mon poil par tout se herisse.[56]

We find that, to pre-empt the pain of such dissolution, the poet engages in a kind of voluntary 'self-mutilation' or 'self-splitting'. He deliberately cuts his first-person identity away from that of some other part of himself, identified as his 'nom', perhaps, or his 'Muse'. It is this part that undergoes metamorphosis as a proxy for the poet, as in the example from Fontaine:

> Par toy [Muse] j'ay un nom qui s'abille
> Tout de plumes, pour son vol prendre,
> Et s'en va leger, & habile
> Loing se faire voir, & entendre.[57]

The poet thus spares himself the pain and risk of transformation. He can even send his 'nom' or 'Muse' out as an emissary into the world to travel, span the globe and run risks while apparently preserving the integrity of his own true identity and remaining safe. Yet the ultimate cost is high: this move creates an irremediable fissure in identity, as the poet's 'ego', the 'je', does not undergo change and is left behind. Without undergoing metamorphosis, the poet's full identity cannot travel and so cannot reach the afterlife.

The associated process of doubling in metamorphosis brings with it a further set of threats to identity. In imitating the image from Horace, the early modern poet's 'je' is mapped on to the precursor poet's 'ego' in a gesture of overwriting that also constitutes a doubling. The precursor's identity is visible behind that of the latecomer, as in a palimpsest. The poet becomes a hybrid, 'biformis', generating the possibility of a second self, a second existence that is projected forward into the afterlife. At issue is the relation that the second self bears to the first. The twin polarities within imitative identity of 'ipséité' ['selfhood'] and 'mêmeté' ['sameness' or 'repetition'] strain against each other and threaten to split apart. For such doubling carries with it the threat of dispossession and estrangement, as well as the promise of escape from the present bounds of identity and the ability to live on as different, better, while remaining the same. When Ronsard draws on Horace's image of transformation in the programmatic poem that concludes the *Bocage* of 1550, he makes explicit the doubling process implicit in *imitatio* and thus his debt to his precursor. At the same time, he ostentatiously refuses to conflate or fuse his first-person identity with that of Horace. He takes care, by the inclusion of a strategic 'ainsi que', to acknowledge a relationship of analogy only, and thus, I think, seeks to disarm the threat to his identity posed by his model:

> J'ai delaissé & court, & Roi, & Prince
> Où j'estoi bien quand je les vouloi suivre,
> Pour recompense aussi je me voi vivre
> Et jusque au ciel d'ici bas remué:
> Ainsi qu'Horace en Cigne transmuee
> J'ai fait un vol qui de mort me delivre.[58]

VI. Making an Ending?

After the process of metamorphosis is complete, what then? What sort of image of continuity do the early modern poets discussed here conjure up when figuring the region that lies over the threshold? In spite of the evidence that tensions and anxieties can be traced in the ways in which they respond to the Horatian image of the passage to the afterlife, the fact remains that in the early 1550s in France, this is overwhelmingly a young man's image, an image developed in order to convey an impression of optimism and self-confidence. While remaining sensitive to its connotations of departure and ending, our poets are eager to recuperate the positive power of the figure of metamorphosis and transformation, and to harness its generative energies for their present and future work. In 'De l'immortalité des poëtes', for example, we find Du Bellay contaminating his imitation of *Odes* II.20 with well-known lines from *Odes* III.30, in order to reorient the focus of his own poem away from the attributes of death and the tomb evident in the final stanza of *Odes* II.20, and towards the assertive prospect of a second, fulfilling, posthumous existence beyond the present:

> De mourir ne suys en emoy
> Selon la loy du sort humain,
> Car la meilleure part de moy
> Ne craint point la fatale main:
> Craingne la mort, la fortune & l'envie,
> A qui les Dieux n'ont donné qu'une vie.[59]

More radical, even shocking, is the graphic 'epilogue' that Fontaine contributes to his version of the Horatian image of metamorphosis. He appears to wish to underscore the notion that the afterlife, thus conceived, represents a beginning as well as an ending, and a time of renewed life and fertility. Through an apparent cross-fertilization between Horace's text and the myth of Leda and the swan, and via a curious change of sex, Fontaine offers us a closing tableau to his poem in which the swan–poet, his metamorphosis concluded, interrupts his immortal flight from pole to pole in order to hatch out the clutch of eggs that (s)he has miraculously produced:[60]

> Des oeufs je ponds
> Polis, blanc, ronds,
> Que bien souvent
> Je vois couvant:
> Attendant que bien tost je vole
> Depuis l'un jusqu'à l'autre Pole.[61]

Here we are confronted, I think, with the recreation in one of the early modern avatars of Horace's image, of the surprise, embarrassment, 'trouble', that provoked us in Horace's original. It is perhaps no surprise that Fontaine's efforts to join the Pléiade poets came to nothing: no trace of any literary acknowledgement of any kind survives.[62]

VII. Downstream Disenchantments

In 1559, the young humanist Jean Passerat, an associate of the Pléiade, published in Paris 'L'A-Dieu a Phoebus et aus Muses, avec une Ode à Bacchus'.[63] The appearance of this publication seems to mark a threshold moment in the afterlife of Horace's image, a point beyond which it is very rare to encounter it in its non-parodic, 'enchanted' incarnation. In the poem, Passerat expresses, as Ronsard's 'Dialogue des Muses et de Ronsard' of 1556 had done, disillusion with the vocation of poetry. More particularly, though, Passerat directs his considerable satirical gifts against the prevalence of metamorphosis as a means of claiming immortal renown within poetic discourse. He mocks the idea of poets taking flight, suggesting that the topos is self-aggrandizing 'mensonge':

> Je connoi maintenant que cest art n'est que songe
> Que plus sçavant y est qui sçait plus de mensonge.
> J'ay trop longtemps ouy rocs & arbres parler;
> J'ay trop veu les chevaus & les hommes voler.
> Je ne pourroy conter combien j'ay veu de choses,
> Souffrir en un instant mille metamorphoses.[64]

The cultural climate in which Passerat is writing has lost its belief in the poetic vocation. Claims to immortality ring hollow: the works of poets asserting that their oeuvre will live forever are being used as grocery-wrappings — or worse:

> J'oublioi le meilleur: chascun d'eus en son livre
> Promet, maugré la mort, se faire à jamais vivre [...]
> Pourquoi doncques voit-on la haulte tragoedie,
> Le poëme heroiq', la basse comoedie,
> L'epigramme & l'eclogue, & odes & sonets,
> Servir aus espiciers pour faire des cornets?
> Ce qui est immortel sert-il à la beurriere?
> Ou (plus grand sacrilege) à torcher le derriere?[65]

In such an environment of disenchantment, however humorously expressed, Horace's vision of the afterlife becomes risible.

★ ★ ★

A long way downstream, faint strains of Horace's swansong can still be heard, but most often, it must be said, in its most melancholy incarnation — in Baudelaire's swan, displaced in Paris, which 'sur le sol raboteux traînait son blanc plumage', or in Mallarmé's 'cygne d'autrefois', trapped, caught, frozen by the 'glacier des vols qui n'ont pas fui'.[66] Perhaps a trace remains of the signs of enchantment — joy, hope, exultation — that we hear in the original swansong of Horace in Tennyson's 'The Dying Swan', in which he describes the wild bird whose 'death-hymn took the soul / Of that waste place with joy / Hidden in sorrow'.[67]

Notes to Chapter 4

1. I wish to thank Luisa Calè, Martin McLaughlin and Agnieszka Steczowicz for their comments on an earlier draft of this paper.

2. For a demonstration of the significant 'work' performed by figures of speech in a classical text, see for example D. A. West's article, 'Multiple-Correspondence Similes in the *Aeneid*', *Journal of Roman Studies*, 59 (1969), 40–49, repr. in *Oxford Readings in Virgil's 'Aeneid'*, ed. by S. J. Harrison (Oxford: Oxford University Press, 1990), pp. 429–44. In the early modern period, one of the writers most alive to the heuristic potential of figures and tropes is of course Montaigne; see Carol Clark, *The Web of Metaphor: Studies in the Imagery of Montaigne's 'Essais'* (Lexington, KY: French Forum, 1978).

3. Theognis in the sixth century BCE suggested that his poetry would bestow the wings of immortal renown upon his *eromenos* Cyrnus (Theognis of Megara, 237–39). Pindar famously associated himself with Zeus's bird, the eagle (see *Olympian odes* 2.88, *Nemean odes* 3.80–82 and 5.21), as did Bacchylides in *Odes* 5.

4. For example, Horace compares the sublimity of Pindar with a swan in flight in *Odes* 4.2, while in Virgil's *Eclogue* 9.36, Lycidas, comparing himself disparagingly with Varius and Cinna, likens himself to a goose and those poets to swans.

5. This form of the image exploits the wider associations of the swan in classical literature with mourning. Ovid, for example, narrates the story of Cycnus who, wandering the banks of the Po and bewailing the death of his friend Phaëthon, was transformed into a swan (*Metamorphoses* 2.367–80). Ovid in fact relates the story of two further characters named Cycnus who are transformed into swans; see *Metamorphoses* 7.372–79 and 12.145 and 580–82.

6. For an example of the poet comparing the process of ageing with transformation into a swan, see Ovid, *Tristia* 4.8.1–4.

7. Two illuminating accounts of *imitatio* as practised in early modern poetry are Grahame Castor, *Pléiade Poetics: A Study in Sixteenth-Century Thought and Terminology* (Cambridge: Cambridge University Press, 1964) and Thomas M. Greene, *The Light in Troy: Imitation and Discovery in Renaissance Poetry* (New Haven and London: Yale University Press, 1982). Hereafter, references to 'imitating' and 'imitation' have the culturally specific connotations of *imitatio*, and do not denote 'copying' in any pejorative sense.

8. For related discussions of the ways in which 'before' and 'after', 'retrospective' and 'prospective', can be culturally reconfigured, see the contributions of Marian Hobson and Wes Williams to the present volume.

9. Imitation of Horace *Odes* II.20 forms part of a broader narrative concerning Horace's remarkable popularity as a model for French vernacular poets in the late 1540s and the 1550s in France. The standard account remains for the present Raymond Lebègue, 'Horace en France pendant la Renaissance', *Humanisme et Renaissance*, 3 no. 4 (1936), 141–64, 289–308, 384–419. See also Geneviève Demerson, *Joachim Du Bellay et la belle romaine* (Orleans: Paradigme, 1996), Paul Laumonier, *Ronsard, poète lyrique: Etude historique et littéraire* (Paris: Hachette, 1909), and François Rouget, *L'Apothéose d'Orphée: L'Esthétique de l'ode en France au seizième siècle de Sébillet à Scaliger (1548–1561)* (Geneva: Droz, 1994).

10. In *Odes* III.30, Horace in his lyric persona famously claims, 'I shall not wholly die ('non omnis moriar') as long as Latin culture endures and I continue to be "spoken"'.

11. Horace, *Odes* IV.2.1–4.

12. For a methodological account of the category of 'textes troublés', see Terence Cave, *Pré-histoires I*, esp. pp. 15–17. For Cave's approach to the afterlife of Goethe's Mignon, see 'Mignon's Afterlife in the Fiction of George Eliot', *Rivista di letterature moderne e comparate*, 56 (2003), 165–82, 'Modeste and Mignon: Balzac rewrites Goethe', *French Studies*, 59: 3 (2005), 311–25, and 'Singing with Tigers: Recognition in *Wilhelm Meister, Daniel Deronda* and *Nights at the Circus*', to be published in the proceedings of a colloquium held at New York University, April 2003, currently in press with Peter Lang; it will also be re-printed in *Retrospectives: Essays in Literature, Poetics and Cultural History by Terence Cave*, ed. by Neil Kenny and Wes Williams (London: Legenda, 2009).

13. On what Cave terms 'la tentation analeptique' and 'la tentation de l'histoire rétrospective' and their implications, see *Pré-histoires I*, p. 17 and p. 177.

14. On the use of 'upstream' and 'downstream' context in Cave's work, see *Pré-histoires I*, p. 17, and 'Locating the Early Modern', in *Theory and the Early Modern*, ed. by Michael Moriarty and John O'Brien, *Paragraph*, 29 (2006), 12–27, (pp. 21–22).

15. On the relationship between Horace and his Greek lyric precursors, see Denis Feeney, 'Horace and the Greek Lyric Poets', in *Horace 2000, A Celebration: Essays for the Bimillennium*, ed. by Niall Rudd (London: Duckworth, 1993), pp. 41–63. Feeney characterizes Horace's claim to join the Greek lyric canon as 'a desperately serious joke' (p. 41).

16. For a typical example, see the lines of Theognis quoted in Note 3 above. On the distinctively Roman aspect of Horace's claim, see Feeney, 'Horace and the Greek Lyric Poets', p. 53 and R. G. M. Nisbet and Margaret Hubbard, *A Commentary on Horace's 'Odes', Book II* (Oxford: Clarendon Press, 1978), p. 336.

17. Many critics have drawn attention to and tried to account for the disturbing aspects of *Odes* II.20, including Olivier Thévenaz in his recent illuminating article, 'Le Cygne de Venouse: Horace et la métamorphose de l'*Ode* II.20', *Latomus*, 61 (2002), 861–88. See also Eduard Fraenkel, *Horace* (Oxford: Clarendon Press, 1957), pp. 299–302; Tenney Frank, 'Horace's "Swan" Song, *Odes* II.20', *Classical Philology*, 16 (1921), 386–87; G. L. Hendrickson, 'Vates Biformis', *Classical Philology*, 44 (1949), 30–32; W. R. Johnson, 'The Boastful Bird: Notes on Horatian Modesty', *Classical Journal*, 61 (1966), 272–75; C. B. Pascal, 'Another Look at the Swan Ode', *Latomus*, 39 (1980), 98–108; E. T. Silk, 'A Fresh Approach to Horace, II.20', *American Journal of Philology*, 77 (1956), 255–63; and James Tatum, 'Non Usitata Nec Tenui Ferar', *American Journal of Philology*, 94 (1973), 4–25.

18. Nisbet and Hubbard, *A Commentary on Horace's 'Odes', Book II*, pp. 332–48.

19. See *Horace: The Complete Odes and Epodes*, trans. by David West, 'The World's Classics' series (Oxford: Oxford University Press, 1977), pp. 74–75.

20. See Nisbet and Hubbard, *A Commentary on Horace 'Odes', Book II*, p. 334. Horace's description of metamorphosis has certain points of contact in its realism with Plato's account in *Phaedrus* § 251–52 of the soul sprouting feathers under the influence of love.

21. *Horatius cum quatuor commentarius* [*sic*]*, videlicet Porfirio, Acrono, Landino, Mancinello* [ed. by Antonio Mancinello] (Milan: Joannes de Legnano, 1508), fol. lxxxvii^r. Landino's commentary was first published in 1482.

22. Fraenkel, *Horace*, p. 301.

23. Renaissance editions read 'ocior' ['swifter'] for 'notior'.

24. For readers of Horace, the comparison is inescapable between the evocation of Icarus in *Odes* II.20 and that at the opening of *Odes* IV.2, where the poet predicts that all those who aim to rival the lyric achievement of Pindar are doomed to lend their name to a glassy sea, as Icarus did.

25. Nisbet and Hubbard, *A Commentary on Horace 'Odes', Book II*, p. 344.

26. Johnson, 'The Boastful Bird: Notes on Horatian Modesty', p. 275.

27. *François Rabelais: Les cinq livres*, ed. by Jean Céard, Gérard Defaux and Michel Simonin ([n. p.]: Livre de Poche, 1994), p. 675. Rabelais draws on Erasmus, *Adagia* I.2.55, 'Cygnea cantio' which itself takes its roots in Plato, *Phaedo* § 85 AB.

28. The dying swan shares the power of prophecy with the sibyls; see Mary McKinley's contribution to the present volume.

29. See Plato, *Phaedo* § 85 AB.

30. The choice of *Odes* II.20 as a model forms part of the wider story of the extraordinary upsurge of interest in imitating Horace's poetry in the vernacular, and in particular his odes, that occurred in France between the late 1540s and about 1560. Lebègue qualifies this period as a new *aetas horatiana*; see Lebègue, 'Horace en France pendant la Renaissance', p. 289. By that point, Horace was already firmly established as a model in the French neo-latin tradition; he was imitated most notably by Jean Salmon Macrin whose book of four Horatian *Carmina* appeared in 1530.

31. 'Contre les envieux poetes à Pierre de Ronsard', ll. 229–34, *Œuvres poétiques*, ed. by Henri Chamard, 6 vols (Paris: Cornély; Hachette; Droz, 1908–31), IV, 53. Hereafter 'Chamard,' followed by the volume number in Roman numerals.

32. See Du Bellay, ed. Chamard, IV, 51. The swan/crow distinction in the context of ideas of

afterlife is already present in Greek poetry. See for example the epigram of Antipater of Sidon concerning the poetess Erinna: 'And she is still remembered, is not shuttered / In the shadows, under night's murky wing. / And we, friend, we hordes of later poets? / — Here we are, lying in heaps, rotting, / Forgotten. Better a swan's low song / Than the cackling of crows / Echoing through the spring clouds.' See *The Greek Anthology and Other Ancient Epigrams: A Selection in Modern Verse Translations*, ed. by Peter Jay (London: Allen Lane, 1973), p. 127. Du Bellay had already used the opposition between swans and crows to distinguish fellow-poets from poetasters in *Vers liriques* I: 'A la Royne', ll. 37–42, *Receuil de Poésie* (1549), ed. Chamard, III, 88. On this trope, see G. H. Tucker, *The Poet's Odyssey: Joachim Du Bellay and the 'Antiquitez de Rome'* (Oxford: Clarendon Press, 1990), pp. 32–36, and 'Oubli et écriture chez Joachim Du Bellay', *Revue des Sciences Humaines*, 256 (1999), 35–48.

33. Du Bellay, *Œuvres complètes*, ed. by Olivier Millet and others (Paris: Champion, 2003–), vol. II, ed. by Marie-Dominique Legrand and others, p. 153.

34. See Ode XI, 'Pour le tombeau de Joachim Du Bellay', *L'Olimpe de Jaques Grevin de Cler-mont en Beauvaisis. Ensemble les autres Euvres Poëtiques duduct Auteur* (Paris: Robert Estienne, 1560), p. 189. On relations between Grévin and Du Bellay, see Lucien Pinvert, *Jacques Grévin (1538–1570): Etude biographique et littéraire* (Paris: Fontemoing, 1899), pp. 335–37.

35. See the emblem 'Insignia poetarum', in Andrea Alciato, *Livret des emblemes* (1536), which, like the other emblems discussed here, is accessible via the excellent Glasgow University Emblem website, <http://www.emblems.arts.gla.ac.uk>.

36. For the allusion to Nestor, see Homer, *Iliad* 1.249.

37. Icarus appears in the emblem-books published in France of Alciato, Corrozet, La Perrière and Sambucus. He also features in the woodcuts completed from Ovid's *Metamorphoses* by Bernard Salomon (*c.*1506–61) and Virgil Solis (1514–62). Images of the woodcuts of the *Metamorphoses* can be viewed via the *Ovid Illustrated* site, devoted to the reception of the *Metamorphoses* in image and text, hosted by the University of Virginia; see <http://etext.virginia.edu/latin/ovid/about.html>.

38. On the relation between Arcadelt, the Cardinal de Lorraine and the Pléiade poets, see Jeanice Brooks, 'Italy, the Ancient World and the French Musical Inheritance in the Sixteenth Century: Arcadelt and Clereau in the Service of the Guises', *Journal of the Royal Musical Association*, 121: 2 (1996), 147–90.

39. Arcadelt's madrigal was included in *Il primo libro di Madrigali*, published in Venice by Antonio Gardano in 1539.

40. For an analysis of the madrigal and its sexual connotations in cultural context, see Laura Macy, 'Speaking of Sex: Metaphor and Performance in the Italian Madrigal', *The Journal of Musicology*, 14 (1996), 1–34.

41. There is a document of 1555 recording Arcadelt as the Cardinal's *maître de chapelle*, but it is likely that he came to France in 1551. See Brooks, 'Italy, the Ancient World and the French Musical Inheritance in the Sixteenth Century', pp. 152–53.

42. On Arcadelt's settings, see Brooks, art. cit. p. 161 and p. 169, and Kate van Orden, 'Les Vers lascifs d'Horace: Arcadelt's Latin Chansons', *The Journal of Musicology*, 14 (1996), 338–69.

43. On the relations between Fontaine and the Pléiade, see Richmond Laurin Hawkins, *Maistre Charles Fontaine Parisien* (Cambridge, MA: Harvard University Press, 1916), pp. 143–94.

44. Petrarch had already famously explored the bafflingly various potential of metamorphosis in Canzone 23 of the *Rime sparse*, the longest poem of the collection, charting the lover–poet's transformations under the influence of love, including (in the third stanza) metamorphosis into a swan, resembling that of Cycnus grieving at the death of Phaëthon; see *Petrarch's Lyric Poems: The 'Rime sparse' and Other Lyrics*, trans. by Robert Durling (Cambridge, MA: Harvard University Press, 1976), p. 63.

45. *Les Ruisseaux de Fontaine* (Lyon: Thibauld Payan, 1555), pp. 133–34. The play on cigne/signe here prefigures Ronsard's similar play in his last poem, composed just before his death, the sonnet 'Il faut laisser maisons et vergers et Jardins' included in the *Derniers vers*, which prepares the ground for, a long way downstream, 'Le vierge, le vivace et le bel aujourd'hui' of Mallarmé.

46. Ronsard, *Œuvres complètes*, ed. by Paul Laumonier, rev. by I. Silver and R. Lebègue, 20 vols (Paris: Hachette; Droz; Didier, 1914–75), VII, 121. Hereafter 'Laumonier,' followed by the volume number in Roman numerals.

47. 'Salmonii Macrini Iuliodunensis Ode in Olivam Ioachimi Bellaii Andensis', ll. 7–12, in Du Bellay, Œuvres complètes, ed. by Olivier Millet and others, vol. II, ed. by Marie-Dominique Legrand and others, p. 160.

48. The Horatian phrase here, 'Metior at modulo meo me' (Epistles I.7 l.98) came to mean, 'to be content with one's own condition': thus Macrin's apparently modest phrase is in fact an elegant assertion of independence.

49. Jean Salmon Macrin, Odes I.31, ll. 65–68, Epithalames & Odes, ed. by Georges Soubeille (Paris: Champion, 1998), p. 362. Macrin's comparison is inspired by Virgil, Eclogues 9.35–36.

50. See Livy, Book V.47 and Plutarch, Camillus § 27.

51. See esp. Peter Sharratt, 'Du Bellay and the Icarus Complex', in Myth and Legend in French Literature: Essays in Honour of A. J. Steele, ed. by Keith Aspley, David Bellos and Peter Sharratt (London: Modern Humanities Research Association, 1982), pp. 73–92; Marc Eigeldinger, 'Le Mythe d'Icare dans la poésie française du XVIe siècle', Cahiers de l'Association Internationale des Etudes Françaises, 25 (1973), 261–80.

52. Du Bellay, ed. Chamard, I, 124.

53. Ronsard, ed. Laumonier, II, 150–51.

54. Marina Warner, Fantastic Metamorphoses, Other Worlds: Ways of Telling the Self (Oxford: Oxford University Press, 2002).

55. Cf. Ronsard, 'Les Vers d'Eurymedon et de Calliree' (1578), ll. 49–54, in which Charles IX–Eurymedon, addressing Anne d'Acquaviva–Calliree, describes the transforming power of Love, which leads to etiolation of the body as the spirit moves heavenwards. See Ronsard, ed. Laumonier, XVII, 146.

56. Fontaine, Ode XIII, 'L'Auteur presagit, & quasi prevoit son immortalité, par sa Muse', Les Ruisseaux de Fontaine, p. 153.

57. Fontaine, Ode IV, 'L'auteur à sa Muse', Les Ruisseaux de Fontaine, p. 133.

58. Ronsard, ed. Laumonier, II, 202.

59. Du Bellay, ed. Chamard, III, 53.

60. The way in which Fontaine's swan–poet takes on the female reproductive role hints at the problematic status of female figures within the lyric canon (and within predominantly masculine lines of filiation more generally). Horace, too, is alert to this. It is not only in order to hint at sexual orientation that Horace qualifies Sappho as 'mascula' (Epistles I.19.28); it also suggests her ambiguous, marginal position as a woman within the lyric tradition.

61. Fontaine, Ode XIII, 'A Monsieur le Cardinal de Chastillon. L'auteur presagit, & quasi prevoit son immortalité, par sa Muse', Les Ruisseaux de Fontaine, p. 156.

62. On the relations (or lack of them) between Fontaine and the Pléiade, see Marcel Raymond, L'Influence de Ronsard sur la poésie française (1550–1585), 2 vols (Paris: Champion, 1926), I, 56–63.

63. See Les Poésies françaises de Jean Passerat, ed. by Prosper Blanchemain, 2 vols (Paris: Lemerre, 1880), I, 78–92.

64. Op. cit., p. 80.

65. Op. cit., p. 86.

66. See Baudelaire, Les Fleurs du Mal (Paris: Garnier, 1961), pp. 95–96; 'Le Vierge, le vivace et le bel aujourd'hui', Œuvres de Mallarmé, ed. by Yves-Alain Favre (Paris: Garnier, 1985), pp. 68–69. On the relation between Baudelaire and Horace, see Katherine Elkins, 'Stalled Flight: Horatian Remains in Baudelaire's "Le Cygne"', Comparative Literature Studies, 39 (2002), 1–17. See also Timothy Hampton, 'Virgil, Baudelaire and Mallarmé at the Sign of the Swan: Poetic Translation and Historical Allegory', Romanic Review, 73: 4 (1982), 438–51.

67. Poetical Works of Alfred Tennyson (London: James Finch and Co, [n. d.]), pp. 35–36.

CHAPTER 5

❖

'Ô Courbes, méandre...': Montaigne, Epicurus, and the Art of Slowness

John O'Brien

L'essentiel consiste à déjouer la puissance herméneutique du récit.[1]

Ô Courbes, méandre,
Secrets du scripteur,
Est-il art plus tendre
Que cette lenteur?

Even more than Valéry, whom I have just purposely misquoted,[2] Montaigne is inveterately restless: travel, journeying, moving fitfully from place to place or topic to topic are well-known features of his writing, licensed by a perception of universal flux and instability. Certain forms of movement in the *Essais*, notably staggering, lurching and zigzagging, have received attention elsewhere.[3] Not all varieties of Montaignian motion are, however, so dramatic or eye-catching and it is precisely those quieter movements that will be the subject of the present investigation. Taking its cue from the opening lines of Valéry's 'L'Insinuant', it will concentrate on some of the procedures of indirection, with their explicit or implicit associated images of winding and meandering, an art of slowness coupled with a tenderness appropriate to a 'tendre negotiateur' (III. 1, 791) and the delicate, tentative, probing nature of his enterprise.

This contribution will accordingly be heuristic to the extent that it attempts to follow a particular sequence of images and ideas, in the hope, perhaps, of understanding something of the nature of the 'route par ailleurs' that Montaigne evokes briefly but pointedly in 'De l'experience' (III. 13, 1068).[4] The heuristic nevertheless needs a methodology if it is not to fall into the random,[5] and the approach adopted here is positioned in respect of Terence Cave's pre-histories. It will be suggested that the 'pre-historical' approach holds four advantages, two belonging to pre-history properly speaking, two relating to its afterlife. First, it allows us to preserve the plurality of the trace, and its movement from multiplicity to multiplicity without passing through the One (the unity that makes plurality intelligible as a version or inversion of itself). Secondly, such pluralization is itself evidence of what Terence Cave calls '[ce] mouvement de transvaluation qui permet d'entretenir [...] deux attitudes, ou même plusieurs attitudes, radicalement différentes' and this movement of transvaluation might be 'le signe d'un malaise foncier et perturbant dans la pensée de l'époque pré-cartésienne',[6] a disturbance that makes itself felt with each iteration. Thirdly, pre-histories emphasize that the trace remains resistant to its own assimilation into the larger stories that will be told about it. Finally, they stress that the past is not an extension of ourselves and our projections. This last statement needs a word of explanation. The recent re-branding of the Renaissance, Classicism and (to some extent) the Enlightenment as 'early modernity' is indicative of our own allegiances, desires and anxieties. For by labelling such periods and their texts 'early modern', it is ourselves we seek within them and correspondingly we valorize those works, such as the *Essais*, that we believe to show us ourselves. From Libertinism to Post-Modernism, Montaigne has been our forerunner and ensign bearer, the one who reaches forward proleptically towards *our* future and acts as the source of our intellectual identity. A further point of interest of the 'pre-historical' perspective is thus that it presents us with a Montaigne who is not an *alter ego* of ourselves.

This is nowhere truer than when dealing with the pre-history of pleasure, for which the essayist can supply abundant material. Strowski famously posited a three-stage Montaigne, a Stoic, a Sceptic and an Epicurean, and even though this clean tripartite division has been discredited,[7] the fact remains that there is a high incidence of pleasure-related vocabulary in his writing. I want to concentrate on those occurrences where the name of Epicurus is mentioned.[8] Instances of naming have a special role to play in the *Essais* — think of the incidences of the name of Socrates or of Pyrrho — and the conjunction of a name and a concept — Epicurus and *volupté* or *plaisir*, in this case — has a particular point to make. An initial distinction needs to be made between Montaigne's reaction to Epicureans and Epicureanism in general, and his attitude towards Epicurus in particular. In the 'Apologie', Epicureans are classed along with Stoics as dogmatists ('ces deux grandes sectes dogmatistes', II. 12, 592 and implicitly 502), and Howard Jones has pointed out that Montaigne expresses reservations about a variety of Epicurean doctrines, from epistemology to physics (especially the notion of *clinamen*).[9] On the other hand, the essayist expressly states that Epicurean atomism is not to be taken at face value (II. 12, 511) and Jones also goes on to concede that he deliberately misquotes Lucretian Epicureanism to bolster his own views; instances where the essayist does so in respect of Scepticism deserve fuller investigation. Mediated by way of Seneca, with the support of Diogenes Laertius, Epicurus the man, by contrast, receives largely favourable endorsement from Montaigne and he is one of a number of writers and thinkers that are read through a third party in the *Essais* (Xenophon read alongside but also through Plutarch is another),[10] so that the tinting and highlighting they receive by this process seep into the writing of the *Essais*. Unsurprisingly given the Classical intermediaries, in all the cases concerning Epicurus that will be considered in this paper, the context is that of letter writing. This feature is not accidental: Pyrrho is silent; Socrates speaks; Epicurus *writes*. All three modalities are of significance in Montaigne's work, with its characteristic concern for the pleasures and hazards of communication.[11]

The first instance of the letter occurs in chapter I. 33, 'De fuir les voluptez au pris de la vie'. It begins with a short series of *sententiae* that Montaigne summarizes in French, before quoting in Greek; they are two in number, 'qu'il est heure de mourir lors qu'il y a plus de mal que de bien à vivre; et que, de conserver nostre vie à nostre tourment et incommodité, c'est choquer les loix mesmes de nature' (p. 218). The adversative conjunction 'Mais', echoed structurally by the later 'Si est-ce que', then adds a further thought that Montaigne believes to be without precedent: death as a means of distancing oneself from 'cette vie voluptueuse et pompeuse' (p. 218). Yet he has now found just this precept in a passage in the twenty-second letter of Seneca to Lucilius, which he proceeds to quote. He then adds a rather longer paraphrase of an incident from Jean Bouchet's *Annales d'Aquitaine* in which St Hilary writes to his daughter Abra, praying for her death as a release from 'l'appetit et l'usage des plaisirs mondains' (p. 219). The prayer is subsequently granted.

Montaigne strips away the accretions of St Hilary's letter as recorded in Bouchet, so that Senecan Stoicism and early Christianity look similar in their *rigorisme*. Yet the harmonics they seem to compose are disturbed by a further set of alignments. Between Seneca's letter to Lucilius and St Hilary's to Abra sits Epicurus's to Idomeneus, the source of a quotation in Seneca to the effect that no man is so cowardly that he would not prefer to fall once rather than be forever on the brink. Montaigne has just discovered this Epicurean maxim and the tone of his discovery is surprise; his term is 'estrange', a word he reserves for incidents encompassing the extraordinary, the odd, even the perplexing (it is used, for example, to describe the Martin Guerre case in 'Des boyteux'). If this Epicurean instance seems odd to the essayist, what follows is odder still, for the letter of St Hilary is prefaced by the remark, 'Si est-ce que je pense avoir remarqué quelque traict semblable parmy nos gens, mais avec la moderation Chrestienne' (p. 219). Given that St Hilary is in fact granted a double prayer — the death, first, of his daughter and then of his wife — moderation hardly seems the appropriate description. Here again, however, Montaigne offers revealing terminology interestingly resonant of the 'estrange' of previous sentences. The death of his daughter causes the saint 'une singuliere joye'; when his wife dies soon after, 'ce fut une mort embrassée avec singulier contentement commun'. 'Singulier': 'singular, special of its kind, uncommon'; 'singulier': 'singular, strange'. In speaking of two closely related instances, one from philosophy, the other from theology, Montaigne is allowing us to take the full measure of his chapter title: pleasures must be avoided at all costs, at any price. The strange, extreme steps to which a mature understanding of pleasure propels philosophers and theologians are symptomatic of the risk that it involves. A few chapters earlier, in 'De la moderation', Montaigne had noted, in a statement that is not itself unproblematic,[12] 'les sciences qui reglent les meurs d'hommes, comme la theologie et la philosophie, elles se meslent de tout. Il n'est action si privée et secrete, qui se desrobe de leur cognoissance et jurisdiction' (p. 198). In the circumstances, perhaps it is moderation to flee pleasures at the expense of one's life; yet such moderation will always remain 'singulier'.

'L'extreme fruict de ma santé c'est la volupté' (III. 13, 1103): 'the uttermost, ultimate fruit', but also 'the extreme fruit', 'furthest from the mean', as Cotgrave puts it. Once again, the implied yet ambivalent superlative dominates the discussion of pleasure, on this occasion associated with Epicurus only by juxtaposition. For in the lines immediately preceding this statement about health as pleasure, Montaigne had quoted from Seneca's eighteenth letter to Lucilius, to make two antithetical points: in one case, he follows Epicurus in not looking at what one eats but with whom one eats; in the other case, his practice is opposed to Epicurus's:

> comme Epicurus jeunoit et faisoit des repas maigres pour accoustumer sa volupté à se passer de l'abondance, moy, au rebours, pour dresser ma volupté à faire mieux son profit et se servir plus alaigrement de l'abondance... (p. 1103)

Montaigne paraphrases and shortens a longer passage from Seneca, which the essayist's brother-in-law, Pressac, renders as follows in his translation first published in 1582:

> Ce maistre de volupté Epicure avoit certains jours, ausquels il traittoit maigrement et eschartement sa faim, pour esprouver si en ce mauvais traittement il se trouvoit à dire quelque chose de l'entiere et pleine volupté, ou combien il y avoit à dire, et si c'estoit quelque chose qui meritast qu'on mist grande peine à la reparer. Luy-mesme dit cela en ses epistres que [sic] il escrit à Carinus...[13]

Seneca's letter explains the background to Epicurus's dietary habits as part of his ascesis, summarizing a letter of the Greek philosopher in the process. Both are embedded in the *Essais*, yet in a way that shifts the emphasis from Epicurus's experimentations to Montaigne's; the balanced parallelism of *clausulae* underscores the antithesis of meaning, with 'moy au rebours' thrown into particular relief as the pivotal moment of difference. That shift is suggestive. As an extension of his enquiry (rather than the reverse), the *scripteur* now posits himself as the focus of attention and multiplies instances of the first-person singular engaged in the processes of *essai* that are the subject of his writing, in other words, the testing out of hypotheses drawn from his reading (in this case, a twofold reading) balanced against the data of experience and judgement, and the activity of registering the provisional results of his enquiry in the very form he will entitle *Essais*. Here too, meandering indirection is important to this process: as Seneca speaks through Epicurus, so Montaigne speaks through both, immersing himself in others after the manner of Perseus, king of Macedon, mentioned approvingly at an earlier stage in 'De l'experience' (III. 13, 1077); the doubling or tripling of voices becomes a characteristic of writing *essais*, creating the layered tonalities that distinguish the Montaignian *je* as the focus of enunciative dissonance rather than as the source of settled univocality.[14]

The point of the art of slowness — the process of indirection — and its associated technique of tender handling of materials in this section of 'De l'experience' becomes clearer if one considers two flanking passages in the *Essais* where statements of a similar nature are made. The first occurs at a moment in 'De la ressemblance des enfans aux peres', which outlines the varying attitudes of Montaigne's uncles towards doctors and medicine, leading the essayist to comment on his own attitude towards health:

> [Je] trouve la santé digne d'estre r'achetée par tous les cauteres et incisions les plus penibles qui se facent. [...]. C'est une pretieuse chose que la santé, et la seule qui merite à la verité qu'on y employe, non le temps seulement, la sueur, la peine, les biens, mais encore la vie à sa poursuite [...]. La volupté, la sagesse, la science et la vertu, sans elle, se ternissent et esvanouissent [...]. Toute voye qui nous meneroit à la santé, ne se peut dire pour moy ny aspre, ny chere. (p. 765)

This is the 1580 text, which remained unchanged until after 1588, when, between the first and second sentences quoted, Montaigne inserted a passage that he found in Diogenes Laertius's life of Epicurus:

> Et suyvant Epicurus, les voluptez me semblent à eviter, si elles tirent à leur suite des douleurs plus grandes, et les douleurs à rechercher, qui tirent à leur suite des voluptez plus grandes. (p. 765)[15]

The interdependence of pleasure and health is echoed by the interdependence of pain and pleasure, now regarded as complementary, not antithetical. It is the first step towards questioning the polar oppositions that governed standard thinking about pain and pleasure by showing that the antitheses are implicated in each other or are extensions of each other, stretching elastically in such a way that demarcation lines between them soften and become difficult rigorously to maintain.

A similar point emerges from the second flanking passage, near the close of 'De l'experience' and again a late addition:

> [La philosophie] faict bien l'enfant, à mon gré, quand elle se met sur ses ergots pour nous prescher que [...] volupté est qualité brutale, indigne que le sage la gouste [...]. Ce n'est pas ce que dict Socrates, son precepteur et le nostre. Il prise comme il doit la volupté corporelle, mais il prefere celle de l'esprit, comme ayant plus de force, de constance, de facilité, de varieté, de dignité. Cette cy va nullement seule selon luy (il n'est pas si fantastique), mais seulement premiere. (III. 13, 1113)

The allusion of the opening sentence is to Seneca's letter no. 92. On this occasion, Seneca is made subservient to Socrates whose preference for pleasure — intellectual primarily, but corporal also — is prized over the Stoic's condemnation of it. In the process, the hierarchy of pleasures becomes distinctly precarious, malleable and moveable rather than rigid and fixed. And, equally as part of that process, Socrates is *named*, whereas Seneca is merely alluded to.

What is happening in these three passages? In the first two, the naming of Epicurus, and the quotation of his work, filtered through a third writer, are linked to a re-evaluation of pleasure and its extension by Montaigne, first to the crucial concept of health and then to a wide range of abstract qualities: wisdom, knowledge and virtue. In the last passage, pleasure now speaks in the name of Socrates,[16] and despite the concession that for Socrates intellectual pleasure is preferred to other kinds, Montaigne is quick to emphasize that intellectual pleasure is not the only form, just the first. Socrates validates the forms of pleasure with which the name of Epicurus has been hitherto associated. Released from its Stoic constraints, pleasure, named and identified as such, can then be predicated of an early modern investigator who, elsewhere, himself registers that predication by setting 'ma volupté' alongside 'la volupté' and 'nos voluptés'.

A further element must be added at this point. A common thread that runs through the last three passages we have been studying is reference to Plutarch, in each case to the 'Banquet des sept sages', specified contextually by naming one of the sages — Chilo, Solon and Epimenides, in that order. Yet beyond this particular chapter of the *Moralia*, a wider degree of engagement between Montaigne and Plutarch may be inferred. The emphasis on health, which is debated in Plutarch's

'Banquet', is also prominent in his 'Regles et preceptes de santé' and its connection
with pleasure is an issue likewise discussed in that chapter, but in cautious terms.
Preceding that chapter is a better known and much longer one, 'Qu'on ne sauroit
vivre joyeusement selon la doctrine d'Epicure', with its all-out attack by Plutarch
on Epicurean pleasure. In its implicit reversal of these Plutarchan positions about
pleasure, Montaigne's work can be termed paradoxical, in the sense analysed by Ian
Maclean and Agnieszka Steczowicz,[17] for paradox is one crucial way in which the
premises of the endoxical can be challenged. In Montaigne's formulation of his
position, in the resonance of two chapters from the *Moralia* that inform key passages
on pleasure and health, never directly evoked, but present through theme and idea,
in the specific textual configurations that give substance to his argument, he offers a
subtly inflected, but robust challenge to the prevailing orthodoxy about Epicurean
pleasure. In his version, it is possible to live joyously according to Epicurus's doctrine;
and if that proposition causes us surprise, we might recall that 'inopinatum', the
surprising, the unexpected, is one common Renaissance translation of 'paradoxon',
dating back to Quintilian.[18] The significance of the hidden texts is thus that they
underline a connectivity that is arguably assumed but not fully spelt out, yet at the
same time facilitate the marking out of a space of investigation in the *Essais*, a space
that re-writes concepts and their meanings. The detour via texts whose familiarity
is taken for granted epitomizes Montaigne's serpentine, indirect approach to the
whole problem of intellectual spaces and the concepts that inhabit them. Moreover,
that sideways, crab-like motion is, one might argue, a sign of the literary which
characteristically groups together an archipelago of texts not always aligned in
direct causation, but set out horizontally, in a collapsed genealogy of traces which
intersect, cross over and resonate within each other. It is therefore also a sign that the
enquiry is being conducted in terms that are specific to Montaigne's own project,
in which a recognizable type of humanist discourse — ethical and philosophical, in
this case — is held in tension with, fruitfully crossed with, a discourse that appears
to be supplementary to it, a discourse of difference and singularity, the product of
a differentiated *scripteur*.

But a word of caution needs to be entered here. This re-invention of Epicurus
is a paradox without guarantees. Does Montaigne, for example, see pleasure as the
'beginning and end of the happy life' or the 'first and innate good', as he would have
read in Diogenes Laertius's biography of Epicurus and discerned from Lucretius?[19]
He does not say and we are not in a position to assume it.[20] A retrospective
reading of Montaigne's Epicurean reflections might wish to see in them the royal
road to full-blown heterodoxy, or use occurrences of *volupté* and Epicurus in the
Essais to suggest the writer's attachment to a particular school of thought: this is
Villey's move, in calling the final phase of the writer's work Epicurean. More flat-
footedly, a positivist reading might even suggest that Montaigne's affinity with
Epicurus derives primarily from the fact the Greek philosopher too suffered from
'extremes douleurs de la colique' (II. 8, 401; cf. II. 11, 424). In his recent British
Academy lecture on Montaigne, Terence Cave proposes a distinction that is useful
here: what the essayist does can be described as a break-*out*, but not necessarily as
a break-*through*.[21] It is a symptom that a 'downstream reading' of desire will take

as a cause, locatable at a particular historical juncture (which is then taken as the origin of a master-narrative).[22] In its Montaignian context, however, the process of re-valorizing pleasure is quieter, less clear-cut, less self-proclaimingly dramatic, but no less decisive: it is a process of naming and associating, of omitting and substituting, a process of weaving indirection and subterranean textual echoes by which an early modern thinker attaches to a *je*, 'par maniere d'essay' (I. 28, 183–84), the expression of pleasure, a pleasure that can be traced and analysed in 'les profondeurs opaques de ses replis internes' (II. 6, 378) through the corporal and intellectual colourings and textures of an individual subject.

'De la cruauté' shows this process of omission and substitution, of texturing and colouring at its most elegant. The opening pages of the chapter recognize that 'en fermeté et rigueur d'opinions et de preceptes, la secte Epicurienne ne cede aucunement à la Stoique',[23] and that, in Cassius's words to Cicero (*Fam.* xv.19), the lovers of pleasure are in reality lovers of justice and practise all the virtues (II. 11, 422–23). The following lines likewise refer positively to 'cette brave et genereuse volupté Epicurienne' (p. 424), a phrase which, in context, introduces the notion of pleasure into the attainability of virtue, as gauged by Montaigne in the paired reactions of Cato the Younger and Socrates in the face of death. In each case, the description is heavily pleasure-laden: Cato finds 'je ne sçay quelle esjouissance de son ame, et une émotion de plaisir extraordinaire et d'une volupté virile' (p. 424) in his suicide, while Socrates displays 'je ne sçay quel contentement nouveau et une allegresse enjoüée en ses propos et façons dernieres' (p. 425). A further pair is subsequently adduced from Montaigne's reading of Diogenes Laertius: Aristippus and Epicurus. The first preaches in favour of pleasure, yet does nothing with the three girls he is given by the tyrant Dionysius. The second receives the following comment:

> Et Epicurus, duquel les dogmes sont irreligieux et delicats, se porta en sa vie tresdevotieusement et laborieusement. Il escrit à un sien amy qu'il ne vit que de pain bis et d'eaue, qu'il luy envoie un peu de fromage pour quand il voudra faire quelque somptueux repas. Seroit il vray que, pour estre bon à faict, il nous le faille estre par occulte, naturelle et universelle propriété, sans loy, sans raison, sans exemple? (II. 11, 428)

Compared with the expansive analyses of Cato and Socrates, this passage can at first sight appear bland, not least because the acknowledged founder of 'la secte de philosophie qui a le plus faict valoir la volupté' (II. 12, 493) has, unlike his companion philosophers in previous examples, no pleasure-filled vocabulary to describe him. In fact, the careful phraseology here contains particular resonances. The concession of the first line appeals to a common Renaissance perception about Epicurus's beliefs. It is immediately qualified by the emphasis on his personal abstemiousness, consistent with the stringency of Epicureanism mentioned on the first page of 'De la cruauté'; while the reference to Epicurus's meagre diet prefigures the parallel insistence on his frugal eating habits in 'De l'experience'. As a result, by a neat reversal of expectation, Epicurus now emerges demurely, along with Aristippus, as a model of private ethical rectitude, whatever his public persona.

Yet there is more than dutiful asceticism here. The inference that, in his closing sentence, Montaigne draws from this letter from Epicurus to an unknown recipient moves in a new direction.[24] It opens up the possibility of a natural goodness that is universal, without antecedents, a goodness that precedes any prescriptive codification and exceeds accepted patterns of thinking or moral behaviour. The essayist makes a similar point about the Brazilian cannibals in the 'Apologie', using strikingly similar vocabulary, with the same rhythmical anaphora of 'sans'.[25] This sentence by Montaigne, in its tentative question form, suddenly imagines a world different from our own; briefly but significantly, it ventures into another intellectual space, steps outside — breaks out — of the received wisdom and the fixed paradigms of the universe Montaigne inhabited with his contemporaries. To reduce Epicurus to the promoter of pleasure or the advocate of irreligion is in that light to miss both his personal qualities and what those qualities weightily betoken: the chance to move beyond the *episteme*, to make an excursus into a conceptual 'païs au delà' (I. 26, 146), which in turn queries the basis on which current epistemic stabilities are built. Thus pleasure does not disappear from the picture for all that. It re-appears, in fact, in the narrator's self-description which surrounds and is intertwined with the philosophical instances he has been discussing. He prefaces his remarks on Aristippus and Epicurus by asserting in deliberately provocative style what he knows to be a risky admission, that his own concupiscence is 'moins desbauchée que [s]a raison' (II. 11, 428); and, from his own self-knowledge and experience, he opposes the accepted view that pleasure, particularly sexual 'volupté', is an imperious mistress, while conceding that Venus cannot be controlled. The essayist makes himself the voice of pleasure, transferring to himself the narrative of 'volupté' that is absent from his characterization of Epicurus and combining it with a frank assessment of his own virtues and vices. Emphasizing the contingency of his own 'vertu, ou innocence, pour mieux dire, accidentale et fortuite' (p. 427) and reinforcing this happenstance by the claim that '[c]e que j'ay de bien ... [j]e ne le tiens ny de loy, ny de precepte, ou autre aprentissage' (p. 429), he becomes, along with the Brazilians and Epicurus, a native of the new world his questing and questioning sentence had speculatively conjured up.

We have not yet done with Epicurus, pleasure and letters, however; for, as Montaigne warns us in 'Des boyteux', every medal has its reverse. Sandwiched between Plutarch's 'Qu'on ne sauroit vivre joyeusement selon la doctrine d'Epicure' and his 'Regles et preceptes de santé' is a short chapter which also deals with Epicurus: 'Si ce mot commun, Cache ta vie, est bien dit'. It is a text that informs Montaigne's reflections at the start of 'De la gloire': 'Cache ta vie', he explains, is one of the principal Epicurean doctrines, forbidding its followers from engaging in public office; and, he adds, this must necessarily presuppose Epicurean disdain of 'la gloire, qui est une approbation que le monde fait des actions que nous mettons en evidence' (II. 16, 619). However, Epicurus's dying words show precisely the opposite concern, and Montaigne proceeds to quote, from Cicero's *De finibus* ii.30.96, Epicurus's letter to Hermarchus in which the philosopher expresses pleasure in his own published work,[26] and then, from the same source, Epicurus's will which leaves specific instructions and bequests for the posthumous celebration of his birthday and allowances to encourage his fellow philosophers to gather in honour of his memory.[27] If the reader follows Montaigne's cue and delves further into Plutarch's chapter on 'Cache ta vie', s/he would find a parallel attack on Epicurus's notion that the recollection of past pleasures (rather than of past virtues, as Plutarch would have it) overcomes present pain. Never one to pass up the chance to attack Epicurus, Plutarch adds to this the following barbed comment:

> Et toutefois encore confessoit Epicurus, que de la gloire il naissoit je ne sçay quoi de volupté: et comment eust-il peu faire de moins, veu que lui-mesme l'appetoit si furieusement, et haletoit apres si desesperément ...[28]

In this instance, the cluster of texts around Epicurus's final letter and dying words in 'De la gloire' paint a picture of a philosopher too greatly enamoured of personal and literary immortality to be truly admirable.[29] Yet after Montaigne's rehabilitation of Epicurus and pleasure, this causes the reader discomfort and perhaps bewilderment. Some explanation is provided by the essayist's accompanying gloss, a gloss that has itself become much quoted: 'nous sommes, je ne sçay comment, doubles en nous mesmes, qui faict que ce que nous croyons, nous ne le croyons pas, et ne nous pouvons deffaire de ce que nous condamnons' (II. 16, 619).[30] The formulation, prim and crisp, offers a principle for understanding the contradictions of human nature, a principle fully applicable to Epicurus.

More importantly and pointedly, however, this philosopher now joins a select number of critical figures in the *Essais* who are characterized by doubling and disjunction,[31] transposing them into a hermeneutic crux: Epicurus, here in 'De la gloire', wavering rejecting and yet yearning for glory; Pyrrho, whose ambition to 'se faire homme vivant, discourant et raisonnant, jouïssant de tous plaisirs et commoditez naturelles' is vigorously commended in the 'Apologie' (p. 505) and yet whose conduct is criticized in 'De la vertu' for being incompatible with the ordinary pace of human life (p. 706);[32] and, most stridently of all, Socrates, the disparity between whose face and nature is the subject of extensive commentary and investigation in 'De la phisionomie'.[33] In each case, disjunction creates a puzzle, an enigma, something which reflects in its structure the dislocation of form, the forking paths, the divergent trajectories that typify the *Essais* as a whole, and which compels the reader to exercise judgement in decoding what the enigma might mean (and we might conveniently recall at this point that enigma appears in the same section of the *Institutio oratoria* as irony, both being for Quintilian forms of 'allegoria', the trope *par excellence* of encoding).[34] For to name Epicurus, to name Epicurean pleasure, precisely because it is connected with the 'singulier' and 'extreme',[35] is to increase the risk of being misread by the implications a downstream interpretation will draw out of that naming. Montaigne, as we have seen, moves against the *doxa* in believing that it is possible to live happily according to the doctrine of Epicurean pleasure. Epicurus, however, is a double-edged figure for Montaigne, finding pleasure in both spurning and seeking glory. So what, given this double-edged evidence, are we to think of Epicurus? In a downstream reading, this set of problems presents a hermeneutic dilemma: how are we to interpret the fact that Montaigne uses Epicurus to attack standardized condemnations of pleasure and its viability, and yet locates in the same Epicurus a doubleness that makes him resistant to being turned into an unambiguous figurehead? By presenting such a downstream reading as involving the hermeneutical problem of a paradox about the viability of pleasure that turns into an enigma about Epicurus, Montaigne points up the hiatus between naming and meaning, between Epicurus and his significance, between *volupté* and its afterlife. Foregrounding the problem of its own construction and puzzling interpretation, this reflexive dimension of the Montaignian trace is what permanently questions the later history into which it is inserted and opens up the gap between the phenomenon (here, Epicurus) and its appearing (its afterlife). When the trace returns, it returns not as one among others but as an interpretative dilemma that cannot be written out, in both senses of that expression.

This conclusion holds implications for the image of the sinuous line with which we began. 'L'appartenance historique d'un texte n'est jamais droite ligne,' Derrida writes.[36] In 'De la vanité', Montaigne goes further and deeper: 'Je ne trace aucune ligne certaine, ny droicte ny courbe' (III. 9, 985). 'Ny droicte': so the narrative *je* who speaks his desires in the *Essais* is neither a straightforward Epicurean voluptuary nor a figure of ourselves, postmodern characters in Freud's drama of desire. 'Ny courbe': and yet Montaigne's writing about desire does make history (rather than just reflect it) by, in this case, re-inscribing antitheses, unsettling boundaries, re-positioning hierarchies; and so in a sense it does ironically anticipate the downstream (mis) reading which will allot Montaigne a place in a story which is not fully his. The 'route par ailleurs' to which the essayist alludes in chapter III. 13 is thus a road that is itself conceivably double in nature, neither straight nor curved, looping forwards and backwards, moving towards and away from, with only the assurance that the journey will involve an art of slowness, and that therein lies its tenderness.

> Ô Courbes, méandre,
> Secrets du scripteur,
> Je veux faire attendre
> Le mot le plus tendre.[37]

Notes to Chapter 5

1. *Pré-histoires I*, p. 177. This seems an opportune moment to record a debt of institutional and personal gratitude towards Terence Cave. As Visiting Professor for three years at Royal Holloway (2002–05), he conducted a highly successful seminar on methodology and interdisciplinarity, uniting interests from across the Arts Faculty and creating an outstanding forum for intellectual debate. As a friend and *seiziémiste* colleague, he has long been, and remains, a constant source of inspiration and encouragement.

2. Paul Valéry, 'L'Insinuant', first stanza, in *Charmes, Œuvres*, ed. by Jean Hytier, 2 vols (Paris: Gallimard, Bibliothèque de la Pléiade, 1957), I, 137. The second line reads in the original: 'Secrets du menteur'. On this complex area in Montaigne, see Gisèle Mathieu-Castellani, *Montaigne ou la vérité du mensonge* (Geneva: Droz, 2000).

3. John O'Brien, 'Question(s) d'équilibre', in *Lire les 'Essais' de Montaigne*, ed. by Noel Peacock and James Supple (Paris: Champion, 2001), pp. 107–22.

4. On the 'route par ailleurs', see now André Tournon, *'Route par ailleurs': Le 'nouveau langage' des 'Essais'* (Paris: Champion, 2006).

5. Cf. Jacques Derrida, 'La Double Séance', in *La Dissémination* (Paris: Seuil, 1972), p. 303: 'Toute méthode est une fiction [...] cela n'exclut pas une certaine marche à suivre'. The present discussion attempts to follow a certain set of steps.

6. Cave, p. 49.

7. See now, for example, the comments of Michel Magnien and Catherine Simonin-Magnien in their introduction to *Montaigne, Les 'Essais'*, ed. by Jean Balsamo, Michel Magnien and Catherine Simonin-Magnien (Paris: Gallimard, 'Bibliothèque de la Pléiade', 2007), p. xx: 'On voit [...] à quel point il peut apparaître délicat de parler d'une "évolution" qui aurait conduit le penseur, *via* la "crise sceptique" de 1576, d'un raidissement stoïque initial à une nonchalance épicurienne.'

8. On Epicurus and Epicureanism, see *The Cambridge History of Renaissance Philosophy*, ed. by Charles B. Schmitt, Quentin Skinner and Eckhard Kessler (Cambridge: Cambridge University Press, 1988), pp. 374–86; Howard Jones, *The Epicurean Tradition* (London: Routledge, 1989). For Montaigne himself, see Simone Fraisse, 'Montaigne et les doctrines épicuriennes', in *Actes du VIIIe congrès de l'Association Guillaume Budé* (Paris: Les Belles Lettres, 1969), pp. 677–85; Donald Stone, 'Montaigne and Epicurus: A Lesson in Originality', in *Mélanges sur la littérature de la Renaissance à la mémoire de V.-L. Saulnier* (Geneva: Droz, 1984), pp. 465–71 (usefully compares Montaigne's Epicurus with Valla's *De voluptate* and Erasmus's *Epicureus*); Daniel Ménager, 'Les Citations de Lucrèce chez Montaigne', in *Montaigne in Cambridge*, ed. by Philip Ford and Gillian Jondorf (Cambridge: Cambridge French Colloquia, 1989), pp. 25–38; Marcel Conche, *Montaigne et la philosophie* (Paris: PUF, 1996), pp. 79–109; Eric MacPhail, 'Montaigne's New Epicureanism', *Montaigne Studies*, 12 (2000), 91–103; George Hoffmann, 'Epicure — Epicurisme' in *Dictionnaire de Michel de Montaigne*, ed. by Philippe Desan (Paris: Champion, 2004), pp. 332–35. Montaigne's marginalia to Lucretius have been edited by Michael Screech, *Montaigne's Annotated Copy of Lucretius. A Transcription and Study of the Manuscript, Notes and Pen-Marks* (Geneva: Droz, 1998). Succinct accounts of problems with Epicurus's pleasure principle are to be found in Terence Irwin, *Classical Thought*, 'A History of Western Thought', vol. 1 (Oxford: Oxford University Press, 1989), ch. 8, 'Epicureanism', pp. 145–63, especially 158–63, and R. W. Sharples, *Stoics, Epicureans and Sceptics* (London: Routledge, 1996), pp. 82–99. For editions of Epicurus, Cyril Bailey's *Epicurus* (Oxford: Clarendon Press, 1926) is, despite its age, still serviceable; a more modern edition, with a commentary, is provided by Marcel Conche, *Epicure: Lettres et maximes* (Paris: PUF, 1987).

9. Jones, p. 160. For a counter-view, see George Hoffmann, 'The Investigation of Nature', in *The Cambridge Companion to Montaigne*, ed. by Ullrich Langer (Cambridge: Cambridge University Press, 2005), pp. 171–77 on Epicurean physics.

10. See '"Auteur de merveilleux poids": Montaigne and Xenophon', *Montaigne Studies*, 17 (2005), 17–34.

11. Gisèle Mathieu-Castellani, *Montaigne*, and '"Oser dire tout" ou "ne dire qu'à demi"? Parole ouverte et parole entrouverte dans les chapitres V et IX du livre III (et quelques autres...)' in *Le Livre III des 'Essais' de Montaigne*, Cahiers Textuels no. 26, ed. by Pascal Debailly (Paris: Université Paris 7, 2003), pp. 133–51; Jean-Yves Pouilloux, 'Dire à demi' in *Essais, Livre III, Montaigne* (Paris: Armand Colin, 2002), pp. 57–68.

12. See Tournon, pp. 39–41.

13. Geoffroy de La Chassaigne, souldan de Pressac, *Epistres de Seneque Senateur Romain* (Rouen: Jean Berthelin, 1604), fol. 44[r]. On this translator, see Jean Balsamo, 'Deux Gentilshommes "nécessiteux d'honneur": Montaigne et Pressac', *Montaigne Studies*, 13 (2001), 141–73.

14. Cf. André Tournon, 'Soit que je sois autre moy mesme...', in *Self and Other in Sixteenth-Century France*, ed. by Kathryn Banks and Philip Ford (Cambridge: Cambridge French Colloquia, 2004), pp. 189–212.

15. From Diogenes Laertius, x.129 or Cicero, *Tusc.*, v.33.94.

16. See Elizabeth Guild's reading of Socrates and desire in 'Sur des vers de Virgile', 'Vous ne pouvez le savoir — car vous vous détournez', *Paragraph*, 29 (2006), 53–66 (pp. 63–65).

17. *Heterodoxy in Early Modern Science and Theology*, ed. by John Brook and Ian Maclean (Oxford: Oxford University Press, 2005), pp. xiv–xx; Agnieszka Steczowicz, 'The Defence of Contraries: Paradox in the Late Renaissance Disciplines' (unpublished doctoral thesis, University of Oxford, 2004).

18. Quintilian, *Institutio oratoria*, ix.2.23. The tradition of the *Suda* (Suidas) sheds further important light on the meaning of *paradoxon*. In that dictionary, *paradoxon* is given the synonyms *aprosdokêton*,

thaumaston; when these terms are translated into Latin in Portius's edition of the *Suda* (Geneva: Pierre de la Roviere, 1619), they are rendered 'Inopinatum. Insperatum. *A communi mortalium opinione remotum, ac* admirandum' (italics in original). *Paradoxon* is immediately preceded in the *Suda* by the phrase *para doxan*, the synonyms for which are *para prosdokian, par'elpida*, all three being rendered in Portius's Latin respectively 'Praeter opinionem. Praeter expectationem. Praeter spem'. This suggests a very close connection, almost a contamination, between *paradoxon* as a rhetorical figure of the unexpected, *paradoxon* as the wondrous (deriving from Cicero's translation of the Greek term *paradoxa* as *admirabilia* in *De finibus* iv.74), and *paradoxon* as a proposition that runs counter to commonly-held opinion (as illustrated by Cicero's *Paradoxa Stoicorum* which indeed provides the definition of such paradoxes as 'admirabilia contraque opinionem multorum'). This connection is itself reflected in dictionaries of the period, most revealingly in Henri Estienne, *Thesaurus Graecae Linguae* (Geneva: [Henri Estienne], 1572), *s.v.*, 'Qui est praeter seu contra omnium opinionem, Inopinatus. Vnde & Admirabilis, item Incredibilis ex consequente redditur. [...]. Item *Paradoxon* schema Rufiniano, quum aliquid praeter expectationem auditoris profertur'. Estienne's careful distinctions are repeated word for word in subsequent dictionaries indebted to him, for instance *Lexicon Graecolatinum recens constructum* (Lyons: Barthélemy Vincent, 1583), *s.v.* Earlier dictionaries are generally content to restrict themselves to the *admirabilia* definition only, usually citing Cicero as their source, e.g. Mainus's *Lexicon Graecum* (Paris: Aegidius Gormont, 1523), *s.v.*, and the *Dictionarium Latino-Graecum* (Paris: Charles Estienne, 1554), *s.v.* For a more detailed account of the *admirabilia* tradition, see Chapter 1 of Agnieszka Steczowicz's thesis. I am grateful to the author for letting me see this chapter of her work, which confirms my own research. See also Letizia Panizza, 'The Semantic Field of "Paradox" in 16th and 17th Century Italy: From Truth in Appearance False to Falsehood in Appearance True; A Preliminary Investigation', in *Il Vocabulario della 'République des Lettres'*, ed. by Marta Fattori (Florence: Olschki, 1997), pp. 197–220.

19. Diogenes Laertius, x. 128–29; Lucretius, *De rerum natura*, ii. 258: 'progredimur quo ducit quemque voluptas'.

20. A passage in the 'Apologie', for instance, approves of Epicurean 'indolence' (absence of pain) as the culmination of pleasure (pleasure aspires to its own abolition), but not if 'indolence' dulls pain, which must be felt to the same degree as pleasure; the *je* specifically gives this as his own judgement and experience, adding, post 1588, the *sententia* that '[l]e mal est à l'homme bien à son tour' (II. 12, 493). Conche, *Montaigne et la philosophie*, p. 79, offers a different view of Montaigne and Epicureanism, starting from the post-1588 statement, 'en la vertu mesme, le dernier but de nostre visée, c'est la volupté' (I. 20, 82), in order to build the picture of an end-orientated pleasure in the *Essais*. Conche stops short, however, of labelling Montaigne a full Epicurean.

21. Terence Cave, 'Master-Mind Lecture: Montaigne', *Proceedings of the British Academy*, 131 (2005), 183–203 (p. 196).

22. On the notion of 'downstream reading', see Terence Cave, 'Locating the Early Modern', *Paragraph*, 29 (2006), 12–26 (p. 21).

23. A related point emerges when Montaigne is discussing the contrasting values of Plutarch and Seneca: 'l'autre [=Seneca] les [= opinions] a Stoïques et Epicuriennes, plus esloignées de l'usage commun, mais, selon moy, plus commodes [C] en particulier [A] et plus fermes' (II. 10, 413).

24. Diogenes Laertius, x. 11.

25. The point in this [C] addition bears on peace of mind: 'Ce qu'on nous dict de ceux du Bresil, qu'ils ne mouroyent que de vieillesse, et qu'on attribue à la serenité et tranquillité de leur air, je l'attribue plustost à la tranquillité et serenité de leur ame, deschargée de toute passion et pensée et occupation tendue ou desplaisante, comme gents qui passoyent leur vie en une admirable simplicité et ignorance, sans lettres, sans loy, sans roy, sans relligion quelconque' (II. 12, 491).

26. The idea occurs more than once in the *Essais*. In III. 4, 834, Montaigne merely notes that 'Epicurus mesme se console en sa fin sur l'eternité et utilité de ses escrits', but in II. 8, 401, there is a much longer paragraph comparing intellectual and biological progeny in respect of Epicurus who 'avoit toute sa consolation en la beauté de sa doctrine qu'il laissoit au monde'.

27. The will is also preserved in Diogenes Laertius, x. 16–22, but Epicurus's final letter is there addressed to Idomeneus. For a recent discussion of the will, see James Warren, *Facing Death: Epicurus and His Critics* (Oxford: Clarendon Press, 2004), pp. 162–73. Warren explains plausibly

why the will is in this form. For Cicero's reactions to the will and especially the letter, see *De finibus*, ii.30.99–31.101: 'nihil in hac praeclara epistula scriptum ab Epicuro congruens et conveniens decretis suis reperetis. ita redarguitur ipse a sese, convincunturque scripta eius probitate ipsius ac moribus'.

28. Plutarch, *Œuvres morales*, trans. by Jacques Amyot (Paris: Abel L'Angelier, 1603), I, 907 (first edition, 1572).

29. Further twists to this part of the tale are provided by chapter I. 39, 247–48, where Epicurus and Seneca are enlisted approvingly as spokesmen of 'la vraye et naifve philosophie' against 'gloire', and, shortly afterwards, by Montaigne's concession in 'De ne communiquer sa gloire' that 'il semble que les philosophes mesmes se défacent plus tard et plus envis de ceste-cy [= la gloire] que de nulle autre', adding '[a]pres que vous avez tout dict et tout creu pour la desadvouer, elle produict contre vostre discours une inclination si intestine que vous avez peu que tenir à l'encontre' (I. 41, 255).

30. For other famous doubles in Montaigne, cf. III. 11, 1034 (the understanding): 'c'est le soulier de Theramenez, bon à tous pieds. Et il est double et divers, et les matieres doubles et diverses'; II. 12, 581: '[A] Voylà comment la raison fournit d'apparence à divers effects. [B] C'est un pot à deux anses, qu'on peut saisir à gauche et à dextre'; and II. 17, 654: '[C] La raison humaine est un glaive double et dangereux'. In III. 13, 1077, actions are described as 'doubles et bigarrées à divers lustres'. Montaigne's self-description in III. 9, 964, 'Moy à cette heure et moy tantost sommes bien deux', suggests division rather than doubling. On this whole issue, see Jean-Yves Pouilloux, 'Pot à deux anses', *BSAM*, 43/44 (2006), 75–85.

31. Cf. Richard Parish's illuminating account of this trope, '"Je t'aime moi non plus": Disjunction and the Discourses of Love in the Seventeenth Century', *Seventeenth-Century French Studies*, 24 (2002), 17–28. Despite its specific focus, this article offers important methodological considerations susceptible of wider application.

32. Compare what Montaigne says about Epicurus in 'De l'yvrongnerie': 'quand Epicurus entreprend de se faire mignarder à la goute, et, refusant le repos et la santé, que de gayeté de cœur il deffie les maux, et, mesprisant les douleurs moins aspres, dedaignant les luiter et les combatre, qu'il en appelle et desire des fortes, poignantes et dignes de luy [...] qui ne juge que ce sont boutées d'un courage eslancé hors de son giste?' (II. 2, 347).

33. For a representative set of attempts to interpret this dichotomy in 'De la phisionomie', see John O'Brien, 'Montaigne and the Exercise of Paradox: *Essais* III. 12', in *Montaigne in Cambridge*, pp. 53–67; Marie-Luce Demonet, 'Le Signe physionomique dans le livre III des *Essais*', in *Des signes au sens: Lectures du livre III des 'Essais'*, ed. by Françoise Argod-Dutard (Paris: Champion, 2003), pp. 151–78; and André Tournon's two rather different readings in *Essais de Montaigne, Livre III* (Paris: Atlande, 2002), pp. 163–66, 171–74 and *'Route par ailleurs'*, pp. 76–79.

34. Quintilian, *Institutio oratoria*, viii.6.52–54.

35. Montaigne's reluctance even to name Epicurean books in 'Sur des vers de Virgile' ('Car il faut laisser à part les escrits des philosophes qui ont suivy la secte Epicurienne', III. 5, 858), owing, Villey reasonably surmises, to their insistence on pleasure as the supreme good, is evidence of the risky character of Epicureanism, the danger of its being misunderstood by the readers the chapter is discussing.

36. Jacques Derrida, *De la grammatologie* (Paris: Minuit, 1967), pp. 149–50.

37. Paul Valéry, 'L'Insinuant', final stanza, with modification of the second line quoted.

CHAPTER 6

❖

Diderot and Montaigne:
Portraits and Afterlives

Kate E. Tunstall

Portraiture and self-portraiture is a genre with a particularly pertinent role to play in any study concerned with the notion of 'afterlives', as the portrait painter or writer might be said to aim, by means of representation, to confer a posthumous existence on himself or his subject. Although Diderot was not much given to self-representation (unlike his one-time friend, Rousseau, author of the autobiographical *Confessions*), he was often represented by others during his lifetime, most notably in painted portraits.[1] In the *Salon de 1767*, he discusses two of these portraits, one by Michel Vanloo (Louvre), the other by Mme Therbouche (lost), and as he does so, he also writes what might be described as self-portraits.[2] One of the most interesting aspects of these discussions and these textual self-portraits is that, at the same time as they look towards the future, offering images of Diderot for posterity, they also look back, as Diderot suggests a genealogical history for himself as a writer and philosopher. He evokes Plato, Aristotle, Seneca, Diogenes the Cynic and, most importantly for my purposes here, Montaigne. I want to explore how Diderot's writing of and about his portraits evokes the self-portraits offered by Montaigne in the *Essais*, and so, how in attempting to shape his own afterlife, Diderot draws on and gives new shape to Montaigne's.

It is a commonplace of literary history to observe that Diderot shares something with Montaigne, and yet few critics have made any serious attempt to describe exactly what that might be.[3] Walter E. Rex, for example, limits himself to observing that, 'Of all French writers, the one whom Diderot most resembles is Montaigne',[4] thereby neatly demonstrating Philip Knee's more recent claim that, 'ce qui frappe le plus dans le traitement par les commentateurs du rapport entre Diderot et Montaigne est le caractère allusif de leurs remarques et finalement le peu d'attention qu'ils accordent à un rapport que la plupart jugent pourtant très significatif'.[5] And although Jerome Schwarz has devoted much attention to the relationship between the two writers, his book offers in the end little more than the vague terms 'affinity' and 'shared humanism' to describe it, along with a compendium of references to the *Essais* in Diderot's work, which (though useful) might be thought of as a series of, 'Voylà d'où il le print!' (II. 12, 546).[6] If we are to give a meaningful description of Diderot's relationship to Montaigne, we must, I think, carry out some detailed analysis of the texts.

Terence Cave proves inspirational here, not only for his work on Montaigne, but also for his approach to textual analysis, with its fine-tuned attention to verbal rhythms, logical *volte-face* and in particular, intertextual echoes. This essay attempts this kind of analysis for Diderot's texts on portraiture from the *Salon de 1767* with the aim of moving beyond another of Rex's passing observations, namely that the commentary on the Vanloo portrait has 'a hint of Montaigne'.[7]

It might be said, however, that anyone writing a self-portrait in eighteenth-century France would be bound to make reference to Montaigne, the *Essais* having come to be seen primarily as an examination of the self and an exercise in self-representation.[8] By the mid to late seventeenth century, Pascal's question, 'Qu'est-ce que le moi?', in fragment 688 of the *Pensées* seemed almost immediately to trigger a reference to Montaigne (it comes in the following fragment),[9] and by the latter part of the eighteenth century, Rousseau's introspective writing, be it the *Rêveries* or the *Confessions*, is full of echoes of the *Essais*.[10] Moreover, in the context of writing about painted portraits in particular, a reference to Montaigne might even be thought *de rigueur*, owing to his use of the verb 'peindre', albeit metaphorically, in his celebrated claim, 'c'est moi que je peins' ('Au lecteur', p. 9).[11] I shall return to the question of reception history in a moment, but it is important to be clear here that in the *Salon de 1767*, the relationship between Diderot's writing about his painted portraits, his textual self-portraits, and those of Montaigne, is no simple cultural reflex.

Diderot writes in imitation of Montaigne, deliberately and carefully orchestrating quotations or near quotations of the *Essais*, echoing them not simply in the themes he explores, but also in the very texture, lexical and syntactical, of his writing. He explores themes familiar to any reader of the *Essais*, such as friendship and the relationship between the friend and the self, the flux and change of the world as it relates to the possibility of knowledge and of self-knowledge, and he does so in a style of writing that shares with Montaigne's such features as the constant shifting between opposing points of view and the important use of 'if' clauses. Moreover, Diderot's imitation shows him 'thinking with'[12] and writing with Montaigne about what is involved in genealogies and afterlives.

It has often been observed that the *Essais* seem on a number of occasions to be concerned with their own afterlives and to project their own future readers and readings, a phenomenon present to some degree in 'Au lecteur', and which Terence Cave has distinctively called 'downstream context'.[13] He distinguishes this notion from reception history, in which, by contrast, a 'threshold' has been crossed such that the text arrives in a context, the contours of which the author could not possibly have foreseen.[14] Certainly by 1767, a number of thresholds have been crossed, not least that of the emergence of a 'public space', so that Montaigne could not have predicted a review of a *salon* art exhibition as a possible context for reading 'Au lecteur' (though he might, I suppose, have been amused by the reading, as we'll see).[15] But what of Diderot's backward look, his suggestion, via the references to Montaigne, that the late sixteenth century is his 'upstream' context? As will be shown, it is shot through with comedy and paradox. Diderot subtly quotes 'Au lecteur' so as to make the comic suggestion that Vanloo and Therbouche have made him look as Montaigne explicitly stated he had not made himself look in the *Essais* (though Montaigne says that in other circumstances, he would have done). Moreover, though presented as better likenesses of himself than the paintings, Diderot's self-portraits, with their thematic and syntactic echoes of Montaigne, paradoxically make him look — or rather sound — like someone else.[16] In the *Salon de 1767*, Diderot imitates Montaigne in order to project genealogies and afterlives for both himself and for Montaigne, as well as to undermine them.

I. The Self and Change

Diderot's commentary on the Vanloo portrait is remarkable for the multiplicity of points of view he adopts on the representation of himself. He begins with the single word 'Moi', a monosyllable isolated by a full stop, suggesting perhaps the shock of self-recognition. Yet in what follows, Diderot's relationship with the portrait turns out to be a rather complex affair: he praises it for being a good likeness; he censors it for not being a good likeness; he criticizes it for being too good a likeness; and finally he disregards it on the grounds that a painted likeness is impossible because his face is constantly changing:

> J'avais en une journée cent physionomies diverses, selon la chose dont j'étais affecté. J'étais serein, triste, rêveur, tendre, violent, passionné, enthousiaste. [...] les impressions de mon âme se succédant très rapidement et se peignant toutes sur mon visage, l'œil du peintre ne me retrouvant pas le même d'un instant à l'autre, sa tâche devienne beaucoup plus difficile qu'il ne la croyait. (IV, 532)

This idea of constant physiognomic change echoes Diderot's materialist vision of nature and the universe, found in texts such as the *Lettre sur les aveugles* (1749), *De l'Interprétation de la nature* (1754) and the *Rêve de d'Alembert* (1769). It might also be said to echo Montaigne's conception of his 'moi' which is likewise always on the move:

> Je ne puis asseurer mon object. Il va trouble et chancelant, d'une yvresse naturelle. Je le prens en ce point, comme il est, en l'instant que je m'amuse à luy. Je ne peints pas l'estre. Je peints le passage : non un passage d'aage en autre, ou, comme dict le peuple, de sept en sept ans, mais de jour en jour, de minute en minute. (III. 2, 805)

The problem with Vanloo's portrait of Diderot is that the painter has attempted to 'pein[dre] le passage', an impossible project for the painter who, according to Diderot, 'n'a qu'un instant' (IV, 496), and for whom there is no equivalent to the rhetorical figure of *amplificatio*, which characterizes Diderot's self-description — 'serein, triste, rêveur, tendre, violent, passionné, enthousiaste' — as well as that of Montaigne:

> Je donne à mon ame tantost un visage, tantost un autre, selon le costé où je la couche. Si je parle diversement de moy, c'est que je me regarde diversement. Toutes les contrariétez s'y trouvent selon quelque tour et en quelque façon. Honteux, insolent; chaste, luxurieux; bavard, taciturne; laborieux, delicat; ingenieux, hebeté; chagrin, debonaire; menteur, veritable; sçavant, ignorant, et liberal, et avare, et prodigue, tout cela, je le vois en moy aucunement, selon

> que je me vire; et quiconque s'estudie bien attentifvement trouve en soy, voire
> et en son jugement mesme, cette volubilité et discordance. Je n'ay rien à dire de
> moy, entierement, simplement, et solidement, sans confusion et sans meslange,
> ny en un mot. (II. 1, 335)

In contrast to Diderot's list in which the adjectives are arranged in an order that is apparently random, Montaigne's list consists of pairs of antonyms ('Honteux, insolent; chaste, luxurieux; bavard, taciturne; laborieux, delicat; ingenieux, hebeté; chagrin, debonaire; menteur, veritable') and a final trio ('liberal, et avare, et prodigue'), and this binary and ternary structure is then reflected in reverse order in the adverbs ('entierement, simplement, et solidement, sans confusion et sans meslange').[17] Yet, ordered or not, such lists enable the writers to 'pein[dre] le passage' of their 'moi', while a painter has to make do with, as it were, 'un mot'.

Is the snapshot portrait necessarily lacking in resemblance, however? A close reading of Diderot's text reveals that the answer to this question is both 'yes' and 'no'. As such, the text on the Vanloo portrait reveals another characteristic, reminiscent of Montaigne's writing: contrariety.

II. Contrariety, 'Que Sais-Je?', 'Qui Suis-Je?'

It used often to be claimed that Diderot was illogical or incoherent, but Rex has persuasively argued for what he calls a 'dynamics of contrariety' in Diderot's writing, situating him in a rhetorical tradition next to La Fontaine, Molière and Voltaire.[18] The absence of Montaigne from the tradition identified by Rex is peculiar, however, especially since, as we have just seen, Montaigne uses the word 'contrariétez' to describe his temperament, and he also uses the adjectival form, 'contraire', to describe his way of thinking: 'Maintes-fois (comme il m'advient de faire volontiers) ayant pris pour exercice et pour esbat à maintenir une contraire opinion à la mienne, à mon esprit, s'applicant et tournant de ce costé-là, m'y attache si bien que je ne trouve plus la raison de mon premier advis, et m'en depars' (II. 12, 66). Perhaps Rex thought Montaignian contrariety too bound up with scepticism, and he wished to avoid opening the rather vexed question of Diderot's scepticism.[19] Yet it is possible to avoid that debate without also avoiding a fruitful, comparative analysis of Diderot and Montaigne's writing, an analysis of which is all the more important because Diderot draws on Montaigne not for any philosophical position but for his writing style, as he makes clear in the *Essais sur les règnes de Claude et de Néron* (I, 1133).

Montaigne's art of writing is an art of contrariety, or rather, to borrow Terence Cave's more precise description, it makes extensive use of the figure of *antiperistasis*,[20] an analysis of which enables Cave to short-circuit the question of Montaigne's relationship to scepticism, a question even more vexed than that of Diderot's relationship to scepticism.[21] Cave explains the term as follows: 'l'antipéristase [...] n'est pas un simple contraste ou même une *coincidentia oppositorum* ou un paradoxe, mais un mouvement de transvaluation qui permet d'entretenir successivement — sinon simultanément — deux attitudes, ou même plusieurs attitudes, radicalement différentes'.[22] The most striking example of this kind of writing is to be found in the 'Apologie de Raimond Sebond', a text which has at its centre an unresolved and indeed insoluble tension, as Cave explains: 'l'outrance des arguments sceptiques provoque d'abord un mouvement contraire vers la sécurité de la censure; mais ensuite dès que l'intensité de la rhétorique autoritaire s'est épuisée, les figures mêmes de cette rhétorique réapparaissent dans un autre discours où leur valeur est inversée'.[23] This antiperistatic mode of writing, which is provoked in Montaigne by the question 'que sais-je?', is also to be found in Diderot, where it is provoked by the question, 'qui suis-je?', itself a version of the Delphic injunction to 'know thyself', to which Montaigne's *Essais* might also be said to respond. A close analysis of the Vanloo commentary enables us to track the switch-back dynamic of Diderot's writing.

If Diderot begins the commentary on his portrait with the recognition, 'Moi', he immediately follows it up by calling that recognition into question: 'J'aime Michel, mais j'aime mieux la vérité' (IV, 531). This version of the famous Latin *sentential*, perhaps first uttered in Greek by Aristotle, 'Amicus Plato, sed magis amica veritas',[24] suggests that the portrait is not a true likeness and that his friendship with the painter, Michel Vanloo, will not prevent him from taking a critical stand on it. Indeed, in the rest of the text Diderot no longer refers to the figure in the portrait as 'Moi', but rather in the third person. In the next sentence, however, the portrait is nonetheless described as 'assez ressemblant', and Diderot reports what 'he', the figure in the portrait, could say to someone who did not recognize him in it: 'Il peut dire à ceux qui ne le reconnaissent pas comme le jardinier de l'opéra-comique : "c'est qu'il ne m'a jamais vu sans perruque"' (ibid.). A reference in the first person reappears here ('ne m'a jamais vu'), though it does so in the reported direct speech of the 'le jardinier de l'opéra-comique',[25] and what he says upsets the opposition between the self, the friend and truthful representation contained in the opening phrase, for his remark about the wig suggests, on the contrary, that only a friend would have seen the true Diderot, because only a friend would have seen him without his wig on, and thus only a friend could paint a true likeness of him. Diderot's reaction to his painted portrait is in the first few sentences already quite complicated.

In what follows, Diderot affirms the resemblance, denies it, reaffirms it and denies it once again:

> Très vivant, c'est sa douceur avec sa vivacité. Mais trop jeune, tête trop petite. Joli comme une femme, lorgnant, souriant, mignard, faisant le petit bec, la bouche en cœur. Rien de la sagesse de la couleur du *Cardinal de Choiseul*. Et puis un luxe de vêtement à ruiner le pauvre littérateur si le receveur de la capitation vient à l'imposer sur sa robe de chambre. L'écritoire, les livres, les accessoires aussi bien qu'il est possible, quand on a voulu la couleur brillante et qu'on veut être harmonieux. Pétillant de près, harmonieux de loin, surtout les chairs. Du reste de belles mains, bien modelées, exceptée la gauche qui n'est pas dessinée. On le voit de face. Il a la tête nue. Son toupet gris avec sa mignardise lui donne l'air d'une vieille coquette qui fait encore l'aimable, la position d'un secrétaire d'Etat et non d'un philosophe. (ibid.)

As Rex has also observed, the rhythm of the phrases which affirm the resemblance is very different from that of the phrases which deny it: Diderot defends his friend's portrait of him in short, almost staccato sentences — 'Très vivant, c'est sa douceur avec sa vivacité', 'Pétillant de près, harmonieux de loin, surtout les chairs' — and criticizes it in longer sentences with verbs and dependent clauses — 'Son toupet gris avec sa mignardise lui donne l'air d'une vieille coquette qui fait encore l'aimable, la position d'un secrétaire d'Etat et non d'un philosophe'. Indeed, it almost sounds as though there are two different voices in the text, a sense that is confirmed by a letter from Diderot to Sophie Volland, in which he reports his wife's reaction to the portrait: she said he had, 'l'air d'une vieille coquette qui fait le petit bec et qui a encore des prétentions'.[26] In the Vanloo commentary, this censorious voice fades in and out, seemingly at the mention of Diderot's bare head. Such back and forth between opposing points of view is not resolved in the text, instead it is simply displaced, as Diderot now shifts both focus and genre, away from a critical appreciation of his friend's painting to an anecdote, recounting what happened during the sitting.

While there seemed to be two different voices in the critical appreciation of the portrait, in addition to the reported speech of the 'jardinier de l'opéra-comique', the anecdote about the creation of the portrait makes it clear that, in addition to Diderot and Vanloo, a third person was also involved: the painter's aunt, Mme Vanloo. And from now on, though Diderot tacitly accepts the point of view of the censorious voice (also that of his wife), he makes it clear that the responsibility for the rather over-dressed, effeminate, coquettish figure does not lie with the painter nor indeed with himself, but with Mme Vanloo: 'la fausseté du premier moment a influé sur tout le reste. C'est cette folle de Mme Vanloo qui venait jaser avec lui, tandis qu'on le peignait, qui lui a donné cet air-là et qui a tout gâté' (ibid.). He claims that by starting off the sitting by chatting to him, she made him look like that. This is, of course, implicitly to accept that the picture is a true likeness, albeit one in which he is wearing a rather unfortunate expression, and he thereby adds another contradictory element to his commentary.

Diderot thus claims that the portrait is both a likeness and not a likeness; he claims with the 'jardinier de l'opéra-comique' that it is a likeness, which only he and his friends will recognize; with his wife, he claims that it is not a likeness at all; and finally he claims that it is a true likeness, but of a 'false' expression, the responsibility for which lies with the painter's aunt. Diderot refuses to pass judgement decisively one way or another, shifting instead between different opinions, different voices, different verbal styles, all of which might be said to echo his changing facial expressions.

It is not only in its exploitation of contrarieties, however, that Diderot's writing might be said to resemble that of Montaigne. Diderot also makes much use of 'if' clauses, a feature of the *Essais* that Cave has analysed particularly in the context of Montaigne's statements about religious faith.[27] Yet 'if' clauses are also one of the distinctive marks of 'Au lecteur', central to which is the question of self-representation. And it is this text that Diderot cites in both the commentary on the Vanloo portrait and that on the Therbouche portrait. The way he does so puts Montaigne's 'if' clauses to comic purpose.

III. Fictional Self-Portraits

In 'Au lecteur', Montaigne famously presents himself between two hypothetical alternatives:

> Si c'eust esté pour rechercher la faveur du monde, je me fusse mieux paré et me presanterois en une marche estudiée. Je veus qu'on m'y voie en ma façon simple, naturelle et ordinaire, sans contention et artifice: car c'est moy que je peins. Mes defauts s'y liront au vif, et ma forme naïfve, autant que la reverence publique me l'a permis. Que si j'eusse esté entre ces nations qu'on dict vivre encore sous la douce liberté des premieres loix de nature, je t'asseure que je m'y fusse tres-volontiers peint tout entier, et tout nud. ('Au lecteur', p. 9)

If he had been addressing himself to the public or if he had been living in another historical moment or in another country (most probably, the New World),[28] Montaigne says that he would either have presented himself better dressed, 'mieux paré', or not dressed at all, 'tout entier, et tout nud'. But instead, writing for 'parens et amis', and living in the late sixteenth century in France, he says he has decided to present himself in his, 'façon simple, naturelle et ordinaire, sans contention et artifice'. What is remarkable about the two texts from Diderot's *Salon de 1767* is that they echo this text in such a way as to make the comic suggestion that the portraits of Diderot done by Vanloo and Therbouche are in some way realizations of Montaigne's two self-portraits that might have been.

As we have seen, Diderot is represented in the Vanloo portrait 'en robe de chambre', a mode of dress which is judged to be much too luxurious for a 'pauvre littérateur' and which suggests an attempt to impress the spectator: 'qui fait [...] l'aimable'. On its own, it would be difficult to argue that this constitutes an intertextual reference to 'Au lecteur', in which Montaigne explains how, if he had been seeking 'la faveur du monde', he would have been 'mieux paré'. However, when Diderot subsequently recounts how, by contrast, he came to appear naked in the Therbouche portrait, the intertext is clear, and its presence retrospectively suggests that it was also to be heard in the Vanloo commentary. Describing the circumstances of the sitting for Mme Therbouche, Diderot writes:

> Lorsque la tête fut faite, il était question du cou, et le haut de mon vêtement le cachait, ce qui dépitait un peu l'artiste. Pour faire cesser ce dépit, je passai derrière un rideau, je me déshabillai, et je parus devant elle en modèle académique. 'Je n'aurais pas osé vous le proposer, me dit-elle, mais vous avez bien fait, et je vous en remercie'. J'étais nu, mais tout nu. Elle me peignait, et nous causions avec une simplicité et une innocence dignes des premiers siècles. (IV, 726)

The echoes of 'Au lecteur' are subtle but clear here. Diderot's reference to 'une simplicité et une innocence dignes des premiers siècles' recalls Montaigne's 'la douce liberté des premières loix de la nature', and Diderot's phrase, 'j'étais nu, mais tout nu', echoes Montaigne's 'tout entier, et tout nud', both in terms of content and form, as Diderot's repetition of the adjective 'nu' is a variation on Montaigne's repetition of the adverb 'tout'. To a reader attuned to these intertextual echoes, Diderot is suggesting that Therbouche has done a portrait of him which realizes the self-portrait that Montaigne said he could only have done for himself if he had been living in the New World. Yet the responsibility for this portrait does not lie entirely with Therbouche for, as Diderot explains, it was his idea to get undressed — 'Je n'aurais pas osé vous le proposer, me dit-elle'. Moreover, the idea that Diderot appears in it as the naked Montaigne is a suggestion achieved not by the painting itself, but by Diderot's writing. Diderot's descriptions of his portraits thus transpose into the indicative the two conditional self-portraits of Montaigne, the one in which he was dressed to impress and the other not dressed at all.

Diderot's reaction to the Vanloo portrait is, as we have seen, marked by a kind of switch-back logic reminiscent of Montaigne's sceptical writing, but, recalling 'Au lecteur' more specifically, the Vanloo commentary also contains its own 'if' clause. Where Montaigne's actual self-portrait is framed by two hypothetical ones, Diderot's description of his actual painted portrait by Vanloo, which he presents as a realization of the first of Montaigne's fictional self-portraits, is itself followed up by a fiction:

> Si elle [Mme Vanloo] s'était mise à son clavecin et qu'elle eût préludé ou chanté *Non ha ragione, ingrato, un core abbondonato* ou quelque autre morceau du même genre, le philosophe sensible eût pris tout un autre caractère, et le portrait s'en serait ressenti. Ou mieux encore, il fallait le laisser seul et l'abandonner à sa rêverie. Alors sa bouche se serait entr'ouverte, ses regards distraits se seraient portés au loin, le travail de sa tête fortement occupée se serait peint sur son visage, et Michel eût fait une belle chose. (IV, 531–32)

Diderot's 'if' clause introduces an alternative, imagined set of circumstances, in which he would have looked like a *philosophe*, gazing into the distance, his mind on higher things, and it is this fictional painting that Diderot would have wanted left to posterity. As a textual self-portrait, written in the past conditional, it is what he himself offers to posterity as 'une belle chose'.

It does not last long, however, since a few lines later, Diderot replaces it with a different self-portrait, this one written in the imperfect: 'J'avais un grand front, des yeux très vifs, d'assez grands traits, la tête tout à fait du caractère d'un ancien orateur, une bonhomie qui touchait de bien près à la bêtise, à la rusticité des anciens temps' (IV, 532). For the first time in the text, we have a description of a facial expression, which Diderot claims he really had at one moment in the past, and which recalled a figure of the past, 'un ancien orateur', Seneca perhaps. Within the text, the reference to 'la rusticité des anciens temps' looks forward, anticipating the Therbouche portrait, which, as we have seen, Diderot says shows him behaving with an innocence and simplicity 'dignes des premiers siècles'. Yet when we read this self-portrait à la Seneca in relation to the Therbouche commentary, it becomes difficult to take it entirely seriously, as Diderot will go on to undermine the connotations of the 'premiers siècles' and present them in a comic light. Moreover, such a comic presentation will involve the further use of 'if' clauses.[29]

One of the ways in which Diderot praises the Therbouche portrait and suggests that it is suitable for posterity comes in a report of what his daughter said about it: '[Le portrait] était si frappant que ma fille me disait qu'elle l'aurait baisé cent fois pendant mon absence, si elle n'avait pas craint de le gâter. La poitrine était peinte très chaudement, avec des passages et des méplats tout à fait vrais' (IV, 726). In contrast to his wife's reaction to the Vanloo portrait, his daughter's reaction to the Therbouche one is very positive, and most importantly for our purposes, it consists of a fiction, which recounts how she would have kissed the portrait, if she had not been afraid to ruin it. His daughter's hypothetical reaction is then doubled by another, this time his own to Mme Therbouche. Having stripped naked for her, Diderot imagines the following:

> Comme depuis le péché d'Adam, on ne commande pas à toutes les parties de son corps comme à son bras ; et qu'il y en a qui veulent quand le fils d'Adam ne veut pas, et qui ne veulent pas quand le fils d'Adam voudrait bien ; dans le cas de cet accident, je me serais rappelé le mot de Diogène au jeune lutteur : 'Mon fils, ne crains rien ; je ne suis pas si méchant que celui-là.' (p. 726)

His naked portrait, which, 'si elle n'avait pas craint de le gâter', his daughter would have kissed in his absence (after his death?), and which is then presented as an imitation of Montaigne's fictional naked self-portrait, is itself 'gâté' here. Instead he imagines how he might have behaved, a post-lapsarian man, sexually aroused at an inappropriate moment (during the sitting, but also perhaps as a result of his daughter's kisses), a Diogenes figure, joking about the unpredictable motions of his naked body. Moreover, this fiction also undermines his earlier self-portrait as Seneca, bringing back into view but with altered connotations, the references to 'la bêtise' and to 'la rusticité des anciens temps'.

Diderot realizes Montaigne's fictional self-portraits here, only to replace them with fictions of his own. And these fictions comically undermine both Montaigne's desire to present himself naked to his readers and Diderot's realization of Montaigne's desire, as well as Diderot's textual imitation.

IV. Ifs and Afterlives

I have been arguing here that Diderot's description of his naked portrait constitutes one of Montaigne's afterlives, but what of the afterlives of Diderot-as-Montaigne? There is space for only one brief example here, but it is a particularly suggestive and comic one.

It is to be found in Eric-Emmanuel Schmitt's play, *Le Libertin* (1997), which was made into a film in 2000 (by Gabriel Aghion, with Vincent Perez in the role of Diderot),[30] in which we see Diderot, Schmitt's eponymous *libertin*, sitting naked for his portrait with Mme Therbouche (played by Fanny Ardant in the film version). She asks him to look at her; he refuses, muttering: 'Comme depuis le péché d'Adam, on ne commande pas toutes les parties de son corps', and then declaring: 'N'ayez pas peur, je suis moins dur que lui'. Schmitt and Aghion realize here for their 'Diderot' what was presented by Diderot himself as a past conditional (and change its sexual orientation): 'dans le cas de cet accident, je me serais rappelé le mot de Diogène au jeune lutteur : 'Mon fils, ne crains rien ; je ne suis pas si méchant que celui-là'. In so doing, they imitate to some degree (though no doubt unknowingly) Diderot's earlier realization of Montaigne's past conditional. Posterity, it seems, delights in turning 'if' clauses into statements of fact.

We are a very long way downstream here; indeed we have made it into the wider waters of afterlives and reception histories beyond what Montaigne himself imagined. Montaigne's naked self-portrait, evoked in 'Au lecteur' as something that might have been, but never would be, as a possibility that had already been ruled out, has crossed thresholds, causing it to mutate almost beyond recognition, but also enabling its possibilities to be explored. Perhaps Montaigne would have been able to predict that his past conditional would one day be turned into a present indicative, since it might be argued that he did so himself, in 'De la force de l'imagination', in which he refers to rebellious members,[31] and in 'Sur des vers de Virgile', which, as Cave has also remarked, 'seems to put into practice Montaigne's desire to show himself naked to the reader'.[32] But he could not have predicted that a later reader, writer and imitator would combine his conception of the self as constantly changing with his antiperistatic mode of writing in order to convey the inevitable one-sidedness of any portrait or indeed self-portrait, nor that a later writer would draw on 'Au lecteur' in order to endorse a real painted portrait of himself naked. Still less could he have imagined that his naked self-portrait would finds its way into a twentieth-century depiction of an eighteenth-century *libertin*. Montaigne has, so it would seem, arrived in the New World.

Notes to Chapter 6

1. See Jeannette Geffriaud Rosso, *Diderot et le portrait* (Pisa: Libreria Goliardica, 1998).
2. All references are to Denis Diderot, *Œuvres*, ed. by Laurent Versini, 5 vols (Paris: Robert Laffont, 1994–97).
3. For recent attempts to do so, see Philip Knee, 'Diderot et Montaigne: Scepticisme et morale dans *Le Neveu de Rameau*', *Diderot Studies*, 29 (2003), 35–51; Knee, *La Parole incertaine: Montaigne en dialogue* (Québec: Les Presses de l'Université Laval, 2003); Kate E. Tunstall, 'The Judgement of Experience: Reading and Seeing in Diderot's *Lettre sur les aveugles*', *French Studies* (forthcoming, 2008). Parts of the present essay first appeared in French in 'Paradoxe sur le portrait: Auto-portrait de Diderot en Montaigne', *Diderot Studies*, 30 (2007), 197–210.
4. Walter E. Rex, *Diderot's Counterpoints: The Dynamics of Contrariety in his Major Works* (Oxford: Voltaire Foundation, 1998), p. 308.
5. Knee, 'Diderot et Montaigne', p. 35. See also Roselyne Rey's passing reference in the conclusion to her study of *Le Neveu de Rameau*: 'si la lecture des moralistes est toujours profitable, ce n'est ni vers Pascal ni La Rochefoucauld qu'il faut se tourner, mais vers Montaigne' ('La Morale introuvable' in *Autour du Neveu de Rameau*, ed. by Anne-Marie Chouillet (Paris: Champion, 1991), 59–87, pp. 86–87).
6. Jerome Schwarz, *Diderot and Montaigne: The 'Essais' and the Shaping of Diderot's Humanism* (Geneva: Droz, 1966).
7. Rex, *Diderot's Counterpoints*, p. 28.
8. See, for example, Angelica Goodden, *The Backward Look: Memory and the Writing Self, 1580–1920* (Oxford: Legenda, 2000).
9. Terence Cave observes: 'la juxtaposition de 688 et 689 établit une relation *a posteriori* entre 'moi[S]' et Montaigne, comme si la question 'Qu'est-ce que le moi ?' conduisait tout naturellement à une réflexion sur Montaigne' (*Pré-histoires I*, p. 118).
10. See, for example, Colette Fleuret, *Rousseau et Montaigne* (Paris: Nizet, 1980); Knee, *La Parole incertaine*, pp. 129–59.
11. We might also think of his phrase 'se peindre de la plume' (II. 17, 653).
12. The idea of the *Essais* as a text to 'think with' is expressed by Terence Cave in 'Locating the Early Modern', *Paragraph*, 29 (2006), 12–26 (p. 24).
13. Ibid., p. 21.

14. Ibid. The idea of the 'threshold' or 'seuil' is important in Terence Cave's approach to literary history, as the sub-title to *Pré-histoires I* reveals.

15. For an analysis of the emergence of the public space of the art exhibition, see Thomas Crow, *Painters and Public Life in Eighteenth-Century France* (New Haven and London: Yale University Press, 1985).

16. Such a claim echoes that of Jean Starobinski in 'Diderot et la parole des autres', *Critique*, 28 (1972), 3–22.

17. For a study of *amplificatio* in early modern French writing, see Terence Cave, *The Cornucopian Text: Problems of Writing in the French Renaissance* (Oxford: Clarendon, 1979); Rowan Tomlinson, 'Thinking with Lists: Description and Cognition in French Vernacular Writing (1548–1600)' (unpublished D.Phil. thesis, Oxford, 2008). There is no equivalent study for the eighteenth century.

18. Rex, *Diderot's Counterpoints*, pp. 1–25.

19. See, for example, the differing critical responses to Diderot's reference to 'la balance de Montaigne' at the end of the *Lettre sur les aveugles* (I, 184). For Richard Glauser, Diderot is adopting a sceptical position on the evidence of the senses ('Diderot et le problème de Molyneux', *Les Etudes philosophiques*, 3 (1999), 383–410), whereas for Andrew Curran, such a reference is purely ironic (*Sublime Disorder: Physical Monstrosity in Diderot's Universe* (Oxford: Voltaire Foundation, 2001), p. 77).

20. *Pré-histoires I*, pp. 35–39.

21. Cave remarks: 'On a parlé inlassablement du mouvement qui porte Montaigne, à travers ce qui était censé être une apologie de Sebond, à mettre en avant des arguments radicalement opposées à ceux du théologien. On s'est demandé non moins inlassablement si Montaigne était réellement un 'sceptique chrétien' ou un libre penseur avant la lettre. La figure de l'antipéristase offrirait peut-être le moyen de sortir de l'impasse' (*Pré-histoires I*, pp. 48–49).

22. *Pré-histoires I*, p. 49.

23. *Pré-histoires I*, p. 44.

24. For a study of this phrase, derived perhaps from Aristotle, see, for example, Henry Guerlac, 'Amicus Plato and Other Friends', *Journal of the History of Ideas*, 39 (1978), 627–33.

25. This is a reference to *Le Jardinier et son seigneur*, a comic opera by Philidor (whom Diderot perhaps knew for his chess-playing also) and Sedaine, first performed on 18 February 1761, at the Foire Saint-German.

26. Letter to Sophie Volland (11 October 1767), cited in Rex, *Diderot's Counterpoints*, p. 30.

27. Terence Cave, ' "Si je n'avois une certaine foy": Montaigne lecteur de Ronsard', in *Lire les Essais de Montaigne: Perspectives Critiques*, ed. by Noel Peacock and James J. Supple (Paris: Champion, 1998), pp. 183–94; *Pré-histoires I*, pp. 53–59.

28. See Montaigne's chapter 'Des cannibales' (I. 31).

29. For Pierre Hartmann, Diderot's self-portrait is suspect because he describes his works as 'tristes': 'Mais que diront mes petits-enfants, lorsqu'ils viendront à comparer mes tristes ouvrages avec ce riant, mignon, efféminé, vieux coquet-là !' (*Diderot: La Figuration du philosophe* (Paris: José Corti, 2003), p. 121).

30. I should say that, beyond what it permits us to observe here regarding 'if' clauses and afterlives, the play, or rather its film adaptation, has little to recommend it.

31. 'On a raison de remarquer l'indocile liberté de ce membre, s'ingerant si importunement, lors que nous n'en avons que faire, et defaillant si importunement, lors que nous en avons le plus affaire' (I. 21, 102).

32. 'Problems of Reading in the *Essais*', in *Montaigne: Essays in Honour of Richard Sayce*, ed. by Ian MacFarlane and Ian Maclean (Oxford: Clarendon Press, 1982), p. 154.

CHAPTER 7

❖

Diderot's *Neveu de Rameau*

Rear-Mirror View (I), or,
Using What is in Front and in the Future to
Understand What is Past

Marian Hobson

It is not usual to use future events to explain, or, less aggressively phrased, to interpret past ones. Many would say that the whole idea is quite ridiculous.[1] Would not that imply that an effect has preceded its cause, that something lying in the future has in some way brought about the cause-paths that lead to it? In this paper I shall deny that such a procedure is ridiculous, or faulty. To react in this way is to rely on a view of causation and indeed a concept of time which are entirely partial, and in addition, largely inappropriate for the kind of explanation one would be seeking in matters of intellectual and cultural history. Such a reaction introduces a confusing simplification into what is taken as context: it limits history to time lines, interpretation to biography, and our heavily striated culture, which has losses, loop-backs, and sudden jumps forward, to sedately progressive accumulation.

My argument will be based on a case study, Diderot's *Le Neveu de Rameau*. But to begin with, the 'rear-mirror' view advocated for this text needs to be compared briefly with two other accounts of interpretation and its temporality, neither of which are linear. First of all, Terence Cave's concept of 'pre-histories'. With this, as with its parallel and opposed concept of 'afterlives', Terence Cave has made room for an account of a text which does not treat it as a settled and limited item so much as a cultural force, one that has a history and a future, and one whose histories and futures are themselves embedded in the looking back and looking forward which is interpretation. Such an account then must also refuse the singularity of the moment, though not the singularity of the text (he calls it a *hapax*).[2] However, the 'rear-mirror' view I am proposing will in fact be resistant, in the final case, to that enabled by 'pre-histories', because while accepting the advantages this offers, it cannot make use of the parallel and opposed concept 'afterlives', at least as far as I can see it cannot. For 'rear-mirror view' is cast so as deliberately to elude what the use of pre-histories and afterlives would seem to entail: the reciprocal structure of temporality round the moment, or the text, in question.[3] This reciprocal structure would make of time a chiasmus: AB BA, where the future bears the reversed shape of the past. And this structure when itself considered as an operation in time, gives the second account of interpretative temporality mentioned above: that of a dialectic. Ideas negated by their opposites when active in time create something different, something which has absorbed the opposite, not left it as a sediment, but made of it a synthesis (A, ¬A: B).

This eluding may be felt to be perverse. One of the most probing articles ever written on *Le Neveu* pointed out how predominant was the figure of the chiasmus.[4] And Hegel, as we shall in rather passing fashion see, himself inserted allusions and quotations from the dialogue into his phenomenology of the spirit, into the history of development to the dialectic. But the 'rear-mirror view' allows a taking seriously of something somewhat different, that the common factor in spatial and temporal location in the word 'before' gives us: something is before us, we can see it, because it has already happened, we have just been through it. What we can't see is what is coming, because it is coming up on us from behind, overtaking us, like our view of a car in a rear-mirror.[5]

I will refer both explicitly and implicitly to Michael Dummett's four articles on time in justification of what some would claim to be my anachronistic approach.[6] However brief, these remarks and the above preliminaries will then underpin the attempt in the second part of this paper to construct a context and if possible assign a shape to the object of the study, Diderot's *Le Neveu de Rameau*.

But first, why does it need a context? This powerful and mysterious dialogue, written at some point in the later part of his life (1713–84), does not seem to have been known during his lifetime by any of his close circle or family (though it could be that this statement will have to be corrected at some point in the future of scholarship). It is scurrilous — a satire in *both* the senses current in the eighteenth century (its subtitle on the holograph reads 'satire seconde'): a genre that castigates vices of individuals, remorselessly named in this case, and a *Satyra*, a stew or mixture of different elements. And that duality of sense may help us with the shape of the work: the piercing point of a satire is pulled in different directions, blotched though not too much blunted by the mix the work contains: of levels of discourse, of topics discussed, of genres. For the work is strange in its form: a dialogue, yes, but a *narrated* dialogue, ME recounting his habit of walking in a public garden, the Palais Royal, and then an occasion, a chance meeting with an acquaintance, HIM, nephew of the great composer Rameau, in a café.[7] ME can discuss with himself in a park-like space both open and confined by social limits; if, or when, the weather has changed, he repairs to a closed and noisy café where on this occasion a conversation is engaged whose rhythm is much less sedate. For it runs through a set of remarkable discussions of public and moral questions: the effects of a capitalistic society on happiness and morality, music, the nature of genius, the current state of the Parisian Opera, the relation between truth, beauty and goodness, etc. etc. It also contains the narrated description of a remarkable series of turns, both in the sense of comic acts and near-medical seizures, that HIM performs or undergoes. However hard ME, the somewhat staid philosopher tries, he fails to find a breaching point in the arguments and attitudes of HIM, a down and out, a failed musician sleeping with the horses in stables, not always sure of his next meal, hanging on to the rich — celebrities as they would now be called — who have little personal but a good deal of financial worth, to whom the eighteenth-century equivalents of the *Sun, Hello, the News of the World*, pay court in order to help spend their money, and to laugh at them behind their back.

This group, for the most part consisting of enemies of the *Encyclopédie*,[8] is then taken apart into its constituent elements; they are the butt, the point of the work's satire. However, this satire is performed by a mouthpiece, HIM, who although actually of the group, is one who is so irregular, so much a loose cannon, that he can speak for just one, for himself. He is thus other than their anti-*Encyclopédie* party-line, and can the more effectively send them up, while not speaking from the place of the *Encyclopédie*'s supporters. The discussion even refers to Diderot as if he were exterior to the conversation, as if he were not ME, however close to Diderot's own career the references to ME are. So the point, the acuteness, of the satire is as if diffused; at least we are not able to follow any clear-cut scratch of malice back to what was certainly the seed of the work: the production of Palissot's comedy *Les Philosophes* in 1760 which represented the *philosophes* as madmen (the character representing Rousseau comes in on all fours munching a lettuce) or unscrupulous con-men (Diderot–Dortidius is represented as tricking a patron out of money, and dissecting another's body.)

If then the origins of Diderot's text were in a counter-satire, written as a kind of response to *Les Philosophes*, its point was felted round like the old way of carrying pens. For one person only seems to have known about it while Diderot was alive. No one else claims to have seen it.[9] This is not totally surprising given its scurrilous nature:[10] it contains for example a wonderful scene in which the rich tax-farmer, i.e. capitalist, named, has to be rescued in the middle of the night from beneath his overweight starlet-mistress, also named, who has been suddenly smitten with the desire to make love. But in *Les Salons*, and the great ones are written in the decade after the probable beginning of the *Neveu de Rameau*, then circulated in the manuscript journal *Correspondance littéraire* quite widely among a selection of the European courts, Diderot had not stepped back from circulating dirty stories told against others, even those he was beholden to. So the theory of self-censorship through worries about obscenity and satire does not seem to explain much, even if it may explain a little.

Moreover, even if the dialogue starts as a private satire countering *Les Philosophes*, it is not really clear when it was written: the fact that it contains a multitude of risqué items of news which actually occurred in very different years during the 1760s and 1770s doesn't help in the dating of it, except to give possible *termini ab quo* and *ad quem* and to suggest that it may have been continually added to. Even its genre, however much *satyre*, is uncertain in some ways: to my mind related to the *nouvelles à main* circulating in the graphic eighteenth-century phrase 'sous le manteau', to works like Chevrier's *Le Colporteur*,[11] and to journals like *Le Papillon*,[12] but also to the mysterious co-production by Diderot and Rousseau written at some indeterminate date in the 1740s, *Le Persifleur*.[13] It doesn't seem as if anyone were meant to see it: so far as it is understood today, there seem no complicit references for a special audience, the inner reader is reduced to Diderot. We have a satire seemingly designed for an audience of one.

Yet, like some submarine, the dialogue rises to the surface of European culture, bearing its torpedoes. Its exceptional power was recognized in the most decisive way at the end of the eighteenth century: Goethe, no less, translated and published it in 1805, adding notes to help with the understanding of the items of gossip which play such an important role.[14] He is said to have obtained the manuscript from Schiller, who is said to have received it via Germans working in Russia. There had been copies of the text sent after Diderot's death, with the rest of his library, to Catherine the Great of Russia (she had provided financial support by buying his library and allowing him the use of it during his lifetime) and it is thought that one of these copies was copied and sent to Weimar. The manuscript Goethe translated has since disappeared. And, even more decisive for recognition of its importance, Hegel seized on the translation, apparently at a late stage of the composition of *The Phenomenology of Spirit*, published in 1807,[15] and incorporated into it a discussion of the dialogue as exemplifying the 'unhappy consciousness', the 'self-alienated spirit', in the cursus of consciousness towards Absolute Knowing, which is the subject of his masterpiece.

A further remark needs to be made here. Truth in Hegel's system is but an aspect of something else, the Science of the True, which is located in the future and which teleologically directs the *Bildungsroman* of consciousness, but is also present at each stage of the process, a stage by its nature incomplete, but not relative. For the True is the content of knowledge, and thus in the present absolute — it just is where we have got to; in regard to both past and future, it is an aspect of Absolute Knowing, but no more.

Now, Hegel quotes the text three times and this in itself is more than any other named text. Indeed, most allusions in the *Phenomenology* are not referenced at all. And the place Hegel allots to *Le Neveu de Rameau* in the architectonic of his work suggests that he is in fact doing something more than mention. Hegel's work constitutes and was meant to constitute a hinge between the eighteenth and nineteenth centuries. It sketches a history of previous philosophy and eighteenth-century science, which deliberately opens out onto the now, the new, nineteenth, century, where Absolute Knowing is possible because objective and subjective knowing have been united. In that process, Hegel takes human productions, among them the genre of tragedy and Diderot's dialogue, and by the place he gives these in his series seems to assign them the role of precursor to his own work. But unlike his own work, they do not achieve the resolution of the past and of its conflicts and oppositions; their unresolved action or thought means that those coming before him do not make it all the way to the dialectic. For it is here, of course, that Hegel comes in, and why his system is so powerful: it accounts for itself. In the case of tragedy, we have only a definitive, irremediable break, between antagonists, and in the case of *Le Neveu de Rameau*, only a continual swinging between opposites — the last words of the dialogue are 'He who laughs last, laughs best', HIM is going off to see an opera, and nothing whatsoever has been resolved or resolved on, except that he is 'still the same'. In other words, for Hegel, Diderot's dialogue is placed in the phenomenology of spirit as a kind of pre-dialectic, one that does not achieve *Aufhebung*, one that does not resolve and ingest, that is, subsume what has gone before, but remains constantly starting up again, with no real end in sight. A failed dialectic, in other words, one in which the spirit's rationality and the social world the dialogue presents do not match. Hegel, on the other hand, obviously *did* get there, the process described *is* leading up to the work. (This teleological pattern to the *Phenomenology*, and to Hegel's work in general, has, of course, been attacked, indeed been taken apart, by many, but most especially and powerfully by Derrida in *Glas*.)[16]

Given how little we know about the immediate circumstances of *Le Neveu de Rameau*, and of Diderot's intentions with the text, I propose to examine whether a kind of deferred context in the culture of the very late eighteenth and early nineteenth centuries can be constructed for it, and in particular, whether Hegel's use of it in what was its future can be so construed, *revealing something about the temporality of the satire*. In other words, whether *Le Neveu de Rameau*'s afterlife can illuminate what was its present in the past. But first, the notions of context, and indeed cause, worked with here will need to be made precise.

We tend to think of a cause as starting off a process which follows it.[17] We need reminding that causes are in fact simultaneous with their immediate effects, though obviously preceding their remote effects. But once more, given the paucity of actual information about Diderot's text, that may not be enough. So what kind of view of cause and context might help us with this puzzling work, so evidently important, so mysterious? Where should we look, what kind of information should we be searching for in constructing this view?

First, let's take Diderot's own attitude to the future. He did not believe in the afterlife, yet there is a sense in which he is not his own contemporary, and he must have known it. He was the author of one side of a correspondence about the importance of the idea of posterity to an author or artist (it is true that he was not very keen to have this correspondence published, and gave in to a much more imperious nature, the sculptor Falconet, who had gone ahead with the preparations). The whole purpose of the work he was known for during his own lifetime, the one he devoted more or less twenty years of his life to, the great *Encyclopédie*, was to influence the future, the immediate future, by changing attitudes in the present. His dramatic works and their associated theories had a huge and immediate impact in Germany through Lessing, who read them carefully, reported on them regularly, and acted on their recommendations. The influence in France percolated more slowly, and in the provinces rather than in Paris. It may be that some of what seems like strange carelessness with his own texts, as if Diderot were relying on the future to thresh things out for him, was in fact partly bad luck — for instance, the failure to get a proper edition started; or was due to, among other things, the fact of his working on communal projects where someone else was probably looking after the paper work — for instance, first the *Encyclopédie*, then the *Histoire des deux Indes*, the great anti-colonial work edited by the Abbé Raynal. Both these are works in which his contributing role is far from being always clear. But it must have also been, in part at least, a reliance on the future as the temporal zone of his reputation, because his work would, to some degree, have led to that future. There would be a kind of panning out, in which if he were lucky, for luck would be needed, there would be some kind of justification of his endeavours. Now that reliance on the possibility of an afterlife in men's minds is, it seems to me, related to the view of truth expressed as follows by the philosopher Michael Dummett: 'We could never have come to understand what it would be for the statement to be true independently of that which we have learned to treat as establishing its truth: there simply was no means by which we could be shown this.'[18] I am giving here Dummett's formulation of an 'anti-realist' view of truth about the past, one that does not think that a statement can be true OR false independently of our knowledge. For the statement to be pronounced true or false, we have to have some idea of the conditions which make it so, and 'these conditions do not exist independently of our capacity for knowledge'. We must grasp to some degree what it would be to prove or disprove the statement, and in Diderot's case, the truth conditions, the means by which we judge it true or false, would have been partly developed by his own *Encyclopédie*, and more largely, by the group of philosophers and scientists he had brought together for its production.

I am going to take Michael Dummett's 'learned' in the statement quoted above seriously. Not as implying that the teaching we have absorbed or been subjected to is to be treated as a cause: to do that would be to contradict the position I am trying to advocate. But experience gained from editing two Diderot texts has illuminated these articles of Dummett's for me (there are four articles which relate to time, as well as, much more recently, a book), and that helped in turn illuminate Diderot more generally for me. With a colleague, Simon Harvey, I recently edited the *Lettre sur les aveugles* (1749), which landed its author in prison for its atheist tendencies, and which seems to foreshadow early evolutionary theory, together with the *Lettre sur les sourds et muets* (1751), a text which by its discussion of linguistic relativity, by its use of textual analysis of poems, and especially by its denial that poetry and painting can do the same things, points forward to much of nineteenth-century aesthetics. Both then are ahead of their time. Yet both present the intellectual positions of the text as in relation to, not caused by, groups of intellectuals: in the case of the *Lettre sur les aveugles*, scientists in the wake of Newton, English all; in the case of the *Lettre sur les sourds et muets*, rhetoricians and literary critics, many of them priests, and all of them French. We were obliged to suggest that Diderot himself connects his own speculation with socio-intellectual groups, in ways not previously understood. In other words, he was perfectly aware of the social character of meaning, indeed discusses it at the end of the *Lettre sur les aveugles*.[19]

The Dummett phrase I am leaning on does not imply relativity of values, nor that pedagogical or intellectual contexts cause or create notions of truth and falsehood. But it does imply that truth is not independent of our capacity to understand how we would attain truth. Meaning is given in terms of conditions which we recognize as establishing the truth or falsity of the statement, but for Dummett, for Diderot (and, I should add, for Derrida), those conditions can't obtain independently of our knowledge. We cannot stand outside time, and knowing and thinking are always done at a temporal point, for the past at a different temporal point from the occurrences we are thinking about. When, like Dummett or like Derrida for that matter, one is writing after the mathematical intuitionists (led by the great Dutch geometer and logician, L. J. Brouwer, 1881–1966), this does not have to be slated as relativism; instead, it proposes, and an intuitionist would say entails, a radical redrawing of what a logician is trying to do. They cannot use the excluded middle in argument, except in particular circumstances, because they cannot draw a line round the set of alternatives to be considered; and they insist on constructive proofs, where what is said to exist can actually be exhibited. This radically limits classical mathematics.

Dummett says that those who deny this position, those who are technically called 'realists', want 'to stand in thought outside the whole temporal process and describe the world from a point which has no temporal position at all, but surveys all temporal positions in a single glance; from this standpoint — the standpoint of the description the realist wants to give — the different points of time have a relation of temporal precedence between themselves, but no temporal relation to the standpoint of the description — i.e. they are not being considered as past, as present, or as future.'[20] Dummett's exposition of the anti-realist position proposes that on the contrary, we are inevitably rooted in time, in the present as we speak, indicated by speaking about events in the past in the past tense. And this implies that any statement about the past is exposed to a possibility of correction which is structurally irremovable: 'Of any statement about the past, we can never rule it out that we might subsequently come upon something which justified asserting or denying it, therefore we are not entitled to say of any specific statement that it is neither true nor false; but we are not entitled either to say in advance that it has to be either the one [i.e. true] or the other [i.e. false].'[21] I have already slipped in that Derrida can be included among those who would accept this kind of statement, the kind of statement that has been baptized 'Always possibly not'.[22] There is a fundamental and structural incapacity to rule out possible correction of our statements, which derives from our dual temporality, the duality being that a statement has a tense, and is also made at a point in time — we have talked in the past about the future, as in the future we will talk about the past.[23] This incapacity becomes insecurity in Derrida, where it is rather violently, and very consistently, explored, but is part both of Dummett's thought and, I hope to show, Diderot's practice. It is this, by the way, which makes Derrida's thought look like empiricism at certain points; but it isn't empiricist, for the impossibility of incorrigibility is structural, not each time occurrent and just turning up.

In Diderot's case, it is what was in the future that helped later times-present understand his literary work better, and made genuine progress in their interpretation possible. The twentieth-century 'new novel' and its reflexivity threw a powerful and retrospective light on what it was that the eighteenth-century polymath was doing in some of his writings — in his novel *Jacques le fataliste*, for example. Allowing similar arguments about his scientific speculation is now imperative: in the *Suite de l'Entretien*, the third part of *Le Rêve de d'Alembert*, Diderot suggests the creation of transgenic 'chèvre-pieds', goat-men, to act as servants and labourers. The shock of seeing 'Baba', the goat-sheep, in the Cambridge University farm, made me realize that far from indulging in a *jeu d'esprit*, as I had been taught, Diderot was not merely out of step with, but was far beyond the science of his own time; that he was beyond what most of the then twentieth century expected to be possible.

So, to conclude the first two sections of my argument, the anti-realist or intuitionist notion of truth is both powerful in itself, and relevant to Diderot. It is not a relativist notion of truth, but it does deny that we are 'entitled to say, of any arbitrary statement about the past, that it must be either true or false in itself and independently of our present or future knowledge of its truth value'.[24] We cannot even assert that it is *neither* true *nor* false, and thus remove it from the true/false alternative entirely. This seems to bring us to a view of time as real, in the philosophical sense, whereas for common sense, time is unreal, in that we can step outside of it. For the anti-realist, we cannot look at time from the outside; as a result, the description of reality is not, was not and cannot be complete. And what is here now of the past is traces: 'There is a strong temptation to try and contrast the two positions by saying that, for the anti-realist, the past exists only in the traces it has left upon the present, whereas for the realist, the past still exists as past, just as it was when it is present.'[25] I am now going to argue that such an anti-realist view of truth may be useful in the search for what might help us understand better what seems at present largely hidden: the sense of *Le Neveu de Rameau*. I shall argue that intellectual contexts, some thirty or more years later than its probable composition date, can sharpen both our view of its actual and literal content, and the relations which it has with other of Diderot's writings, with the mysterious *First Satire* (you remember that *Le Neveu de Rameau* is called in one manuscript *Second Satire*) and with his art-criticism, what is known as the *Salons*. Yet where to look, and how to proceed? One cannot just paint a wide picture of intellectual Paris, or even intellectual Europe, in the late revolutionary and early Napoleonic period, and hope that some connections will emerge. There has to be a certain pattern in the *explicandum* which can be used as a base to allow the linking in of the material that is chronologically later, and is to be used retrospectively in the explication. The kind of occurrence of that certain pattern in *Le Neveu de Rameau* is typical of much literary work: something recurs, widely, but is hardly murmured in explicit form in the text; certainly never turned into a label or a theme or any other marking post that might have helped readers. One such pattern is the tension between the individual and the universal.

An example of this:

> MOI: Et pourquoi employer toutes ces petites viles ruses là ?
>
> LUI: Viles! Et pourquoi, s'il vous plaît ? Elles sont d'usage dans mon état. Je ne m'avilis point en faisant comme tout le monde. Ce n'est pas moi qui les ai inventées: et je serais bizarre et maladroit de ne pas m'y conformer. Vraiment, je sais bien que si vous allez appliquer à cela certains principes généraux de je ne sais quelle morale qu'ils ont tous à la bouche, et qu'aucun d'eux ne pratique, il se trouvera que ce qui est blanc sera noir et que ce qui est noir sera blanc. Mais, monsieur le philosophe, il y a une conscience générale, comme il y a une grammaire générale, et puis des exceptions dans chaque langue que vous appelez, je crois, vous autres savants, des...aidez-moi donc...des....
>
> MOI: Idiotismes.
>
> LUI: Tout juste. Hé bien, chaque état a ses exceptions à la conscience générale auxquelles je donnerais volontiers le nom d'idiotismes de métier.

Moi: J'entends. Fontenelle parle bien, écrit bien, quoique son style fourmille d'idiotismes français.

Lui: Et le souverain, le ministre, le financier, le magistrat, le militaire, l'homme de lettres, l'avocat, le procureur, le commerçant, le banquier, l'artisan, le maître à chanter, le maître à danser, sont de fort honnêtes gens, quoique leur conduite s'écarte en plusieurs points de la conscience générale, et soit remplie d'idiotismes moraux. Plus l'institution des choses est ancienne, plus il y a d'idiotismes ; plus les temps sont malheureux, plus les idiotismes se multiplient.[26]

Here the tension between individual and universal occurs as what could be called a quasi-theme: an almost-a-theme, in a passage where Diderot uses the idea of 'grammaire générale' of the philosopher grammarians of the *Encyclopédie*.[27] Diderot brings it up here comically, part of an attempt to pin down the Nephew's view of morality. The 'general grammar' however is not merely humorous because inappropriate. Nor is it there to suggest fluid relativity of moral codes, that is, each man according to his fancy, in morals as in everything else. Instead, a greater degree of structure is implied. There are two levels of morality, as of grammar, the individual and then the general or universal. So that just as there is a 'general grammar', a deep level syntactic structure, and then 'idiotisms', a particular schema of grammatical exceptions employed by an individual, so there is a 'general morality', or conscience, but then particular schemas of exceptions to that morality, related to an individual taken as representative of a class. The tension then between individual and universal is not a simple injection of a group of individuals into the set formed by their union. Instead, the groups in the chain enumerated by Lui are made of individuals (since at other points in the dialogue, one gets some names). But these individuals are also already representatives — of a type, a character, a métier.

Diderot is not for the most and greater part a writer of philosophy in a technical sense (though of course he *is* a philosopher: he wrote nearly all the philosophical articles for the *Encyclopédie*, as well as many other works), and he is unlike Rousseau, I would argue, in that he does not use the internal textual marks of philosophical writing, that is, the careful thematizing, the strategic summaries, the step-wise progression of the argument. It is because some of his greatest philosophical and scientific writing is in a highly original form, that of strange dialogues, or else is lodged in art criticism, that it has proved hard to submit it to the usual treatments accorded to more straight-down-the-line philosophy. (He is rarely, if ever, on the set-texts of the *agrégation de philosophie*, and never on the written set-text lists.) So what I have called a 'quasi-theme', that of the tension between the individual and the universal in *Le Neveu de Rameau*, is hardly brought out, is not expressed openly. It is there, none the less. And it has an important pattern associated with it, not just in the quotation above, but also more or less everywhere in the text: the lists, usually but by no means always lists of professions. (A student asked me 'why are there so many lists in this book?', thereby putting his finger on a feature that is central, though unremarked and undiscussed by his elders for two hundred years). Lists in the quotation above, 'le souverain, le ministre, le financier, le magistrat, le militaire, l'homme de lettres, l'avocat, le procureur, le commerçant, le banquier, l'artisan, le maître à chanter, le maître à danser', but also in the frequently listed characteristics:

'Rameau le fou, l'impertinent, l'ignorant, le paresseux, le gourmand, le bouffon, la grosse bête', for instance.[28] These easily turn into lists of characteristic types, and thus link with the contemporary pseudo-science of physiognomy, taken apart by Hegel at an earlier moment of the *Phenomenology*.

First, it is to be recognized that these characteristics, or characteristic types, represent a kind of middle. The particular, in ordinary language as well as in logic, falls between the universal and the individual. An almost contemporary context which supports the picking out of this pattern is the role the particular plays in Kant's table of categories, and the way he develops this between the *Critique of Pure Reason* (1781, revised second edition 1787) and the slightly later text, the *Prolegomena to any Future Metaphysics* (1783). (I have discussed this briefly elsewhere, and leave it aside now.)[29] A further confirming point, further downstream in time and in the future of the reception of Diderot's text, is the structural role that movement between the individual, the particular and the universal plays in Hegel's *Phenomenology*, and hence in his treatment of *Le Neveu de Rameau*. Now, this may just be shared training in the logic of the period — both Hegel and Diderot were trained as theologians for a while, though in Hegel's case, almost sixty years later than Diderot. But one thread of the discussion of the universal, the particular, and the individual occurs quite generally after Diderot in a way heavy with consequence: in relation to race, to what is characteristic of race, and in relation to possible forms which are physiologically neutral, so to speak, in regard to race.

An important aspect of this thread is its bringing together of antiquarian interest in Roman remains, of sculpture, and of the studying of what makes Roman sculpture great. The idea of measuring sculpture goes back at least to Ehrard's measurements of the *Apollo Belvedere*, and the *Venus dei Medici*, done in Rome in 1640.[30] What occurs in the eighteenth century is the transfer of this point of view from statues to the human body, and especially to the head. In a famous series of drawings the great Dutch doctor, Camper, whom Diderot met in Holland and whom he appears to have corresponded with, transfers the calibration of the profile from the skull of a snake, to a bird, to a dog, to a monkey, to an African (he states where the dead person came from, as well as owning up to the composite nature of the skull he used), to a European (his word) and finally to the Apollo Belvedere. Here, the Greek sculpture appears as a kind of end-point, outside nature, as Camper says quite clearly in his commentary.

This bringing together, in an as yet un-sorted conglomerate, of evolutionary form in bones and sculpture is heavy with warning. Camper was definitely not a racist in his writings, as can be conclusively shown if they are all read, especially those in Dutch, still today untranslated, but his method and ideas continue through the eighteenth century and into the nineteenth, in ways that do lead to racial theory. It may be of some comfort that there is resistance to a slick transfer from size into racial superiority, and I have collected some highly amusing and very sceptical remarks, from an early edition of the *Encyclopaedia Britannica*, among other places. But once again, there seems no doubt that some of this activity transfers into physiognomy and phrenology, and from there is translated into the crudest sort of race theory.[31]

How does this happen? One way is the relation between sculptures and measurement. Some tourists, at least, made a practice of measuring sculptures on the Grand Tour. A Lady Riggs Miller recounts her measurements of the statues in Florence: she gives the measurements of the *Venus dei Medici*, which are taken off a pamphlet available from the Abbé who showed the collection in the *Tribuna* (still in the Uffizi, though not all the statues are now there).

> Braccia Fiorentine 2, soldi 11, denari 8
> Palmi Romani 6, once 8, Minuti 4
> Piedi Inglesi 4, pollici 11, linée 5
> Piedi Parigini 4, pollici 6, linée 6.

Lady Miller then gives her own measurements of the Venus, in great detail: heel to great toe, her wrist, the thickest part of her arm, her waist, her shoulders across her breast, her throat, her face from chin bone (not including, Lady Miller remarks, her double chin) to the root of her hair, her mouth, and so on. She is not the only tourist to have done this. A hint that the habit is not an upmarket version of graffiti, is the career of her husband, Sir John Riggs Miller, who was involved in attempts to standardize weights and measures. For the great publication of the antiquities dug up in Herculaneum, *Le Antichità di Ercolano esposte*, begun in 1757, gives under some of its engravings of sculptures a scale in both Roman and Neapolitan 'hands' (*palmi*). On reflection, this presentation has a two-way meaning: it enables the viewer to have an idea of the actual size of the sculpture, by relating it to common Italian measures, as a modern photograph may include a scale to help judge actual size; but the sculpture also stands as a norm, ideal and absolute in its proportion in relation to the variety of human measures. So that behind some of the measuring that goes on is an attempt to find a norm, something that could act as a standard for the human frame in its multiplicity.

Yet other drawings, by the architect's draughtsman, Lequeu, for instance, show a further side to this: the development of semi-mechanical aids to proportion from the measurement of sculpture has lead to a banality of feature which in some ways is quite startlingly modern. I can't here go into even some of the problems posed by Lequeu, except to say that at least some of the drawings are forgeries by a surrealist group around Georges Bataille.[32] I have examined the particular manuscript which deals with physiognomy and am pretty confident that the drawings on human proportion at any rate are not fake, though at least one other almost certainly is. The important point for me here is that the measurement of sculpture and the repeated copying of casts as drill in the learning of drawing has led to a kind of norm, something neutral, not to say neutered. This is what this particular work of Lequeu seems to me to show (among other things, of course).

So the pedagogical use of sculpture, the study of proportions can lead to an idea of the Greek statue as a kind of norm. Yet Greek statues came in different sizes, and earlier, mid-century, with Hogarth and others, it was common to oppose the strong muscular statue, Hercules, with the ephebe, the lightly built boy, while in the centre stood the Apollo, as three different possible builds in male Greek statuary. By the end of the century the centre seems to win, and becomes the unmarked, neutral figure from which other shapes and sizes deviate and against which their deviation can be measured. It can then act as the universal, against which the particularities of the characterized Hercules or the ephebe, can be marked.

The relation between proportion in statues and neutrality is confirmed in the nineteenth century by the great Belgian statistician Quêtelet (1796–1874). It is when he writes an introduction to the English translation of his *Treatise on Man* that he makes explicit the link, in a passage which has not been much remarked on. Starting from the study of proportion by the Greek sculptors, he moves to the Renaissance, to Alberti and Dürer. In particular, he describes how artists have developed a system for representation of the human body which involves a proportional averaging. Quêtelet, who in his youth had trained in the art school at Ghent, describes his statistical endeavours in the same terms: 'It is only by long and laborious study, and by the comparison of a vast number of individuals, that it will be possible to succeed in establishing correct average proportions for each age.'[33] From his calculations, he proposed the notion of 'l'homme moyen', of which all members of a given population would be imperfect copies. And from this he could move to a different level, of comparison between different populations. He believed he could reconstruct the dimensions of a series of average men, who could then be compared, which would serve to make comparison between populations. It is important to my argument that a later statistician, Bertillon père, criticized Quêtelet's idea of the average man as representing 'the very type of vulgarity'.[34]

Diderot shows interest in every one of these threads. He was aware of the possible progression from measurement of heads to characterizing them. In the *Voyage en Hollande* he recounts these drawings of Camper, interested more by their transformation through shape than by any incipient racism; but he does also put forward Camper as a kind of detective for nationalities or races: for example, he recognizes Greeks though they have come from Russia.[35] Now the *Satire première*'s subtitle is 'on characters and expressions of character, of profession, etc'. The look of someone, if properly interpreted, can give away his profession, his character, and even his name, as if by the progressive deductions of a police officer, moving through the particularizing (a Greek) to the singular: that Greek. Men and women have amazing variety at the same time as they are under pressure to conform in a kind of socio-biological way to the life patterns of the group to which we belong. Diderot is, in *Le Neveu de Rameau*, worried by the monotony and banality of much of modern life, the pressures to behave like everyone else, coupled with the need to behave unlike anyone else in order not just to make any money, but to survive as a person at all.

Treating concerns that surface chronologically later in the eighteenth century — the measurements of classical statues, their relation to individuals, the way their averaging of individual aspects is used to achieve the 'classical', the normal, the neutral — can act as a context for a series of Diderot's works (*Le Neveu de Rameau*, the *Voyage en Hollande*, the *Satire première*) which are earlier in time. These concerns can provide a kind of nexus or tissue which turns these writings of Diderot into consistent reflection. A reflection which, while not making it into a history of philosophy, except where it is a phenomenology and by the exceptional Hegel, is nonetheless deep, and daunting.

Notes to Chapter 7

1. This paper was first given as a paper at Royal Holloway, University of London, in Terence Cave's seminar, and for any improvements owes a good deal to the remarks of Katharine Ellis and Ahuvia Kahane.

2. *Pré-histoires I*, p. 14.

3. For the problems time brings with it to the physicist, whose equations are reversible in mathematics but rarely so in physical time, see Peter Coveney and Roger Highfield, *The Arrow of Time* (London: W. H. Allen, 1990) (the kaon is one elementary particle which has direction in time).

4. Jean Starobinski, 'Sur l'emploi du chiasme dans *Le Neveu de Rameau*', *Revue de métaphysique et de morale*, 89 (1984), 182–96.

5. The word 'after' in its derivational sense of 'aft', 'behind', holds the same temporal oddity. Ahuvia Kahane after the seminar (see n. 1) quoted to me Oswyn Murray: 'for the ancients, time past lay in spatial terms before us (ante), visible to the human intellect and capable of providing modes of behaviour; time future lay behind us (post), obscure, invisible, unknowable, but not likely to be different from that past which we could see in front of us'; Oswyn Murray, 'Gnosis and Tradition', in *Agon, Logos, Polis: The Greek Achievement and its Aftermath*, ed. by J. P. Arnison and P. Murphy (Stuttgart: Steiner Verlag, 2001), pp. 15–28 (p. 19).

6. Michael Dummett, *Truth and Other Enigmas* (London: Duckworth, 1978). See also his *Truth and the Past* (New York: Columbia University Press, 2004).

7. La Régence, a café until about 1966; afterwards, Japan Air Lines.

8. It has not been generally noticed that at least one of the butts, Etienne-Michel Bouret, *Fermier général* and *Directeur des postes*, had done favours for Diderot in the 1750s, and would do more in the 1770s. See, e.g., Diderot, *Œuvres complètes*, ed. by Roger Lewinter, 15 vols (Paris: Club du livre, 1968–73), II, 886 and VIII, 1020. He died, rumour had it, by his own hand, in 1777. He is connected by marriage with Mme de Pompadour, rather than with the clique of *anti-encyclopédistes*, another reminder that the dialogue's satire is not completely clarified.

9. Naigeon's claim, made many years after Diderot's death, and inaccurate enough about the text to be a lie, is generally discounted.

10. Our understanding of Diderot's relation to satire is at the present date far from perfect. I have the feeling that he himself was in two minds: he didn't like to hurt, on the whole, but had a real satiric gift, and knew it.

11. F. A. Chevrier, *Le Colporteur, histoire morale et critique* (London: Jean Nourse, 'L'An de la vérité' [1762]).

12. *Le Papillon, ou Lettres parisiennes: Ouvrage qui contiendra tout ce qui se passera d'intéressant, de plus agréable et de plus nouveau dans tous les genres* [1746–48?]. Attributed to Mouhy, one of the figures in *Le Neveu*.

13. A journal, or possibly a spoof project for a journal. See Rousseau, *Œuvres complètes*, ed. by Bernard Gagnebin and Marcel Raymond (Paris: Gallimard, 1964), pp. 1103–12. The *Neveu* actually quotes this, though the only copy known is Rousseau's, and Diderot does not seem to have retained or at least preserved a copy. See Marian Hobson, 'Rousseau et Diderot par Rameau interposé', in *Recherches sur Diderot et l'Encyclopédie*, 39 (2005), 7–18.

14. The whole question of the text and its history is best studied in Rudolf Schlösser, *Rameaus Neffe: Studien und Untersuchungen zur Einführung in Goethes Übersetzung des Diderotschen Dialogs* [1900] (Geneva: Slatkine, 1978).

15. The integration of references and allusions into the Hegel text is to my mind still not well understood. The most complete information to date can be found in the edition by Wolfgang Bonsiepen and Reinhard Heede of the *Gesammelte Werke*, vol. 9, Deutschen Forschungsgemeinschaft and Rheinische-westfälischen Akademie der Wissenschaften (Hamburg: Felix Meiner Verlag, 1975).

16. Derrida, *Glas* (Paris: Galilée, 1974).

17. Michael Dummett, 'Can an Effect Precede its Cause?', *Truth and Other Enigmas*, p. 321.

18. Michael Dummett, 'The Reality of the Past', *Truth and Other Enigmas*, p. 362.

19. The title of another article in *Truth and Other Enigmas*. At the end of the *Lettre*, Diderot makes his solution to the Molyneux problem vary according to the education of the blind man whose sight is restored.
20. Ibid., p. 369.
21. Ibid., p. 364.
22. Marian Hobson, *Jacques Derrida: Opening Lines* (London: Routledge, 1998).
23. I would claim that even if the present tense used in a statement is not referring to the time the statement is made, in other words, if it is a kind of timeless present, it is nevertheless inserted, as is every statement, in an implied piece of reported speech which itself is not timeless.
24. Dummett, *Truth and Other Enigmas*, p. 364.
25. Ibid., p. 370. As Dummett's formulation suggests, he is not content with this because in it each position is only characterized in terms of the other. It is worth noting that Terence Cave's concept of 'traces' is different, representing the stage before the history which is being traced has become more clearly visible, self-conscious, so to speak (*Pré-histoires I*, p. 17).
26. Denis Diderot, *Le Neveu de Rameau*, ed. by Jean Fabre (Geneva: Droz, 1950), pp. 35–36. I have modernized the spelling.
27. Discovered with excitement by the young Chomsky in 1966 when he went looking for the antecedents of his own conception of 'deep structure' in language.
28. *Le Neveu*, ed. cit., p. 18.
29. 'L'Analogie des proportions', in *Hommage à Jacques Chouillet*, ed. by Sylvain Auroux, Dominique Borel and Charles Porset (Paris: PUF, 1991), pp. 159–67.
30. The manuscript is in the Ecole nationale des Beaux Arts in Paris.
31. The physiognomist, Lavater, links physiological measurement in particular, and form in general, to what have to be called racist remarks, via a theory of expression. See, e.g., J. C. Lavater, *Essays on Physiognomy*, ed. by Thomas Holloway, trans. by Henry Hunter, 3 vols in 5 (London: John Stockdale, 1810), I, 29. First English edition of this translation is 1788–98; there are two other slightly different translations; first German edition is 1775–78.
32. The standard work is Philippe Duboy, *Lequeu: An Architectural Enigma*, trans. by Francis Scarfe and Brad Divitt (London: Thames and Hudson, 1986). One can prove that the surrealists were interested in the kind of drawing manual that Lequeu's work partly is, though I shall not do that here.
33. M. A. Quêtelet, *A Treatise on Man and the Development of his Faculties*, trans. by R. Knox (Edinburgh: William and Robert Chambers, 1842). Reference is to the reissue by Gregg International Publishers Limited (1973), p. vi. Quêtelet knew the work of Laplace, indeed Laplace himself, and the development of the idea of proportion at the time in relation to maths and sculpture needs examination. His archive in Brussels proves that he was concerned with proportion in sculpture all his life.
34. Quoted in B.-P. Lécuyer, 'Probability in Vital and Social Statistics: Quêtelet, Farr, and the Bertillons', in *The Probabilistic Revolution*, ed. by Lorenz Krüger et al., 2 vols (Cambridge, MA and London: MIT Press, 1987), I, 317–35.
35. 'Il connaissait parfaitement les physionomies nationales. Il dit d'un gentilhomme qui m'avait accompagné de la Russie en Hollande: "Celui-là est Grec" et il l'était; "ce valet qui est derrière lui est Kalmouck" et cela était vrai. Il accusait tous les artistes d'avoir péché sur ce point. Il a écrit un traité de dessin où il indique des principes par lesquels on peut sans interruption aller de la figure des dieux à la figure de telle nation que l'on voudra; de la figure nationale de l'homme, du nègre, à celle du singe et de celle-ci jusqu'à la tête de l'oiseau, du héron et de la grue', *Voyage en Hollande*, in Diderot, *Œuvres complètes*, ed. by Roger Lewinter, XI, 424.

CHAPTER 8

❖

Back to the Future: 'Les Enfantements de Nostre Esprit'

Wes Williams

My title is old-fashioned, in that it has two parts, separated by a colon. If this strikes the reader not just as old-fashioned, but as peculiarly 'eighties' in style, then it strikes the right note. For one of the things I hope to do in the course of this essay is to indulge in some speculative time travel. This will involve, after discussion of one particular chapter in Montaigne's *Essais*, going back to the eighties — the 1980s — and to the film, *Back to the Future*, written by Bob Gale and Robert Zemeckis, directed by Zemeckis, and starring Michael J. Fox as Marty McFly, with the inimitable Christopher Lloyd as Doc. That particular journey is represented by the phrase before the colon in my title, and signals my attempt to bring the keywords of this collection — pre-histories and afterlives — into conversation, each with the other; and both with a further, related, and paired set of terms (outlined below).

The initial return to the 1980s, will, in the course of this paper, be doubled by a further move, signalled by the quotation in my title: 'les enfantements de nostre esprit.' The words are Montaigne's, and direct our attention — albeit by a circuitous route, with a further significant detour following a peculiar echo of Montaigne's phrase as it travels across genres and across time to the 1620s — back to an earlier eighties, namely the 1580s, and back to the chapter from which they are taken: 'De l'affection des peres aux enfans' (II. 8). By way of this repeated, doubling move back to the early modern eighties, I hope, then, not only to tune in to certain textual echoes still resonating on the airwaves, but also — in imitation of both Montaigne and Cave — to 'frotter et limer' a number of texts, images, and films together, bringing them into productively promiscuous interaction, so as to elucidate the peculiar focus of this paper: the 'enfantements de nostre esprit', and the related themes of dedication, and of filiation.

I. 'De l'affection des peres aux enfans'

'De l'affection des peres aux enfans' is the only chapter in Book Two explicitly dedicated, from the outset, to a specific reader. Like the embedded address to Madame de Duras which concludes the mirror essay, 'De la ressemblance des enfans aux peres' (II. 37), like that to the Princesse in the 'Apologie' (II. 12), indeed like all of Montaigne's dedications, apart (perhaps) from the opening 'Au lecteur', it is addressed to a woman; here, one Mme d'Estissac. Recently widowed at the time of writing, Mme d'Estissac was, 'De l'affection des peres...' tells us, an altogether exemplary mother: 'nous n'avons point d'exemple d'affection maternelle en nostre temps plus exprez que le vostre' (386). Unique in her own age, she not only responds to ancient example but also serves as a sign to future readers of the worth, Montaigne suggests, of these 'our times'. Thus the chain of exemplarity serves both to connect the present with past texts and people and to imagine future mothers and children, texts and readers, who, looking back, will recognize the young widow for the marvel that she was.[1]

Mme d'Estissac's son Charles accompanied Montaigne on his trip to Italy in 1580–81, and seems (although this is speculation) to have been something of a surrogate son to Montaigne, who had no son of his own, and had lost five daughters, none of whom survived infancy — leaving infancy being, 'De l'affection...' later suggests, the point at which a father might become interested in his children. There was, of course, the one surviving daughter, whom a Bordeaux copy insertion to this chapter names as Léonor, who outlived the old man, and there was his 'fille d'alliance', Marie de Gournay. But they are part of another story... or rather part of this one, but in ways yet to be fully explored.[2]

At the outset of the chapter Montaigne seems more concerned about the 'sotte entreprise' that is his book than about Madame d'Estissac's child. The 'dessein farouche et monstrueux [later changed to 'extravagant']' of his work, not her son, is his concern; and indeed these features of the text prove, like its 'estrangeté', a cause for serious concern. Montaigne's express hope is that its 'visage si esloigné de l'usage commun', and (another later addition) its being 'le seul livre au monde de son espece', might yet 'luy donner passage' (385). The emendations matter in that they argue a changing cause: the book transmutes from being a wild and monstrous-looking thing requesting sanctuary with an exemplary mother, to being an altogether new kind of creature, and one which more closely represents its progenitor than his other offspring do. The address to the exemplary mother produces (or at very least permits) the elaboration of a topos adumbrated in earlier essays, but only now given specific shape, body, and fully human form: that of the book-as-child. And the later changes to the text serve to mark a measure of Montaigne's pride in the creature he now acknowledges as his own: the 'monstres et chimeres' of 'De l'oysiveté' (I, 8) here take on the shape of the initially 'monstrueux', later 'extravagant', but nonetheless — it is to be hoped — passable, child.[3]

Following these prefatory gestures of dedication, the focus of the writing in the chapter soon shifts on to the child proper, and it becomes clear that in offering this particular piece about the affection of fathers for their children to Charles d'Estissac's mother, Montaigne is also giving the boy a kind of present (albeit one reserved for the future). If the public address to the mother necessarily includes other readers within potential earshot, then privileged among them is the fine young man the boy will turn out to be, if the 'bonnes esperances que donne de soy Monsieur d'Estissac, vostre fils' are anything to go by. As the child is now too young to know of the excellence of his mother, Montaigne writes for the future, so that the man will one day, in reading, recognize what the infant cannot, at the time of writing, see:

> Mais, d'autant qu'à cause de son enfance il n'a peu remerquer les extremes offices qu'il a receu de vous en si grand nombre, je veus, si ces escrits viennent un jour à luy tomber en main, lors que je n'auray plus ny bouche ny parole qui le puisse dire, qu'il reçoive de moy ce tesmoignage en toute vérité. (386)

Direct address modulates into mediated 'tesmoignage'; in so doing it becomes text, ensuring itself a future beyond death. The survival of his writings, and the possibility of future reading of them, is opened up by Montaigne's wishful if-clause. The metaphor of conversational reading is here given body as part of a peculiar practice of resurrective reading. '[C]es escrits' (with their almost possessive deictic) fall into the hands of the child for whom they prove to have in fact been intended, and the young man's eyes seem to hear Montaigne's voice bearing textual witness long after the old man's 'bouche' and 'parole' are gone. The dedication to the mother amounts, then, to a gift to the child, even as the related metaphor of the book-as-child disaggregates: it gives way, or (like a window) gives on to a prospect, a future scene of reading, in which book and child exist together, but separate. In their conversation, written text and human child each represent their respective father and mother, calling to mind in their fortuitous encounter the affection in which all were once held.

It is worth noting that neither of the participants in this recognition scene, staged in an imagined future beyond the death of both of the initial interlocutors of the drama, serves as figure for the other. The constituent parts of the commonplace, the book and the child, are not in conflict, do not compete for attention, do not stand in one for the other; neither usurps the other by forcing it into the position of being vehicle to its tenor, metaphor for its real presence. And neither lives on at the expense of their parent. These points are worth stressing, since later in the chapter (as in the actual, as opposed to the imagined future) things will be different. Montaigne will later argue that children all too often — and, a later addition suggests, especially these days — prey on their elders: they are 'bestes furieuses', whom parents would do well to 'hayr et fuyr pour telles' (392). The 'bestes' here are metaphors, not similes, and as such are fully present in Montaigne's thoughts as they circle the question of the difference between men and beasts, closing in on the specifics of human affection, human kin and kind.[4]

Nor, for all the talk of wild beasts, has Montaigne forgotten the 'enfantements de l'esprit'; indeed the one distinction prepares for the other. For if human children can prove to be beasts, then how much more proper — nobler and more properly ours — are, the essayist argues, children of the mind: 'plus nobles' because there's no physical sex involved in the making of this 'autre production'; 'plus nostres' because there is no gender in this engendering: 'Nous sommes pere et mere ensemble en cette generation' (400). Montaigne's apparently inclusive 'nous' here in fact serves to unmake an 'ensemble' that had thus far generated the text. His making a metaphor of the mother — her double displacement, both from subject to object of the discourse, and from fellow participant in, to occasion for, the drama of 'cette generation' — marks a crucial twist in the plot of this chapter, as the mind, turning and turning about itself, spirits both mother and physical child away. It is a move reinforced in later emendations to the text, where, as we have seen, the writing directs the reader towards 'cette' rather than any other 'generation', to 'ces escrits' rather than to either Mme d'Estissac, or to her child.

Indeed from this point on, the chapter leaves talk of mothers behind, and retells a series of micro-narratives concerning 'cette amitié commune des peres envers les enfans' — by which Montaigne now means, and only means, authors and their works. 'Affection' has modulated, or perhaps matured, into 'amitié'; the 'cette', however, remains: this one, the essayist insists, not that other — less 'noble' and less 'nostre' — one, about which I no longer want, or am able to speak. Along with Epicurus, Lucan, and a host of other men of antiquity, Montaigne reconstructs the pre-history of his chosen topos, and its associated complex of terms: 'affection, amitié, generation, les enfantements (de l'ame, de l'esprit)'. The examples make the case: Labienus had himself walled into his ancestral tomb rather than survive the slaughter by public burning of 'cette sienne si chere geniture'; Lucan, condemned to death by 'ce coquin de Neron', bore witness with his last words, even as the last drops of blood were leaving his veins, to the 'tendre et paternel congé qu'il prenoit de ses enfans' (401). And so it continues, as Mme d'Estissac, the 'exemple d'affection maternelle en nostre temps [le] plus exprez', finds her portrait as it were prefigured in a roll-call of ancient fathers — all of whom bore extraordinary witness (were effectively martyred) to their affection for their children; and all of them — books, not babies — children of the mind.

II. *Back to the Future*

As the chapter 'De l'affection...' lives on, and as Montaigne rethinks and rewrites over time, the insistent refrain which resonates through the text hardens into a question, and so takes on the shape of choice. It is as if Montaigne found himself, eventually, seeking to cut the knot of the metaphor once and for all: 'this child, and not that one: are you really sure?' The list of ancient, exemplary fathers presented by the A-text, and concluding first with the example of Epicurus, is *fairly* confident of the answer when it asks: 's'il eust esté au chois de laisser après luy un enfant contrefaict et mal nay, ou un livre sot et inepte, il ne choisit plutost, et non luy seulement, mais tout homme de pareille suffisance, d'encourir le premier mal'heur que l'autre?' (401). And it is *fairly* sure in the subsequent sentence that it would be proof of 'impiété en Sainct Augustin (pour exemple), si d'un costé on luy proposoit d'enterrer ses escrits, de quoy nostre religion reçoit un si grand fruit, ou d'enterrer ses enfans, au cas qu'il en eut, s'il n'aimoit mieux enterrer ses enfans' (ibid.). Only *fairly*, because in each case the grammar of the proposition allows for doubt; and it is a doubt that persists in still later emendations to the text, as they recalibrate the if-clauses, making the earlier, ancient rhetorical questions read as though they had all, and always, been leading to the question, the choice, which the essayist finally puts to himself: 'Et je ne sçay, si je n'aimerois pas mieux *beaucoup* en avoir produict ung parfaictement bien formé, de l'acointance des muses, que de l'acointance de ma femme' (ibid.; emphasis added). Puts to himself, that is, for the first time in 1588, before adding by hand, on the Bordeaux copy, that curiously insistent intensifier: 'beaucoup'.

In the (almost) concluding moves of 'De l'affection...', then, the insistent conjoined metaphor — that of the brainchild — metamorphoses once again into the drama of forced choice. Which one: book or child? Of course Montaigne doesn't really have a choice, or at least not this one. He, being 'de pareille suffisance', might have made the same decision as Epicurus; but the choice he puts — in that conditional perfectly modulated if-clause — to himself is, as closer reading of the kinds of reversals involved in the shift from ancient example to present and future choice reveals, altogether different. And the quality of this difference becomes clearer when we reconnect these (almost) closing moves with the opening frame of the chapter, and with its initial address, directed neither at the muses, nor at the essayist's own wife, but to the young widow who was Charles d'Estissac's mother. For there, at the chapter's outset, we see Montaigne imagining both book and child together; together, that is, *with* and *in* a future, in which, crucially, the person missing is the author. The natural order of things is such that the child should outlive the man, and both book and child, now man and reader in turn, are here imagined as duly surviving the writer, who, for all that he is dead, still bears witness — 'tesmoignage [...] en toute vérité' — to aspects of the reader's own past experience, experience which he would otherwise have altogether forgotten, since he never really knew he was experiencing it at the time. It's a fantasy, about recognition, about the not-quite-death of the author, and about the recovery of past experience in the present tense of reading.

As it turned out, Charles d'Estissac was killed in a duel on the morning of 8 March 1586. Brantôme and L'Estoile both have their say about the grim business of the affair in which he lost his life, and which historians know as the 'duel des mignons des mignons.'[5] But Montaigne, it seems, prefers not to speak of it; at least not here. The Montaigne who published the first version of the *Essais*, six years earlier, in 1580, could not have known that the young d'Estissac who that same year travelled with him to Italy (where, like so many young French noblemen, he studied the art of duelling) would meet his death in this way. And yet, even in later editions of the text, in Montaigne's life-time and after — which is to say in 1588 and on the Bordeaux copy — the dedication to the boy's mother, like the fantasy about the child's future reading of the old man's words, stands, remains still, unchanged in time.

'De l'affection ...' does not, then, end with the drama of choice. The book survives its father, the boy d'Estissac will never reach adulthood, and the *essai* as form, in Montaigne's hands, of course, never quite concludes; it is, as Cave, following Adorno and others, has taught us, provisional, incomplete, as yet unmade.[6] And even in a more strictly punctual sense this *essai* does not end there. It concludes, rather, with starkly negative counterparts to Mme d'Estissac and her exemplary affection for her son: the 'passions vitieuses et furieuses' of incestuous fathers for their daughters, and the particular example of (and an interrupted quotation from Ovid concerning) Pygmalion.[7] All of which serves to take its readers back to that opening dedication, to begin reading again; and serves, too, to take us, at last, *Back to the Future*.

For readers who know the film, and know it to be an allegory of historical scholarship, as well as a roller-coaster reconfiguration of the Oedipus plot, with a Pygmalion story of sorts thrown in for good measure, some of what follows will be familiar territory. Such readers will know that *Back to the Future*, firstly in the 1985 film, and then in the two sequels, each of which goes further back in historical time, exploring a different genre within film history with each move, represents not only a development of the arguments and structures of Montaigne's chapter 'De l'affection...', but also a kind of shadow image of Terence Cave's own work, as it has developed in the last twenty years or so.[8] Rather than demonstrate how this is so in laborious detail, I should like, briefly, to evoke one particular, exemplary scene from the first (and best) film in the Trilogy. It is a scene which has peculiar resonance in this context — a discussion of pre-histories and afterlives arising out of Terence Cave's work, and my own contribution to an exploration of the thematics of filiation in Montaigne, and in the chapter 'De l'affection des peres aux enfans' in particular — in that it stages that initial, initiatory moment (which I imagine all readers will have experienced in some form) when a terrified young student, time-travelling in search of wisdom, knocks at the Doc's door.

Teenager Marty McFly, having made his way, from the storm, the lightning and the machine-gun fire of a fateful November night in 1985, back to the past, propelled by the plutonium-powered DeLorean cobbled together by his friend the Doc, experiences first of all that *dépaysement* which comes of recognizing that his own home town, Hill Valley, is — thirty years earlier — a distinctly other country. Not least among his disturbing encounters is one with a teenage girl, who, on seeing him, is struck by a *coup de foudre*, as if by lightning, and so falls in burning love with the boy who will one day be her son. One strand of the plot will now have to concern itself with ways in which the young man can reverse the effects of his intervention in the course of history, so as to ensure his own, future, birth. But the principal plot revolves around Marty's other mission: to save the Doc from the death which he, Marty, has just witnessed in the future. Having looked up his address in the phone book, the young man makes his way to the Doc's house (oblivious, for the moment, to the significance of the sign at the foot of the drive, leading back up to the mansion, '1640') and knocks, gingerly, on the door.[9]

There's no substitute for seeing the film, so I won't try to describe the scene which ensues, the scene on which I want to focus, and from which the illustration is taken. Suffice to say that there is an awful lot going on in it, and not all of it has to do with the experience of tutorials with Terence Cave. Most of it has to do in fact with Montaigne, with the temporality of reading, with pre-histories, afterlives, dedication, and with filiation. For alongside the various figures for historical scholarship in this scene — the mind-reading machine, the documentary evidence of images, and the many bits of paper scattered about the study and the garden in the dark — there is a peculiar focus on language, on narrative, and on the pain and the passion of recognition. The scene turns on the collocation 'flux capacitor' and on the narrative of pain associated with its invention. The 'flux capacitor' is the one invention in the room which will turn out to have a history, in that it will eventually enable the Doc (and Marty) to travel through time. But back in 1955 talk

FIG. 8.1: Doc with the mind-reading machine on his head
(Copyright Universal, courtesy of the Kobal Collection)

of the 'flux capacitor' seems simply a waste of time, since the Doc appears to have either forgotten it, or discounted it as just another failed experiment. The narrative of pain — recalled by the young man — is what calls the experiment back to mind and back into history. It is a narrative that Marty remembers having been told in the future, that he recounts, now, to the Doc, and that the Doc then recognizes as having experienced himself, only moments before.

The encounter is a kind of dramatization *avant la lettre* of pre-historical thinking in action; it is also the reverse of the meeting which Montaigne imagines his text having, in some future afterlife, with Mme d'Estissac's son. It is Marty, the student, and not the Doc, the professor, who makes the effort of travelling through time, and so enables the recognition scene to take place; it is the teenager who recalls to the older man the experience of discovering the flux capacitor, an experience he might otherwise have forgotten, or whose significance he might otherwise have discounted. Montaigne knows that teaching, like reading, can be like this, just like this. And the pathos of the resemblance between the scene evoked in the chapter and that represented in the film derives from the fact that the Doc, who occupies of course the position of Mme d'Estissac's son in the parallel, is, in the future, already dead. He has (as Marty knows, since he was there: as a witness) been killed by some comedy Libyan terrorists whom he has hoodwinked out of some nuclear fuel to power the flux capacitor — terrorists could be comedy characters in 1985, and they could be from Libya. This being Hollywood film (subject to the twinned laws of suspense and resolution), and not *essai* (provisional, incomplete, still, even now, in process), the Doc's recollection of the experience of invention which Marty brings with him ensures both that the young man will in fact be born, despite his having tampered with history, and that the Doc will survive beyond that apparent death, in the future. I've ruined the ending for you; but I hope also to have made it even better, by showing how Marty McFly is a kind of Michel de Montaigne in reverse; in photographic terms, the one MM is the negative of the other. The picture, when developed back and forward across time, first upstream and then back down, produces something akin to a likeness, something akin, perhaps, to the 'ressemblance des peres aux enfans'.

III. 'S'il y a quelque loy vrayement naturelle...'

The third and final scene I want to focus on here takes up, one last time, the twinned themes of dedication and filiation with which this paper began, in order to examine once again that peculiar aspect of Montaigne's deployment of the brainchild topos in 'De l'affection...' which concerns our — that is humankind's — resemblance to, and difference from not only our fathers, but also brute beasts. As so often in Montaigne, the fact that this is a theme about which it is not easy to speak is signalled by an if-clause: 'S'il y a quelque loy vrayement naturelle, c'est à dire quelque instinct qui se voye universellement et perpetuellement empreinct aux bestes et en nous (ce qui n'est pas sans controverse)', he begins, before conceding that if such a law exists, then surely, after the desire for self-preservation, the 'affection que l'engendrant porte à son engeance, tient le second lieu en ce rang' (386).

That this is not an uncontroversial question is of course well known to readers of Montaigne. This includes both contemporary, named, readers such as Mme d'Estissac, still clearly in view at this stage of the chapter, and future, as yet unimagined readers, such as a certain young lawyer, anxious about bringing into print the strange legal thought experiment about the difference between men, beasts, satyrs and demons which he had just composed. Keen to gain the attention of his powerful patron, the Maréchal de Saint-Géran, the young lawyer in question, François Hédelin, describes his text, whose full title runs *Des Satyres brutes, monstres et demons. De leur nature et adoration. Contre l'opinion de ceux Qui ont estimé les Satyres estre une espèce d'hommes distincts et séparés des Adamicques*, as both the product of a long-standing tradition of service which is 'naturel en la famille' into which he has been born, and as a sign of a desire for something more: 'l'honneur d'être reconnu autant d'affection que de naissance.'[10] In presenting his credentials in these terms, Hédelin occludes as much as he reveals. He does not name (because he does not need to: the Maréchal will know) his own maternal grandfather, Ambroise Paré, the author of vernacular treatises on conception and childbirth, and of an initially small treatise on monsters, which then grew and grew as the century progressed. Nor does he openly acknowledge the further links in the chain of filiation. For Paré's work served as one of the principal sources for Montaigne's reflections on the force of the imagination; and the force of Montaigne's own imagination can be felt, time and again, in his (Paré's) grandson's treatise. Not least in that dedication to the Maréchal which prefaces the work, in which the young lawyer characterizes his book both as a small child whose 'débileté' and 'difformité' bear witness to its need for protection, if it is to survive at all; and in the address to the reader in which the author offers his text as 'les arrhes d'un plus grand [ouvrage] auquel je suis maintenant comme engagé', and which will give his public 'ce que j'ai pu recueillir des Hippocentaures, Tritons, Néréides, Géants, Pygmées, Acéphales, Arimaspes, Hommes colorés, et de tant d'autres monstres, dont les histoires font mention' (pp. 36–39).

The larger book was never published; but exactly thirty years later, François Hédelin would publish the (very long) text for which he is best known today: the *Pratique du theatre*. By then the Abbé d'Aubignac, he would throw monsters, demons, satyrs and other such hybrid forms off the French stage by casting himself — and by being recognised, at least by some — as the legislator of neo-classical dramatic theory: the unities, *vraisemblance* and the rest. In 1627 however, Hédelin's concern lies not with dramatic illusion and legitimate modes of retelling classical myth in French form, but with credible narratives of a different kind: with pre-history, with what comes after life, and with what it might mean to be in the middle, which is to say, to be human.[11]

The anxiety about the vulnerability of the book–child is one first given voice, as noted above, in Hédelin's preface, which opens with a brief discussion concerning the Spartans' practice regarding certain 'petits enfants' born among them who 'feraient honte à leur parents, ou des délicats qui seraient inutiles à leur république'. Such 'monstres' were, Hédelin reminds us, handed over to a 'certain officier' whose task it was to 'visiter' the children, and to decide between those who could live, and those who should be cast into 'apotèthes ou dépositoires, lieu déstiné pour cette inhumanité.' Montaigne's choice returns, only this time the business of decision is assigned to a public official. This child, or that one: the 'officier' will decide. Hédelin has — as several extended passages of discussion in the treatise proper make still clearer — been back to the past; he has been reading his sixteenth-century authors: Ronsard's 'Hymne des daimons', Montaigne's 'Apologie', and perhaps several other essays which we shall return to in a moment; and, as his prefatory remarks make plain, Amyot's translation of Plutarch's *Lives*. He has privileged among these different pasts the locally appropriate example of the Spartans, with their 'officier', and their concern for what Amyot calls the 'chose publique'. But he has also been reading actively, imitating in the present, adding to his sources: the shame of the parents, and the sense that Spartans are exemplary in something called 'inhumanité', are present neither in Plutarch, nor in Amyot.

We might, I think, legitimately wonder if Hédelin's reworking of the Spartan example and his focussing on something called 'inhumanité' are the result of his having read, closely, Montaigne on the affection of parents for their children, or Montaigne's 'Apologie', or again Montaigne's brief chapter about his meeting with a particular monstrous child (II. 30). Certainly, the turn which the preface takes as it draws its conclusions from the parallel of the Spartans' lives has a certain post-Montaignian twist: 'Or puisque les livres sont les enfants de l'esprit', Hédelin wonders, 'quel jugement dois-je attendre en vous' my patron, my reader? (35). Will you play the role of that 'certain officier', and, throwing my book–child, 'dont le nom et le sujet est si monstrueux, et le discours si faible', into 'quelque depositoire'; will you, extinguishing all hope of my words (unlike those of Montaigne) bearing witness beyond my death, 'me fermer la bouche d'un éternel silence?' (36)

Within the treatise proper, the prefatory conceit of the book as child develops into the more urgent form of Hédelin's enduring, inherited concern with the birth, the representation, and the management of monsters: the argument in the treatise turns on whether any of the various forms of creature believed to be half-man, half-goat or -monkey deserve the name, or enjoy the condition, of human being. His growing conviction, as the treatise progresses, is that to think that they might do so is dangerous error; and that to argue that there is an alternative pre-history of humankind to the one we know (a pre-Adamite history for instance), of which Satyrs would be the living trace, is nothing short of blasphemy. And so Hédelin's treatise turns, again and again, around its central thesis, its revisiting of Montaigne, which is also a return to Augustine, and a turn towards a new orthodoxy in the definition of the terms of what it means to be human: to be human is to be in the middle, to be between the beasts and the angels; so far so Montaigne. But then: to be human is to be subject to sin, and so to mortality; it is to be subject to redemption, and so, to immortality. And thus to even ask the questions — is there another species of middle being? did Christ die for Satyrs? — demonstrates, Hédelin suggests, the monstrousness of any proposition that might grant to such creatures belonging to our group, and to our status, that of being human beings:

> Le Messie est venu seulement pour rendre aux enfants d'Adam la gloire qu'ils avoient perdue par la faute de leur père, et les Satyres, ni quelque autre créature

que ce soit, ne se peuvent arroger aucune participation au mérite de son humanité. Ce mystère requéroit qu'il se fît entièrement semblable à l'homme qu'il voulait rendre digne d'une éternité glorieuse. (71)

The primary narrative of human belonging is, for Hédelin, one of soteriological filiation and divine dedication; a child of Adam, I know I am human in that Christ dedicated himself to me and my kind, took on my humanity, and so redeemed me of my inherited sin. The beginning and the end of the story are set down; we humans occupy the middle ground, and there is no room for anything, let alone anyone, else. And the answer to Hédelin's question about the humanity of Satyrs is found, as it must be, in an alternative narrative of belonging, filiation, and redemption:

> Le Verbe, dit Saint Augustin, s'est revêtu de l'homme tout entier, et n'a rien pris, ne plus, ne moins que lui. Quoi que l'on veuille donc supposer de la nature humaine des Satyres, Jésus-Christ ne s'étant point couvert de leur humanité, ils ne pourraient prétendre leur part aux biens immortels qu'il est venu départir aux hommes: il leur faudrait un autre Jésus-Christ et un autre Paradis. (ibid.)

Separate but equal? Not quite. But the doctrine of excluded, or at least exclusive, middles elaborated here has its political uses. This is not to read Hédelin's treatise as an 'early' working through of a theory of racial difference; for this would be to drown its specific concerns about the workings of the devil and the seeping through into our world of creatures and thoughts generated in what he, like others of his time, clearly thought of as an increasingly threatening, indistinct middle zone of being, in the flow of subsequent history. Rather, it is to suggest that Hédelin's rhetoric of exclusion, of separateness, and of proper and improper filiation, generating as it does arguments, laws, and institutions seeking to define the terms of exclusive belonging, reaches both back and forward — which is to say across — to debates concerning the humanity of people both indigenous, and expatriated, to the New World; across, also to Shylock's speech in the courtroom in the *Merchant of Venice*; across to *Daniel Deronda*... It is an argument which — for all its initial soundings in the *Essais* — leads Hédelin, and others since, some long way distant from Montaigne's thoughts, into a new, and distinctly less brave world.

★ ★ ★

Marty McFly, exiled to his own pre-history, pleads with the Doc first to open the door, then to listen, and finally to believe his — Marty's — story. He does so in order that the Doc can believe in his own seemingly crazy brain-child, the flux capacitor, so that he — Marty — can be born, and so that the Doc need not die, and so that the two of them, the Doc and the young man who is not his son, but is, in a sense, his creation, can live on as friends. Marty's story becomes *vraisemblable* when he recalls a conversation that he and the Doc had shared in the future, the conversation in which the Doc had explained how he got the bump on his head which was the still visible trace of the moment when he came up with the idea for the flux capacitor, which will power them back...

I am not from the future, and the aim of this piece is not to tell Terence that one day, in a tutorial, he will tell me and my then tutorial partner, Lucy Baxandall, about

stubbing his toe while out running, and coming up with the idea of pre-history...
or, later, of realizing while listening to a particular piece of music, the importance of
afterlives, and of the figure of Mignon in particular. Terence is not Mme d'Estissac;
and I am certainly no Montaigne. If I am anyone in this constellation — or should
I say complex? — of characters, it is the monster-monger, claiming that this short
piece is nothing but 'les arrhes d'un plus grand [ouvrage] auquel je suis maintenant
comme engagé', while also shifting any blame and potential shame associated with
it, on to the parents, and the patron: for, 'quelque étrange difformité qui soit' in my
work, Terence, like the Maréchal, has always been, since the early eighties onwards,
up for the conversation, discussion, and reading. For like Mme d'Estissac, like the
Doc, and like the Maréchal to whom Hédelin dedicated his book about monsters
(see above, p. 129), Terence has consistently 'témoign[é] par [ses] paroles quelle
était [sa] curiosité'. And so, like Hédelin, I can say with some confidence that 'cela
même qui m'a donné le courage d'entreprendre ce petit ouvrage, me confirme en
la croyance qu'il ne [luy] sera point désagréable' (36).

Notes to Chapter 8

1. For more on dedications to women readers in Montaigne, see Terence Cave, *Pré-histoires I*, pp.
   39–50; Cathleen Bauschatz, '"Leur plus universelle qualité, c'est la diversité": Women as Ideal
   Readers in Montaigne's *Essais*', *The Journal of Medieval and Renaissance Studies*, 19 (1989), 83–101;
   and for a tremendous, illuminating, account of the figure of Mme d'Estissac and her place in this
   chapter, as of the theme of the text as a kind of 'donation entre vifs' see Natalie Zemon Davis,
   'Art and Society in the Gifts of Montaigne', *Representations*, 12 (1985), 24–32.
2. Others have of course made significant inroads into this story: see, for instance, Philippe Desan,
   'The Book, the Friend, the Woman: Montaigne's Circular Exchanges', in *Contending Kingdoms:
   Historical, Psychological, and Feminist Approaches to the Literature of Sixteenth-Century England and
   France*, ed. by Marie-Rose Logan and Peter. L. Rudnytsky (Detroit: Wayne State University
   Press, 1991), pp. 225–62; and, for a contrastive account, Françoise Charpentier's sharply curious
   'L'Absente des *Essais*: Quelques questions autour de l'essai II. 8 "De l'affection des pères [*sic*] aux
   enfans"', *Bulletin de la société des Amis de Montaigne*, 17/18 (1984), 7–16.
3. For differing responses to Montaigne's use of the book-as-child topos see Robert Cottrell,
   Sexuality/Textuality: A Study of the Fabric of Montaigne's Essais (Columbus: Ohio State University
   Press, 1981), pp. 130–31; Richard L. Regosin, 'Montaigne's Child of the Mind', in *Writing the
   Renaissance: Essays on Sixteenth-Century French Literature in Honor of Floyd Gray*, ed. by Raymond
   C. La Charité (Lexington, KY: French Forum, 1992), pp. 167–81, his *Montaigne's Unruly Brood:
   Textual Engendering and the Challenge to Paternal Authority* (Berkeley: University of California
   Press, 1996) and his earlier *The Matter of My Book: Montaigne's Essais as the Book of the Self*
   (Berkeley: University of California Press, 1977), pp.153–56; Antoine Compagnon, *Nous, Michel
   de Montaigne* (Paris: Seuil, 1980), pp. 215–30.
4. This question, conjoined with the book-as-child topos, is one to which I shall return in part III
   (below).
5. See Lauro-Aimé Colliard, 'Le Thème du duel chez Montaigne: L'Affaire d'Estissac', *Montaigne
   Studies*, 14 (2003), 93–102.
6. See Terence Cave, *How to Read Montaigne* (London: Granta Books, 2007); Theodor Adorno,
   'The Essay as Form', in *Notes to Literature*, ed. by Rolf Tiedemann, trans. by Shierry Weber
   Nicholsen, 2 vols (New York: Columbia University Press, 1991–92), I, 3–23; Claire de Obaldia,
   The Essayistic Spirit: Literature, Modern Criticism and the Essay (Oxford: Clarendon Press, 1995).
7. For two contrastive discussions of this theme, see Constance Jordan, 'Montaigne's Pygmalion:
   The Living Work of Art in "De l'affection des pere [*sic*] aux enfans"', *Sixteenth-Century Journal*,
   9: 4 (1978), 5–12; Patrick Henry, 'Pygmalion in the *Essais*: "De l'affection des pères [*sic*] aux
   enfans"', *The French Review*, 68: 2 (1994), 229–38.

8. The Trilogy has, just this year, been issued on DVD, with extensive outtakes, excerpts from the original screenplay, commentaries from those involved in its production, etc, etc. For details, see <http://www.bttfmovie.com>.

9. The location used as Doc's mansion can be visited: indeed it is now (unlike Montaigne's tower) a National Historic Landmark, and is owned by the City of Pasadena. Known as Gamble House, it was built by American Arts and Crafts pioneers Charles and Henry Greene, for David and Mary Gamble (of Procter & Gamble) as their retirement home in 1908. The '1640' might have alerted Marty that he was crossing a threshold into 'the early modern'.

10. The first (and only) early modern edition of this text came out in Paris, with Nicolas Buon, in 1627. I refer to the modern edition : François Hédelin, *Des Satyres brutes, monstres et demons. De leur nature et adoration. Contre l'opinion de ceux Qui ont estimé les Satyres estre une espèce d'hommes distincts et séparés des Adamicques* ed. by Gilles Banderier (Jérôme Millon: Grenoble, 2003), p. 36.

11. The treatise is little studied. The great exception, and indispensable reading for students of this text, is Amy Wygant's two-part study, 'D'Aubignac, Demonologist, I: Monkeys and Monsters', *Seventeenth-Century French Studies*, 23 (2001), 143–64, and 'D'Aubignac, Demonologist, II: St Anthony and the Satyr', *Seventeenth-Century French Studies*, 24 (2002), 71–85.

EPILOGUE

❖

Time's Arrow[1]

Terence Cave

Acknowledgements

Acknowledgements usually appear at the beginning of a book, but on this occasion
it seemed more appropriate to include them in the Epilogue. That is how they were
presented, in a somewhat different form, at the symposium on 30 September 2006
that provided the starting-point for this volume, and I would like to reiterate here
my warmest thanks to all those who participated in an event that was unusually
lively, focused and productive by any standards, but which was also for me an
extraordinarily moving celebration of the dialogue, both personal and professional,
that makes an academic career much more than just a career. Of the participants
not represented among the contributors to this volume, I am especially grateful
to the following, who played an active part as chairs, respondents and the like:
Kathryn Banks, Jessica Benson, Luisa Calè, Tim Chesters, Richard Cooper,
Miranda Gill, Ann Jefferson, Ruth Livesey, Will McKenzie, Martin McLaughlin,
Will McMorran, Michael Moriarty, Agnieszka Steczowicz, Rowan Tomlinson, and
Valerie Worth. Anna Holland and Richard Scholar have devoted large amounts of
time and meticulous editorial attention to the task of transforming an oral event
into a printed volume; without them, none of it would have happened.

I think of those who were able to be present on 30 September 2006 as a small
but symbolically complete cross-section of all the friends, colleagues and students,
past and present, at home and abroad, whom I have had the privilege of knowing
and talking with over what is now already a half-century (I first went to university
in October 1957). As I cross this threshold — which is after all only an arbitrary
one — into a kind of afterlife, I would like to take the opportunity to thank that
virtual community for all they have taught me, for all their tender or not-so-tender
attention to my thoughts on these and other questions, for taking them much
further than I ever could, and for allowing me to catch a glimpse of what the future
might be in the discipline we share.

The Time Machine

Regardless of all the processes of physical and mental ageing, the memories
that remain with us in later life are subjectively 'natural'. The world of black-
out curtains, air-raid sirens and shelters, D-day convoys parked overnight in our

street (South Court Avenue in Dorchester), rationing, pea–souper fogs, hearing the BBC newsreader (Alvar Liddell?) say 'Paris has been liberated', Charlie Kunz, Flanagan and Allen, *ITMA* and *Much-Binding-in-the-Marsh*, horse-drawn milk-carts, my first bike and a corgi called Skipper and everything else I can remember from my childhood is distant to me but in no way 'foreign'. The foreignness of the past that is palpable to younger generations is more visible to me in movies or in radio recordings of that time, because I experience them in a new context and mediated by a new technology;[2] internally, introspectively, my memories of those or similar happenings, ways of being, epidermal impressions, are simply a part of my home world in a way that the 'pre-war' period, as my parents nostalgically referred to it (or rather they would refer to certain things — clothing, food and the like — as pre-war: it wasn't for them a 'period'), could never be. That pre-war past, when they had a dog called Nipper and bought a new house in Hamilton Crescent in Hounslow, is indeed 'another country', as is *a fortiori* the world of my mother's childhood when she picked blackberries on the common called Heathrow. All that is history.

The point of these remarks is to recall what we all implicitly know: that everyone experiences time-travel, all the more acutely in an era of rapid technological change. We experience it, for example, by comparing the internal, familiar world of the past with the preserved images or documents that bear witness to it: the comparison reveals the unfamiliar amid the familiar; the shock of recognition is also the shock of the uncanny. Its mirror image is the experience I have, say, when I walk into the coffee shop in Blackwell's bookshop in Oxford, expecting to find the Classics department that used to be in that area, and see it as a boy of the 1950s might have seen it, with *wonder*: the very existence of a coffee-shop in this venerable academic bookshop; the strange coffee machines (I didn't travel abroad until I was seventeen); the oddly dressed young people holding tiny gleaming objects to their ears and apparently talking into them, or sitting in front of flattened typewriter keyboards in a metal box with the open lid at right angles; and, if I should glance at a newspaper (strangely shrunk), find anxieties not of an imminent nuclear holocaust but of another, equally apocalyptic, science-fiction meltdown. Defamiliarization, both upstream and downstream, is right there, adjacent to our daily lives, if we care to step into it through the two-way mirror.

Back to the Future provides, among other things, a brilliant set of variations on that fundamental aspect of experience, and Proust, in *Le Temps retrouvé*, saw it as clearly as anyone. I am thinking here in particular of the 'dîner de têtes' in the last volume of Proust's novel, the party where the narrator encounters some strangely familiar figures and eventually recognizes them as people he had known long before, now defamiliarized by time and old age. The sudden displacements brought about by *mémoire involontaire* are the most dramatic manifestation of this effect, but not the only one, and Proust himself was certainly familiar with the notion of time-travel. H.G. Wells' *The Time Machine* was published in 1895 when, as a young writer, Proust was beginning to reflect on problems of time, and in the opening pages of *A la recherche du temps perdu* one finds the following passage (the narrator is speaking of the disorientation that occurs when one wakes up after falling asleep in an unaccustomed position):

alors le bouleversement sera complet dans les mondes désorbités, le fauteuil magique le fera voyager à toute vitesse dans le temps et dans l'espace, et au moment d'ouvrir les paupières, il se croira couché quelques mois plus tôt dans une autre contrée.[3]

Past and Present

The 'anti-realist' view, as characterized by Michael Dummett, that 'the past exists only in the traces it has left upon the present' (see above, p. 114) is hard to resist as a philosophical statement. The Chinese vase or Bronze Age arrowhead we see in a museum is there in the present; similarly, the future plays a role in all our present calculations as it does when the stock market assigns values to 'sugar futures' or 'oil futures'. That we can't actually experience the past or the future in 'real time', as they now say, is a truism. But, as Marian Hobson indicates, those 'traces' Dummett speaks of are not a mere scattering here and there, a barely discernible pattern in the landscape, like the outline of an ancient fortification as seen from the air (or like a pre-history as I have defined it). They fill the whole landscape as far as the eye can see. In that sense (as Dummett also says), the past is never complete. More traces keep being added, the viewpoint shifts, the knowledge at our disposal increases or decreases.

Yet in that landscape of the past, we do in fact — adopting, whether consciously or not, a 'realist' view in the terms of Dummett's opposition — assign broad swathes of territory to the narratives we call 'history', even if the distinction between canonic history and personal or family or social histories is becoming increasingly permeable. Phenomenology has its way of dealing with that problem (as Ben Morgan indicates when he cites Heidegger); but there are other ways, including more immediately accessible ones. We couldn't handle the huge tidal wave of time past that seems to be always on the point of engulfing us unless we had at our disposal efficient cognitive techniques that act like sea-walls or locks (or possibly surf-boards). It isn't, for example, difficult for us — and it isn't an illusion — to conceive of our dialogue with history and its inhabitants as a dialogue with a foreign culture, always translatable, never perfectly translatable.

The question here is whose voice matters most, who holds the floor. Well, we are the ones who are currently on the floor, the ones with the microphone, so I am happy to concede that Ben Morgan is entirely justified in pointing out that I short-change Charles Taylor, and in encouraging us (me) to use the methodologies of pre-history to draw a more nuanced map of the possibilities of thought in the present. Taylor's project (and Stephen Toulmin's, in *Cosmopolis*)[4] of discovering in the past an alternative to the supposedly hegemonic 'Cartesian' model of rationality is in fact one with which I have a great deal of sympathy. But there is a balance to be preserved. The argument I put forward in *Pré-histoires* and elsewhere in favour of trying as far as possible to leave behind the present when studying the traces of the past should be understood in the context of a present-day culture that seems unduly obsessed with its own priorities, and of an academic culture that has sold out to the idea that the only way history (or so-called high culture, for that matter) can be made palatable to students and the society they represent is by using it as a sounding-board for current issues and preoccupations. If that argument were applied to the study of Arabic or Chinese or Kikuyu culture, it would be greeted with scorn, if not outrage. Anthropologists know about this problem, and they know the difference between, on the one hand, admitting that one's interpretation of another culture cannot avoid being grounded to a significant extent in one's own, and, on the other, arguing that *therefore* we should simply give priority to our own concerns. Even if, for each individual, the whole past may be conceived as a subjective field accessible only as traces in present consciousness, that doesn't and shouldn't lead to solipsism or, worse, narcissism. We remember the past collectively, socially, communicatively, as much as we remember it individually and subjectively.

It's not good enough here to use the theoretically self-evident impossibility of ever recovering the real past, the actual experience of people now dead, as an excuse for not making every effort to do just that. There are a lot of things which are impossible to achieve but which are well worth trying for. That is why I continue to defend the supposedly 'humble' interrogation of fragments of the past,[5] in the hope of extracting from them some kind of memorial DNA, the contours of a forgotten melody, the sound of someone's voice saying something that is normal to them but wonderfully strange and *novel* to us. That kind of search isn't antiquarianism: it's passionate, engaged, and founded in an insatiable desire for communication. It also no doubt delivers transferable skills of the kind that are needed to deal with our own world (not least the skills of the linguist, or more precisely the cultural linguist); but that is a kind of practice that is very different from the use of historical materials to reflect, and reflect on, present-day concerns, and it seems to me to be better not to confuse the two. In that sense, I am opposed to the invasion of cultural history by 'ethics', which is not really a practice of ethics but a rather easy intellectual game played in a domain where nothing much is at stake and where we therefore take few risks. It would not be appropriate to cite specific examples here; in any case, the position I'm adopting is general and polemical, not personal, and many of my friends and colleagues do admirable work in areas such as postcolonial and gender studies, where ethics is unavoidably a key issue. My concern is primarily that historical scholarship should not become judgmental in ways that obscure the differently structured sensibilities of those who lived in other periods and cultures. The ethics of cultural-historical study, as I see it, is embodied exclusively in the act of straining to attend to, listen to, the 'others' who inhabit(ed) the past.

The Sibyls and the Swan

This type of argument may be picked up by way of another point, the one raised by Neil Kenny when he speaks of the combination of historical knowledge with 'emotion' and quotes Collingwood on the disappearance from historical materials of what one might call their 'freshness', their original affective colouring. Of course the subjective excitement felt by an inventor or a mathematician or for that matter a composer when he or she realizes that she has made a break-through or discovered a haunting melody is not recoverable. But let no one tell me that I don't have any idea what Archimedes felt when he cried 'Eureka!' My eureka experiences have been pretty minor in comparison with his (and I'm sure my experience of having a bath is quite different), but I've had some all the same, and they seemed important enough to me at the time.[6]

The kinds of feeling that texts from the past may make available to us may not be so basic and transferable as the eureka feeling, which is clearly ancient, programmed into our brains: finding and recognizing the thing that matters is such an essential skill for survival. We have to make the assumption here that the forms of language (including cultural language) used at a given moment in the past are capable of recording at least traces of a mode of feeling now unfamiliar to us, whether it is the experience of love as mediated by a troubadour lyric or a Petrarchan sonnet, the absorbing interest to seventeenth-century French readers of baroque romance, or Montaigne's reflections on sex, religion or politics. The fullest answer to Collingwood (who is mainly concerned with the history of science and of ideas) is in fact provided by the way poems and fictions work, which is itself a special application of the way all language works. They communicate, admittedly often using strategies of indirection in order better to preserve the charge invested in them, but they are there to communicate: they make something happen 'at the other end of the wire', to use an almost outdated metaphor. The something that happens (the output) will never be exactly the same as the input, because the receiver's context is different, but we're used to that in our daily lives (try reading a student's notes on a lecture or tutorial you've just given). When we study and explore such artefacts from the past, we're not handling dead chunks of material from which all the energies drained away in the moment of conception; to look at it that way would be absurd. We're in the privileged position of beings from somewhere else in space who find an artefact from Earth designed to speak to whoever finds it.[7] The speech may be enigmatic, and when we crack the language, the content may be weird, but the act of attending to it will certainly make something happen and we shall equally certainly try hard to use that something to help us reconstruct what it might be like to live on the alien world which we have named Trans-solar III but which its inhabitants modestly call 'Earth'.

'Emotion' then, or 'the affective domain', or 'the passions', are certainly a legitimate object of historical knowledge, not just as a theory but as an integral part of the materials we explore. Here I would tentatively suggest that Neil Kenny's provisional distinction between the cognitive and the affective (p. 16) is not a necessary one, and might even be misleading.[8] There is an important sense in which the cognitive embraces the affective: cognitive psychologists would certainly agree with that, and Lakoff would also be unhappy with a distinction that assigned the cognitive and the affective to different categories. The point of raising that objection here is to create an opening to the way several of the essays in this volume are presented. I entirely concur with Neil's argument that pleasure, joy, excitement, as evinced by texts from the past, may be just as useful as anxiety, fear or disquiet in directing us towards important shifts or disturbances in the weave of history. More broadly, the widely held assumption that the historical is incompatible with the aesthetic (except no doubt in a history of the aesthetic) is one that in my view has impoverished history and left the aesthetic in the privileged but therefore dubious 'category' to which Kant famously assigned it.[9] This is where the sibyls and the swan come in.

Both Mary McKinley's essay and Anna Holland's, in their different ways, make space for the instantly recognizable affective charge of the materials they explore. Aesthetic beauty is an integral part of the history of those materials, not a self-indulgent bonus for the weary researcher or a badge worn by the amateur of fine things to show that she belongs to the elite club. Both the silent choir of exiled sibyls and the not-yet-singing swan are classic figures or topoi of the 'Renaissance' in the full sense of that word: Seznec's study of the survival of the pagan gods provides most of the context one needs in order to understand how such a complex cultural phenomenon as the sculptural ensemble of Saint-Bertrand arose in this period, while the remaking of Horace's uneasy swan represents *imitatio* on its most central ground, vulnerably wresting from the ancient poets their laurels, their claims of immortality.[10] Both examples, therefore, share a particular kind of relation to time. Both look to the future, and thus to duration, yet both are fraught with transience: that aesthetic beauty, the intensity of feelings, impressions and sensations, comes at such a price is the lesson of Wallace Stevens' 'Sunday Morning'. Both the sibyls and the swan are also figures of prophecy, half turned towards the world, half towards the transcendental.[11] Both are enigmatic by vocation, rather than by the accident of a particular expressive form. Both, finally, look simultaneously backwards and forwards, and are thus figures of what this book as a whole is about.

It is clear that, in such cases at least, the distinction between 'pre-histories' and 'afterlives' is invalid, or only valid if one chooses a threshold point which will always be arbitrary (I shall return to this point later). When did the sibyls reach their threshold? With Plutarch's *De Pythiae oraculis*? In the choir of Saint-Bertrand de Comminges, they have certainly passed it in one sense. What do they feel there, those twelve captive pagans groomed to fit into a triumphalist Christian hierarchy? They belong to a pre-history of how humans seek to include the future in the present, yet they seem to inhabit an endlessly recurring afterlife, always rehearsing some *Ur*-foretelling like the pronouncements of Erda in Wagner's *Ring*. The horizon of belief in which they were conceived encloses them within a finite history between human redemption and the Last Judgement, but they have outlived it and still point onward at the beginning of the third millennium.

As a consequence of this positioning 'in the middest', to take up the phrase used by Frank Kermode in *The Sense of an Ending*,[12] both the sibyls and the swan incur the risk of a fall into banality, repetition, or inauthenticity. Horace's self-parody, his rueful humour in imagining his skinny legs, his roughening arms, all the discomforts of an ageing body that Montaigne registers in such lucid detail and that Diderot no doubt also felt when he took his clothes off for Mme Therbouche, all these are familiar enough to us; one is reminded, too, of Ian McKellen as Lear stripping down to the poor forked creature that is 'man'.[13] The would-be swan may fall like Icarus or fail to sing, emitting only some harsh corbine croak. The sibyl's voice may be only the ventriloquism of a venal priestess, a shabby deceit; her profound enigma may be only a two-faced formula allowing the seer to claim later, whatever the outcome, that she foretold the truth. We, the latecomers, the fashionably disillusioned modernists and postmodernists, the tired academics conscious of our own spindly legs and moulted feathers, like to dwell on what we now call the 'downside'. But I still prefer the metaphor 'downstream', which was coined between Marian Hobson, Ahuvia Kahane and me (I'm no longer sure which) at a memorable seminar at Royal Holloway, and which in this case restores the swan–poet to his silver stream and the sibyls to the streaming wind of prophetic inspiration. The moment in the choir as Mary describes it is a moment of hard-won harmony, a vision of repose, an imagined memory: the children in the apple-tree, Montaigne in his orchard;[14] for the swan, there is at least the dream of flight, when the ugly duckling becomes a thing of beauty as it streaks across the sky. In those icons, pre-histories and afterlives are gathered together in an 'anti-realist' present that is pregnant with both past and future.

Method: The Way Round

Echoes of the affective mode sound again in John O'Brien's essay, especially when he speaks of tenderness, by which I take it that he means both the amorous delicacy with which Montaigne attends to the curving stream of his thoughts and a possible method of textual and historical analysis that strives to follow that inimitable example. Here again, time is of the essence. As Kate Tunstall also shows when she juxtaposes Montaigne's verbal self-portrait with Diderot's portraits (and his verbal accounts of them), time takes us and our thoughts and feelings apart, scattering them over a series of discontinuous moments any of which (but not all at once) may be captured by the portrait-artist or photographer. Montaigne handles this by giving licence to the flow and seeking to record, not every moment, but enough over the course of two decades to be, as we would say, statistically viable. This 'recording', which he habitually calls a 'register', is also represented as a listening process: 'il n'y a personne, *s'il s'escoute*, qui ne descouvre en soy une forme sienne, une forme maistresse...' (my emphasis).[15] The recognition scene here, even if the discovery is not an Archimedean eureka moment, is a product of close attention sustained over time and sensitive to the primal randomness of any such sequence. It points towards wholeness while never achieving it and never breaking the fundamental 'anti-realist' rule: don't pretend that you can stand outside time and view it as a single invariable field. Using the inward time machine I refer to in my opening remarks, Montaigne shuttles to and fro between his early and his late thoughts, his old age and his youth, his prime of life and the prime of his writing life (which are separated by the twenty years of composition). So he doesn't have the problem that irritates and amuses Diderot (why did she paint me while I happened to have *that* silly expression on my face?): use of the commonplace metaphor of the (self-)portrait is overwritten by the listening and recording metaphors.

So much for Montaigne, but for us, the relationship between the intractable object of study and the apparently inadequate recording instrument, between literature and its would-be rational counterpart, remains problematic. This problem was already one that much preoccupied Valéry, as for example when he speaks of the art of La Fontaine, commonly characterized as 'natural' and easy-going: 'Et plus la proie que l'on convoite est-elle inquiète et fugitive, plus faut-il de présence et de volonté pour la rendre éternellement présente, dans son attitude éternellement fuyante.'[16] It was also widely discussed in the post-structuralist era, when Derrida's brilliantly creative rewriting of philosophical discourse undermined the antithesis and pointed to the seductive possibility that critical language, being profoundly dependent on the rhetorical resources normally attributed to literature, could itself pretend to literary status. But literary scholars are for the most part ugly ducklings: the best they can do is flap their wings and peer up at the clear blue sky they will never themselves inhabit. Besides which, a few moments with Bourdieu would remind us that the institution we belong to assigns us a different task and therefore a different language. A more accessible model here might, as I suggested earlier, be the anti-Cartesian stance of Charles Taylor and Stephen Toulmin, although they were thinking of broadly ethical questions rather than those of literary or cultural studies. Either way, the question remains: how does one maintain intellectual rigour when the object of one's study is irremediably untidy, multiple, elusively unresolved? This I believe is a fundamental question of research in literary and cultural studies (to which I would happily add history in general, including the history of ideas and philosophy), a question that is never fully answerable and that we nevertheless can't avoid answering in one way or another, even if only by accident rather than by design.

A good place to begin looking for an answer is, once again, John O'Brien's call for tenderness, which is in this context the reverse of an untidy emotion: it betokens the fidelity of a carer, or perhaps of a picture-restorer, although it goes well beyond 'restoration' as such. It also carries with it, as the quotation from Valéry in John's essay indicated, the notion of a discourse that works by indirection. This is what Montaigne calls 'la route par ailleurs', in a phrase that André Tournon has shown to be focal for an understanding of the way Montaigne writes and thinks (see above, pp. 81, 90). It is also, I believe, the way that 'method' and its generalized field 'methodology' are best conceived. Where one's aim is primarily philosophical, theory (of literature, of criticism, of culture and its institutions) is clearly the dominant discipline, if by 'theory' we mean the desire to clarify the ultimate limits of any claim that may be made about the object of study. Yet the reign of theory in the late twentieth century was restless, unstable: it taught us a lot, but it gave us (of course) no infallible answers. And those of us who embarked on academic careers because we felt especially drawn to those strange objects we call literary texts are not primarily philosophers. As a consequence, theory has sometimes been confused in our discipline with method, as if you only have to choose a suitable theory and it will provide you with the analytical tools you need. Method may draw on theories of various kinds, and on philosophical writing, be it that of Hegel, Heidegger, Derrida or Wittgenstein, but that is not where it begins. It begins when you've found a text or corpus of texts or textual problem that you want to investigate and start to look for the analytical tools that are best adapted to those materials. And the materials themselves will always have priority here, not the desire to illustrate or confirm or modify a 'theory'.[17]

This is why I think of method as a 'route par ailleurs', which as it happens is one plausible way of reading the etymology of the word 'method': 'meta-hodos', a path between, a path round, a meta-path.[18] For it to 'go round' at all, there must be materials, a configured landscape of probably untidy and potentially inscrutable objects both shaped and damaged by time. It can't simply swallow and digest them, as the snake would digest the elephant in a Cartesian version of *Le Petit Prince*. It curves round and between them, shuttling back and forth and taking new sightlines at each approach.

Pre-Histories and Afterlives; Doppler Effects and Flux Capacitors

This book contains some wonderful examples of how to shuttle in time: the careful teasing out of trans-historical differences in the first two essays, then the swans and the sibyls, Montaigne's indirection and Diderot's self-portrait. The last two essays contribute another remarkable crossover. Marian Hobson's discussion of Diderot and the goat-men opens up a series that eventually includes evolutionary science and theories we would now call racist; Wes Williams sketches a pre-history of ways of thinking the man–beast monster (it would be tempting to include Horace's swan–man here too).

But is 'pre-history' the right word in such cases?[19] There are certainly some afterlives here, too: the afterlives of the goat-men, for example. But if one adds in other examples more or less at random (Caliban and his kin, Frankenstein's monster, to mention only the most familiar), we return to a point I made earlier, namely that pre-histories only become distinguishable from afterlives if one assigns to a particular text or moment the status of a threshold. There may well be strategic reasons for choosing a threshold, and it is certain that some moments are especially prone to shifts in a given sequence: Diderot's moment, or the one that immediately follows him, provides an obvious example. But all these thresholds remain provisional according to the rule (also from Dummett via Hobson) that new knowledge may change the shape of the past, not as dramatically as Marty McFly, who changes his own present by altering the past, yet no less irrevocably.

The threshold thus has a necessary heuristic value as an interpretative instrument, but it is certainly not a point on a fixed line any more than the place where Zeno's arrow happens to be at a given moment is fixed. One might then conclude that pre-histories and afterlives, together with the thresholds that constitute them as such, should be understood as something like a Doppler effect: a moving object is accompanied by an acoustic trace that changes in relation to the position from which one observes (listens to) it. The interest of such phenomena within the field of history is precisely that they are in movement; the moment one fixes them, they lose their colour and vibrancy, like a nailed butterfly. In that light, pre-histories and afterlives are not symmetrical twins, mirror images perfectly balanced on either side of an interface, but slightly different versions of a single relaying effect within the Janus-faced continuum we call historical time. The Cartesian *cogito* is often regarded as a decisive threshold, a turning-point; but it is at least equally one moment among many in the pre-history of 'modern' ways of thinking about the subject *and* one moment among many in the afterlife of Renaissance scepticism. Mignon only has a determinate threshold thanks to Goethe, and, as I shall try to show elsewhere, one of her distinctive features is that all of her life, all of her lives, come afterwards; another is that she always seems to be heralding something that never arrives (or that arrives a great deal later, in the novels of George Eliot and Angela Carter). She is thus a figure of both pre-history and afterlife, the combination of the two modifying the sense of both.

It would be easy to assume that this way of looking at historical sequences must necessarily impose a nihilistic or at least a radically sceptical vision. Everything, it would seem, is trace, shift, centrifugal drive, or indeterminate flux. But, as *Back to the Future* tells us, a flux capacitor has always already been invented; if it had not, we wouldn't be able to think at all, still less manage the world in our day-to-day lives. In any case, convergence is as likely an event in the stream of time as divergence. Recognition scenes may be temporary and even, in some perspectives, illusory, but they are a tangible event, a happening that makes other things happen (a Doppler shift certainly needs an object to make it happen). There are eureka moments; and there are times when, having traversed the monotony of historical space without encountering more than apparently trivial debris, we come across an inhabited world. Something like that is what Plato must be talking about in his seventh letter, using a characteristically Platonist metaphor of the transcendental:

> as a result of continued application to the subject itself and communion there-with, it is brought to birth in the soul on a sudden, as light that is kindled by a leaping spark [*oion apo puros pêdêsantos exaphthen phôs*], and thereafter it nourishes itself.[20]

Finally, it is important to remember that we also live our lives, as I said earlier, among collective memories as well as personal ones, constantly creating new memories for the future by the meetings and conversations that are such a central part of the work we do together. That is why, in the later part of my career, I have given priority to dialogue about method — what Plato in the same letter calls the 'marvellous pathway' (*hodon* [...] *thaumastên*).[21] When one travels on that pathway, Plato insists, talk matters more than writing: dialogue is both the path itself and the map that sustains the hope of finding a 'way round'. Such was the dialogue among friends that really took place on 30 September 2006.

Notes to the Epilogue

1. My sub-title is borrowed from the title of Martin Amis's novel, which is written in reverse temporal sequence; but it is also meant to evoke 'Zeno's paradox', according to which a flying arrow, when considered at a specific point in its trajectory, is claimed to be stationary.

2. Modern fictional reconstructions of that period, however meticulous about detail, always seem to me fatally flawed: the paint is too fresh, the fabrics wrongly textured and cut, the cars too much like museum pieces, the dialogue liable to slip into phrasings that don't sound right, or if they are right, sound self-conscious and thus potentially parodic. I've never been a great fan of historical novels, except when novelists write about their own recent past (George Eliot is an example).

3. Marcel Proust, *A la recherche du temps perdu*, ed. Jean-Yves Tadié et al., vol. 1 ([Paris]: Gallimard, 1987), p. 5 (and see the note on the passage in this edition). I am indebted to Nicola Luckhurst for finding this reference for me. Proust also refers in passing to *The Invisible Man* ('l'homme de Wells') in *Le Côté de Guermantes*.

4. Stephen Toulmin, *Cosmopolis: The Hidden Agenda of Modernity* (Chicago: Chicago University Press, 1992).

5. See Ben Morgan's reference to humility (above, p. 30). The exercise is actually not so very humble: it's very difficult, and still quite arrogant in its way.

6. An example: when I finally found the text by Jeremy Taylor that George Eliot quotes as the epigraph to Chapter 60 of *Daniel Deronda*, I genuinely believed for a moment that GE herself had directed my eye and hand in surfing through the many thick volumes of his collected works in the Bodleian. I had been about to give up, because it wasn't in any of the expected places, but I found it by serendipity, at the very last moment, among Taylor's sermons. The feeling was the more extraordinary as the sermon is written in breathtakingly beautiful prose and is so germane to Eliot's purpose in the novel that it completely changes the perspective of reading. All that became apparent in a couple of minutes as I stood by the open shelves, my hands covered in dust (most of the volumes hadn't been opened for years, perhaps decades), in Bodley's Upper Reading Room.

7. Some literary works are no doubt designed for very particular readers, or have a local, topical or 'private' scope. Some reach the public domain, if they reach it at all, purely by accident and against the intention of the author. Yet these too are saturated with the energy of wanting to communicate, and (as we know from psychotherapy and similar practices) private intentions often conceal a desire for a more public mode of expression. We have to assume that all artefacts that reach us from the past were designed in the hope of finding a reader and thus of communicating, perhaps with an ideal reader, but failing that, with anyone who will listen with care ('tender loving care', as the phrase goes). Montaigne's *Essais* yet again provide a paradigm here.

8. Neil in fact goes on to make it clear that 'the method of pre-history makes no a priori separation of affect from cognition'.

9. Many of the problems of literary and historical study of the last fifty years (at least) seem to me to arise from the kind of confusion between definitions and categories that Wittgenstein famously lays bare in *Philosophical Investigations*, 65–67 and that Lakoff and others have since sought to avoid. For a wide-ranging account of these issues, see George Lakoff's now classic study *Women, Fire, and Dangerous Things: What Categories Reveal about the Mind* (Chicago and London: Chicago University Press, 1987), especially Part I. A prime example of the confusion I am speaking of here is the long-standing debate about what defines 'the literary' in opposition to the non-literary. It's not surprising that no one has ever agreed on a definition. 'Literature' is not a term to be defined but a category with blurred edges, a set of variously related cultural practices, like the games in Wittgenstein's analysis. Some of these practices share one feature, some another, just as different family members may have one or another of the distinctive features that make it possible to surmise that two people you happen to see, say, sitting on a park bench together, are in fact blood-relations. Likewise, the movie *Blade Runner* may be read as a singularly beautiful poetic variation on the ancient problem of what 'defines' a human being: there is in the end no definition, just — again — categories with blurred edges.

10. See Jean Seznec, *The Survival of the Pagan Gods: The Mythological Tradition and Its Place in Renaissance Humanism and Art*, trans. by Barbara F. Sessions (New York: Pantheon Books, 1953); (original edn in French, 1940). On imitation and vulnerability, see Thomas M. Greene, *The Light in Troy: Imitation and Discovery in Renaissance Poetry* (New Haven and London: Yale University Press, 1982), and *The Vulnerable Text: Essays on Renaissance Literature* (New York: Columbia University Press, 1986).

11. For the swan, see the passage from Rabelais cited in Anna's essay (p. 67).

12. Frank Kermode, *The Sense of an Ending: Studies in the Theory of Fiction* (London, Oxford and New York: Oxford University Press, 1966), p. 7. Kermode borrows the phrase, adapting it slightly, from Philip Sidney's *Apology for Poetry*.

13. I refer here to the Stratford production of 2007.

14. I refer here to the passage from Montaigne I quote in the final pages of *Pré-histoires II* (p. 190). As for the 'children in the apple-tree', I was thinking of T. S. Eliot's *Four Quartets* (and certainly not Miles's punning song in Benjamin Britten's *The Turn of the Screw*).

15. Montaigne, *Essais*, III. 2, 811.

16. Paul Valéry, 'Au sujet d'Adonis', in *Variété* ([Paris]: Gallimard, 1924), pp. 53–54. I don't know whether Valéry was thinking of Montaigne's *Essais* when he wrote this passage, but certain of

his images and turns of phrase are strangely close to the way Montaigne formulates (for example in 'De l'exercitation' and 'De la praesomption') his delicate pursuit of fugitive thoughts and the constant alertness it imposes on him.

17. It would be easy here to make the objection that was widely used in the 1960s and 1970s against those who argued that theory was (at best) an unnecessary complication: 'No one is innocent;' we said, 'your apparently common-sense approach is actually loaded with ideological and theoretical presuppositions.' I'm speaking here, however, not about a choice between a 'theoretical' and a 'non-theoretical' approach, but about whether it is necessary, because we undoubtedly have all kinds of presuppositions, first to construct or adopt a theoretical framework that makes some of them explicit (while others remain hidden...), and then to make everything else subservient to that initial move. I am conscious of stating the antithesis in a somewhat exaggerated form, but the point of doing so is that it helps to clarify an important distinction between method and theory which is by no means always observed or understood.

18. See the phrase 'marvellous pathway' from Plato's seventh letter, quoted on page 144; reference in n. 21 below.

19. I should make it clear here that I am myself applying this word to the series that is sketched out, as it were, between Marian's essay and Wes's; Marian's argument has a distinctive temporal axis of its own which I don't engage with directly here, although it has already deeply affected the way I think about such things.

20. Plato, *Epistle VII*, 341 C-D, trans. by R. G. Bury, in *Plato IX* (Cambridge, MA and London: Harvard University Press, Loeb Classical Library, 2005), pp. 530–31.

21. Ibid., 340 C (pp. 526–29). I have cheated slightly here by claiming that Plato is referring to 'method' as such; but that, I think, is essentially what he means by philosophy in the true sense.

INDEX

❖